Actes du XIVème Congrès UISPP, Université de Liège, Belgique, 2-8 septembre 2001

Acts of the XIVth UISPP Congress, University of Liège, Belgium, 2-8 September 2001

SECTION 14

ARCHÉOLOGIE ET HISTOIRE DU MOYEN ÂGE
ARCHAEOLOGY AND HISTORY OF THE MIDDLE AGES

Sessions générales et posters
General Sessions and Posters

Édité par / Edited by
Le Secrétariat du Congrès

Présidents de la Section 14 :
Alain Dierkens & Johnny de Meulemeester

BAR International Series 1355
2005

Published in 2016 by
BAR Publishing, Oxford

BAR International Series 1355

Acts of the XIVth UISPP Congress, University of Liège, Belgium, 2-8 September 2001
Section 14: Archéologie et histoire du moyen âge / Archaeology and History of the Middle Ages

ISBN 978 1 84171 800 2

© The editors and contributors severally and the Publisher 2005

Avec la collaboration du Ministère de la Région Wallonne. Direction générale de l'Aménagement du territoire, du Logement et du Patrimoine. Subvention n°03/15718

Mise en page / Editing : Rebecca MILLER

Marcel OTTE, Secrétaire général du XIVème Congrès de l'U.I.S.P.P.
Université de Liège
Service de Préhistoire
7, place du XX août, bât. A1
4000 Liège Belgique
Tél. 0032/4/366.53.41   Fax 0032/4/366.55.51
Email: prehist@ulg.ac.be   Web: http://www.ulg.ac.be/prehist

The authors' moral rights under the 1988 UK Copyright,
Designs and Patents Act are hereby expressly asserted.

All rights reserved. No part of this work may be copied, reproduced, stored,
sold, distributed, scanned, saved in any form of digital format or transmitted
in any form digitally, without the written permission of the Publisher.

BAR Publishing is the trading name of British Archaeological Reports (Oxford) Ltd.
British Archaeological Reports was first incorporated in 1974 to publish the BAR
Series, International and British. In 1992 Hadrian Books Ltd became part of the BAR
group. This volume was originally published by Archaeopress in conjunction with
British Archaeological Reports (Oxford) Ltd / Hadrian Books Ltd, the Series principal
publisher, in 2005. This present volume is published by BAR Publishing, 2016.

Printed in England

BAR titles are available from:

	BAR Publishing
	122 Banbury Rd, Oxford, OX2 7BP, UK
EMAIL	info@barpublishing.com
PHONE	+44 (0)1865 310431
FAX	+44 (0)1865 316916
	www.barpublishing.com

TABLE OF CONTENTS / TABLE DES MATIÈRES

SESSION GÉNÉRALE / GENERAL SESSION 14-I

Cave Sanctuaries of the Pechora Pre-Urals: Medieval Chronological Horizon 1
A. Murygin

The Ethnic Picture of the Great Hungarian Plain in the 6th-9th centuries. Methods and Possibilities 9
L. Bende, G. Lorinczy, C. Szalontai

For Hotchpot and the Devil: The Ritual Evidence of Medieval Bronze Cauldrons 13
V. van Vilsteren

Some Aspects of the Medieval Fountains in Viterbo 21
C. De Santis

The Middle Ages in the Viterbese Tuscia Region: The Case Study of Castel D'asso (Viterbo) 27
L. Venturi

Étude anthropologique du cimetière médiéval de Saint-Estève-le-Pont (Berre l'Étang, Bouches-du-Rhône) 31
A. Thomann, S. Bello, L. Lalys, P. Adalian, Y. Ardagna, W. Devriendt, M. Gibert, A. Genot, O. Dutour, M. Signoli

SESSION GÉNÉRALE / GENERAL SESSION 14-II

L'évolution des modes d'inhumation en Picardie (France) entre les IIIe et VIIIe siècles 41
L. Hermann

Woodworking in the Early Middle Ages in Central and Northern Europe: Production and Processing Techniques of Handmade Articles 49
P. de Vingo

Migrated Groups and Local Populations: Integration and Contrast in the Western Alps Between the Roman Period and the Early Middle Ages 57
P. de Vingo

Les fouilles des châteaux forts de Castellnou de Bages, Callús et Boixadors, à la frontière méridionale de la Marche Hispanique 63
A. Caixal Mata, A. López Mullor, A. Pancorbo, J. Fierro-Macía

La céramique mise au jour à la couche d'abandon du château fort
    de Callús (Barcelone, Espagne) 71
A. Pancorbo, A. López Mullor & A. Caixal Mata

The Study of Medieval Architecture from an Archaeological
    Perspective 81
R. Blanco Rotea

SECTION 14 – POSTERS

Morphometric Evaluation of some Bony Segments in a Case of Dwarfism
    of the Late Middle Ages, (Cividale del Friuli, Udine) 89
G. Baggieri, M. di Giacomo

A Specific Burial Custom: The Catacomb Grave 93
L. Bende, G. Lorinczy

CAVE SANCTUARIES OF THE PECHORA PRE-URALS: MEDIEVAL CHRONOLOGICAL HORIZON

Alexandr MURYGIN

Abstract: There are known, as minimum, 6 caves in the Pechora Pre-Ural area, in which the archaeological visiting horizons occurred in the Holocene complex of the quaternary depositions. The medieval cult complexes of findings from the caves included the remains of the ritual fire-places and related to them constructions as well as different material, food and blood forms of sacrifices: arrowheads, decorations, coins irrational cult attributes, implements of labour and household, ceramics, abundant faunal material including mammoth bones and traces of human sacrifice, wooden idols. Two main types of archaeological cave sanctuaries are singled out.

The territory under investigation is situated between the Ural Mountains and the Pai-Khoi mountain range from the east and the Timan mountain-ridge - from the west. This vast Pechora Pre-Ural area corresponds mainly to the Pechora lowland, its largest water artery being the river of Pechora. The Pechora basin covers two, sharply dissimilar on the landscape-climatic conditions, areas - Malo- and Bolshezemelckaya tundra and Pre-Pechora taiga.

In this north-eastern area of Europe the first traces of constructions of, probably, cult character were discovered in the Upper-Palaeolithic site in Medvej'ya pesh'era on the Upper-Pechora, dating back to approximately 16-18 thousand years age (Guslitser, Pavlov, 1988, p.12, 13; Pavlov, Indrelid, 2000, p. 166). But no succession of this tradition with further epochs was traced on this territory.

Constant use of the Pechora Pre-Ural caves specially for performing the heathen rites started, as per archaeological data, only since the second half of the II millennium B. C. and periodically, with different intensity, continued up to the XIII-XIV centuries A.D.

There are known, as minimum, 6 caves in the Pechora Pre-Ural area, in which the archaeological visiting horizons occurred in the Holocene complex of the Quaternary deposits (fig. 1, *1-6*). The caves are associated to the regions with developed karst phenomena and formed in the rocky sections of the rivers and dry valleys.

The cultural layer with authentic sacrifice materials of the Middle Ages is practically completely studied in Kanin and Unyin caves on the Upper-Pechora and Unyia rivers (fig. 1, *1, 2*), in Eshmess cave - on the eastern slopes of the Middle Timan (fig. 1, *5*), Adak cave – on the Usa river (fig. 1, *6*) and Arka cave (fig. 1, *3*) - on the Podcherem river (Kanivets, 1962; 1964; 1971, 1972; Kanivets, Loginova, 1970; Murygin, 1987; 1992; Ryabtseva, Semenov, 1990; Semenov, 1987; Semenov, Ryabtseva, 1986; Pavlov, L'ubashkov, 1998).

The cultural layer of most cave cult sites contained mixed implements of different times. Due to the lack of clear stratigraphic observations its dating, as a rule, is done on the basis of comparative - typological method, though Bronze Age materials occurred lower the Iron Age implements. The problem is in singling out the material implements belonging to separate sacrificial complexes, replacing each other in consecutive order, which is of special interest for investigators when carrying out such an operation within narrow limits of one epoch. Usually only chronological limits of findings as a whole for one or another period of site existence are established with sufficient certainty. It is also impossible, with rare exception, to precisely limit the time of different types of cult articles, to establish their ethno-cultural and spatial conformity with other categories of findings due to chronological amorphity and individuality of irrational cult attributes.

The cultural layer in caves deposited mainly in the Middle Ages, that is V-XIII/XIV centuries A.D. In Kanin, Unyin and Adak caves it had been accumulating throughout all this period, in Arka cave - VI-XII (?) centuries A.D. The material implements of Eshmess cave on coins and radio-carbon dating of the carbonised wood from the cultural layer date back to the X-XI centuries A.D.

In the cultural layer of Kanin cave within the studied area no concrete order in location of medieval implements was observed. They were found all over the grotto area and on the sloping ground in front of it (Kanivets, 1964, p.41-48). In Unyin, Adak and Eshmess caves the medieval findings were concentrated, as a rule, in accumulations near one of the grotto walls (Kanivets, 1987, fig.1, 2). The concentration of sacrifices not only in the entrance part of the cave grotto, but also in the well lighted surface area was well traced in Unyin and Eshmess caves (Kanivets, 1962, p.116; Murygin, 1987, p.38; 1992).

In Kanin, Unyin and Adak caves the remains of fire-places, related to ritual fire, were discovered (Kanivets, 1962, fig.7, 8, 10; 1964, fig. 10, 12; 1971, Album, fig. 54). In Kanin and Unyin caves stone planks or clay layers, and the remains of wooden constructions are related to the largest fire-places (Kanivets, 1962, p.116, 117; 1964, p.46, 47). In Eshmess cave the remains of burnt wooden construction, may `be - planking made of boards or blocks were discovered (Murygin, 1987, fig.2; 1992).

The sacrifice materials of the Middle Ages consist mainly of bone, rarely - metallic, arrowheads, different bronze,

Figure 1. Location of cave sacrificial places of the Pechora Pre-Urals. 1 - Unyin cave, 2 - Kanin cave, 3 - - Arka, 4 - Sed`yusskaya cave, 5 - Eshmess cave, 6 - Adak cave.

silver, glass decorations, Middle-Asia and Germanic silver coins, implements of labour and household, clay utensils, animal bones etc (fig. 2-5).

Specific peculiarity of sacrificial implements are the articles for direct cult purposes (fig. 2; 3 *2, 9-19*). They are represented by cast and punched depictions of real and fantastic animals, anthropomorphic and zoo-anthropomorphic figurines; the same in graffiti (scratched depictions). Many figurines are accompanied by depiction of interiors. Fragmentarity is typical for depictions from sacrificial places; many decorations are represented by separate parts of more complex articles which are broken maybe intentionally. Many findings consist of blades and fragments or metal scraps. These features of cult ceremonial rites are not occasional and characterise one of the sides of archaic beliefs and sacred actions of local tribes. Osteological materials take considerable part in the total amount of findings from the cave sacrificial places. Two wooden idols found standing in Eshmess cave grotto are unique (fig. 6). They are well preserved. According to radiocarbon analysis data, one of them dates back to 1060±40 or 890 A.D. (fig. 6, *1*), while another - 1010±40 or 940 A.D. (fig. 6, *2*).

In spite of functional identity of sites as places for performing ancient heathen rites, there exist differences between them in materials for primary utilitarian purposes, the composition of irrational cult attributes, and the choice of sacrificial animals.

Of greatest diversity are bone articles from Kanin and Unyin caves. There prevail bones of bears, fur and ungulate animals, with the presence of bones of domestic animals, birds of prey and fish (Kanivets, 1964, table 7, p.126). In Eshmess cave there are no bones of ornithofauna, domestic animals and bears, but bones of fur animals prevail. Specific weight of one or another animal species from caves mainly corresponds to the quantitative correlation of the remaining skeleton fragments (Kanivets, 1964, table 5, 6).

The correlation of leading species of the Holocene fauna from the caves is also inadequate. Kanin and Unyin caves

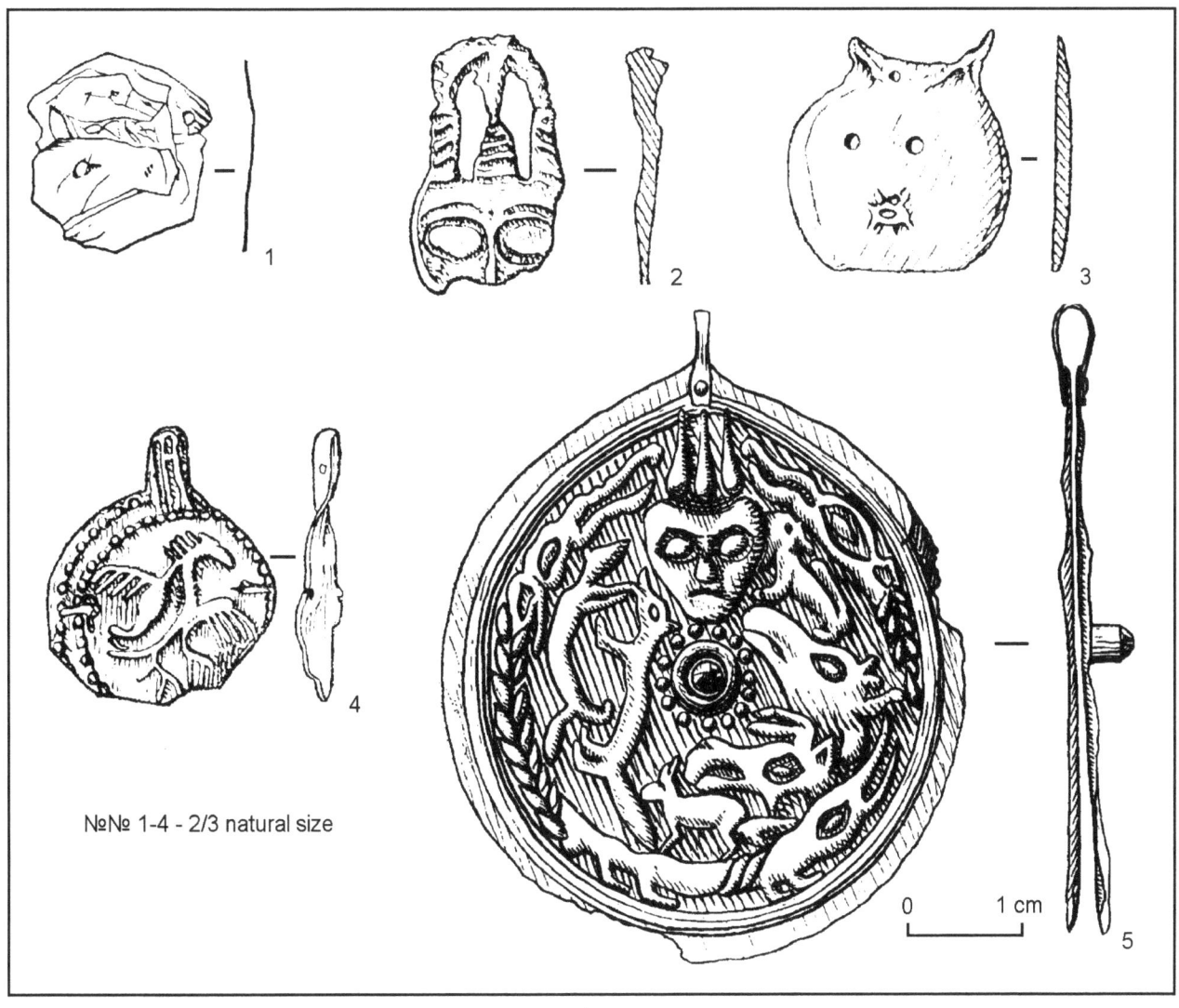

Figure 2. Cult artefacts from Kanin (1-4) end Unyin (5) caves (after Kanivets, 1962; 1964). Bronze, silver, glass.

are similar in the composition of the main species of sacrificial animals, though each has its own peculiarity.

Kanin cave differs by high content of bear bones (*Ursus arctos* L.; 38.3%), among which in greatest number are the fragments of skull and close lying cervical vertebrae (87.7% of the number of bear bones). Not numerous are the bones of elk (*Alces alces* L.; 15.53%), beaver (*Castor fiber* L.; 9.9%), reindeer (*Rangifer tarandus* L.; 5.74%). In the group of "fur" animals in greatest number are the bones of hare (*Lepus timidus* L.; 6.53%) and squirrel (*Sciurus vulgaris* L.; 6.46%). In only one case on the number of species (10 pieces), with small number of bone remains (2.96%) glutton (*Gulo gulo* L.) is noted.

In characterising the ideology of the Pechora Pre-Ural population very important are the findings of the mammoth bones (*Mammuthus primigenius* Blum.) in the medieval layer of the Kanin cave. They are represented mainly by tusk fragments (129 pieces) and teeth parts (29 pieces). The remaining skeleton fragments are rare (3 pieces). These findings are evidently not occasional; we may find explanations in the mythology of the Ob-Ugric and other northern peoples. By the way, a part of a mammoth tooth was found in the horizon of later sacrifices of Adak cave (Kanivets, Loginova, 1970, p.35).

For Unyin cave characteristic are reindeer bones (*Rangifer tarandus* L.; 33.1%). Less represented are the bone remains of beaver (*Castor fiber* L.; 14.3%), bear (*Ursus arctos* L.; 12.4%) and elk (*Alces alces* L.; 4.73%). On the number, from "fur" animals marten (*Martes martes* L.; 10.12%) and squirrel (*Sciurus vulgaris* L.; 5.0%) are singled out. As a reminder of vanished long ago ceremonial rites of human sacrifices which in ancient times existed in many peoples, including Finno-Ugric ones, are, evidently, findings of parts of human fingers (3 phalanges) and teeth (9 pieces) in the medieval layer of Unyin cave. They belonged to not less than two individuals (Kanivets, 1964, p.130, 131). Human sacrifices are also known from the materials of different epochs and kinds of archaeological sites on other Ural regions (settlements, burial grounds, fire-places) (Goldina, 1985, p.99-107). The motif of such a heathen rite has remained in the ethnography and folklore of the Ob-Uric peoples (Lepekhin, 1805, p.376, 377; Karjalainen, 1922, s.134-139; Kannisto, 1958, s.256-258; Kerezsi, 1990, s.18-23 and others). It existed, probably, in the post-archaeological

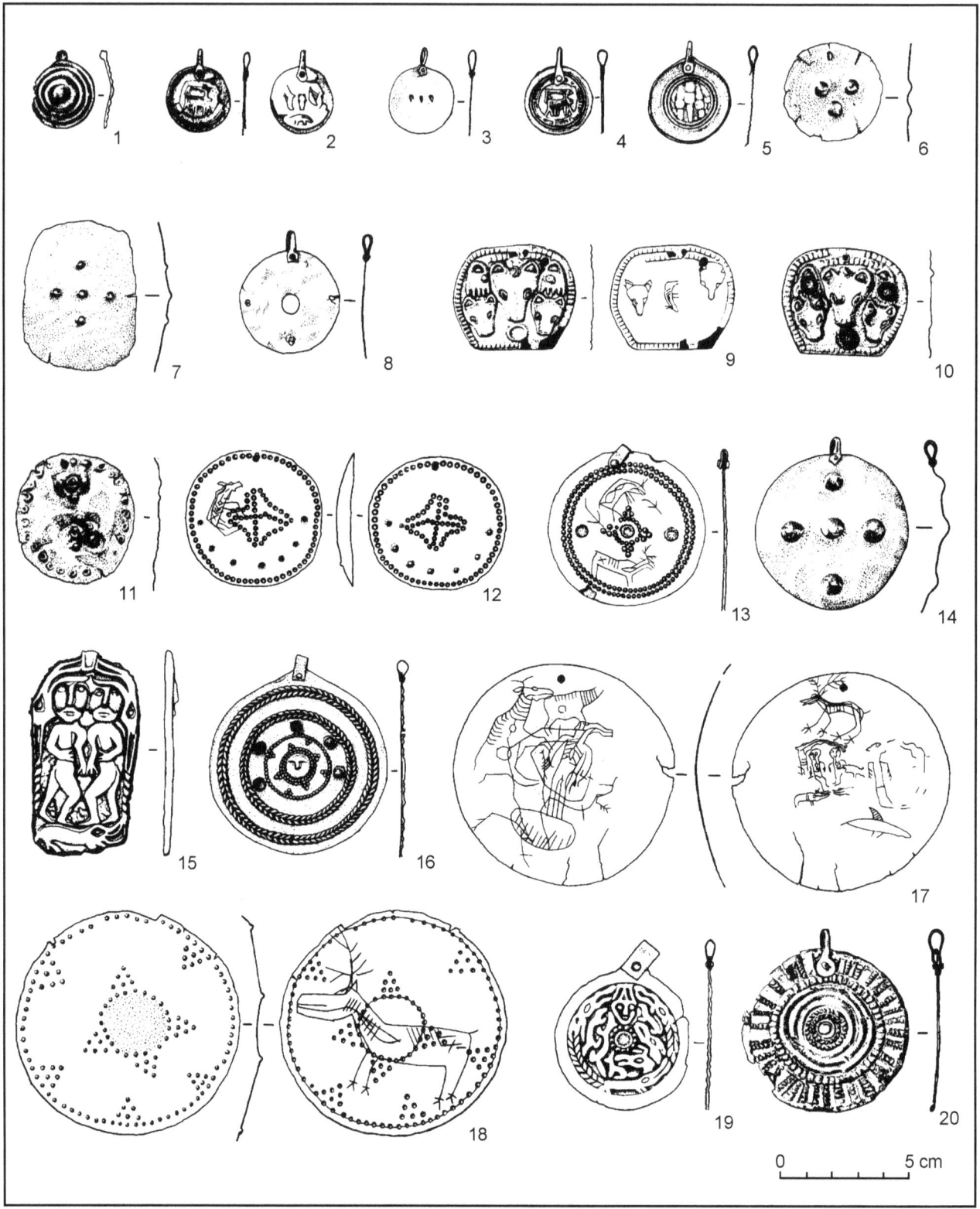

Figure 3. Cult artefacts from Eshmess cave. Bronze, silver, gilding.

period as well, but, evidently, later it acquired greater symbolic meaning and became a component part of heathen mystery.

The osteological material from Eshmess cave is notable for absolute prevailing of beaver (*Castor fiber* L.; 81.8%) bones. Most of them are skulls or their fragments (93.3%). The reindeer (*Rangifer tarandus* L.) bones are not numerous (5.5%). We should recognise considerable difference of Eshmess cave on the character of sacred actions performed with the beaver given preference to as compared to other sacrificial animals.

Moreover, Eshmess cave is different from other cave cult sites by the absence of abundant offerings of different decorations, implements of labour and household,

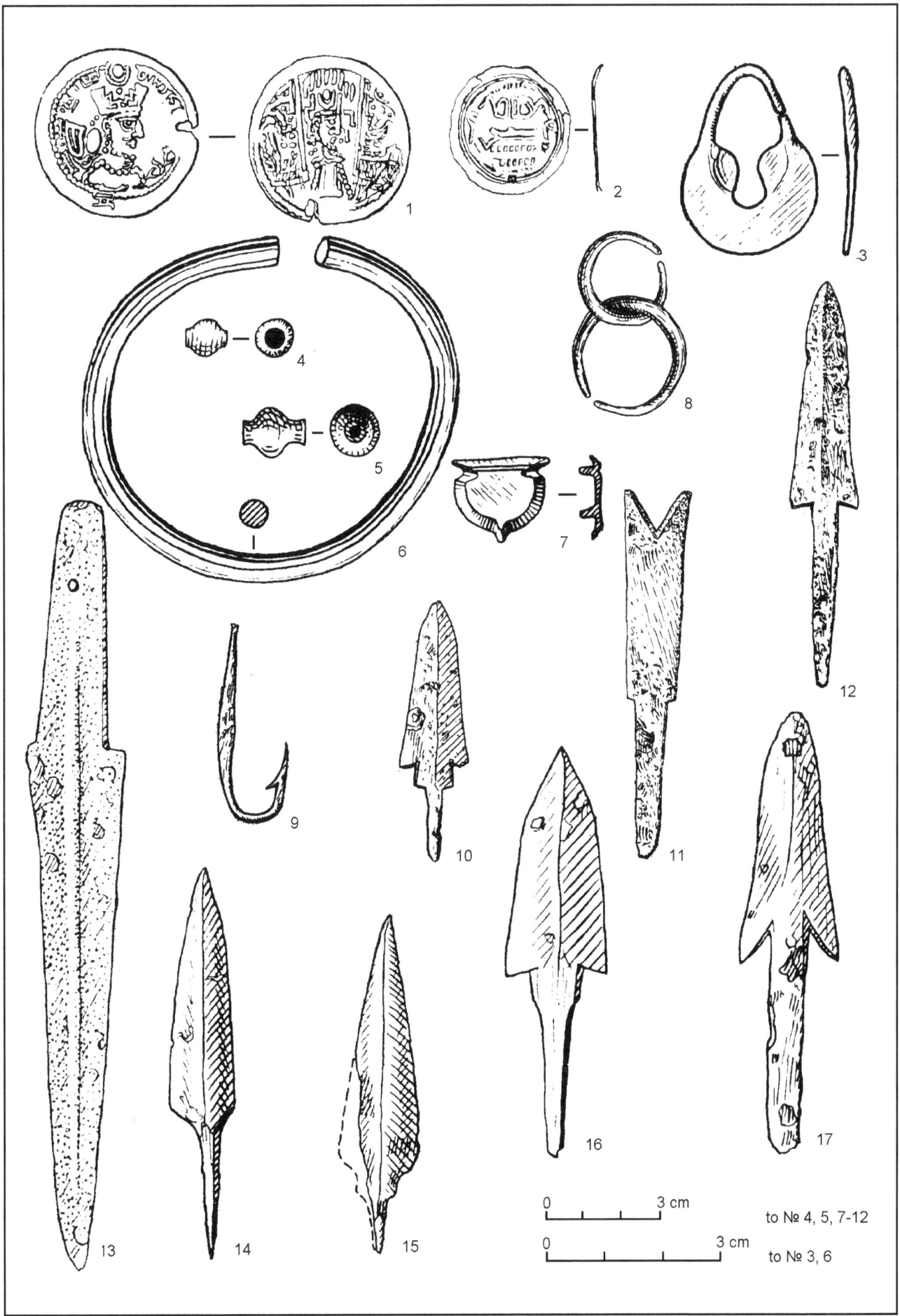

Figure 4. Implements of sacrificial places (after Kanivets, 1962; 1964). 1-3, 6, 7, 13-17 - Kanin cave; 4, 5, 8-12 - Unyin cave (1, 3, 4 - silver; 2 – silver, bronze; 5-8 - bronze; 9-17 - iron).

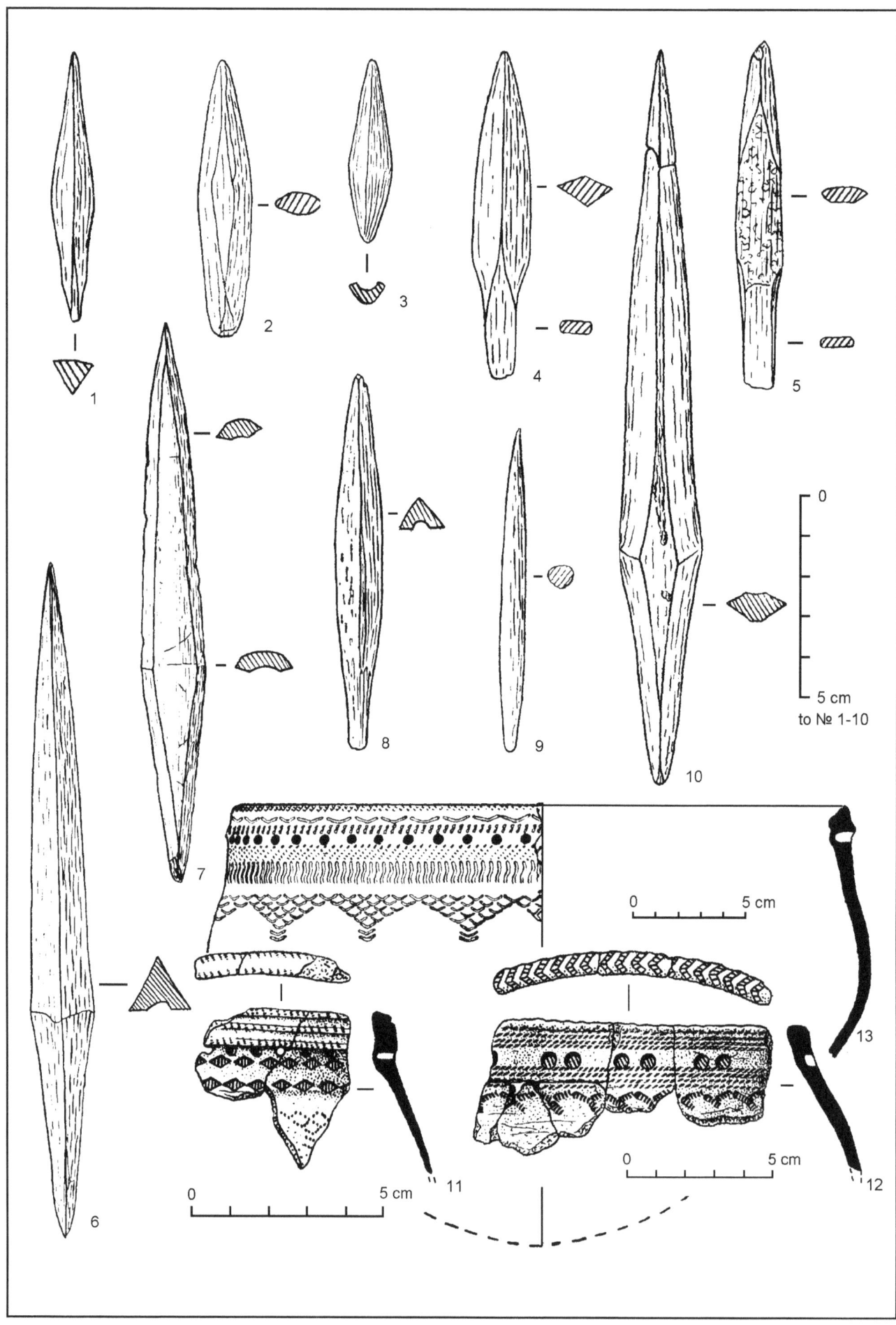

Figure 5. Implements of sacrificial places (after Kanivets, 1962; 1964). Unyin cave (1-12), Kanin cave (13). 1-10 – arrowheads, 11-13 – vessels (1-10 - bone, 11-13 - ceramics).

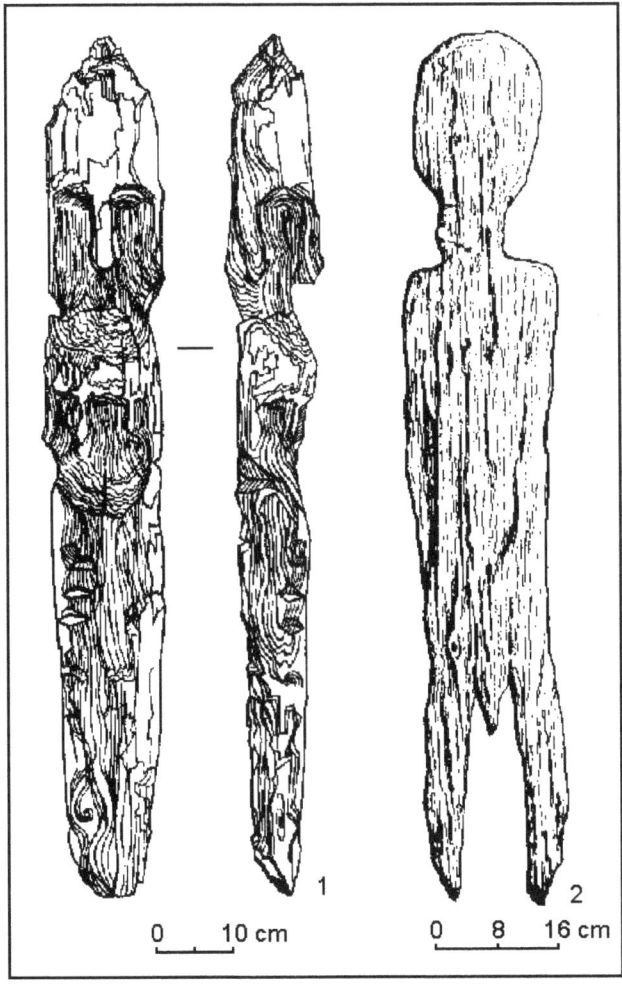

Figure 6. Eshmess cave. Idols. Wood.

ceramics, not numerous and similar bone remains, limited number of entire implements, and by its location in the secluded place far from the central river mains of the Pechora Pre-Ural area.

As said above, different metallic articles found at the grotto entrance of Eshmess cave were concentrated in a compact group. Possibly, at one time there was a ritual box for ritual articles being brought and kept there. Peculiarities of the archaeological material from Eshmess cave allow us to suggest that silver and bronze articles with clearly expressed solar and cosmological symbolics are not occasional or arbitrary set of articles. Uniformity of Eshmess metal manifested through morphological peculiarities and articles' semantics makes it possible to reconstruct their total character as a specially chosen cult complex created within a homogeneous group of tribes of the Pechora Pre-Urals and representing some finished whole. What is characteristic, one of silver pendants with gilding remains shows a man in a ritual ("dancing") pose, hands up, knees bent (fig.3, *11*). Evidently, this pendant is a stylised figurine of a mediator between the world of people and the world of spirits – "Eshmess shaman", a man performing ritual actions in front of idols asking for well-being for his people from spirits-protectors. The articles making a cult complex could quite well be of different time, different origin, but had their own sense, quite understandable and closely related to the world view of the mediator and his kinsmen.

The offerings to wooden idols standing in Eshmess cave consisted of bone arrow-heads and meat of sacrificial animals, with beaver prevailing. Maybe, Eshmess cave was used for the intercourse with the heavenly upper world and the underground kingdom, embodied in the zoomorphic images of a solar reindeer and bear (fig.3, *9, 10, 18*). The central part in the ritual action, evidently, took the intercourse with the world of the Universe, the address to the Mistress of the Universe, Mother-Mistress of the nature, animals and people, that was manifested in some attributes of the cult (fig.3, *16, 19).*

As distinct from Eshmess cave, the material complex of findings from Kanin, Unyin and Adak caves was formed throughout the V-XIII/XIV centuries A.D. It contained more numerous and diverse material, in composition and cultural respect, greatly differing from that of Eshmess cave (Kanivets, 1962, table I-XI; 1964, fig.34-45), which makes it difficult or, more probably, practically impossible to single out a separate cult complex functionally identical to the Eshmess one. Evidently, Kanin, Unyin and Adak caves should be combined into a special group of cult sites of the Pechora Pre-Ural area, where sacrifices were performed by different groups of population of the North Urals throughout a lone period of time.

The difference in materials of cave sacrificial places makes it possible to single out two main types in this category of medieval archaeological sites of the Pechora Pre-Ural area. The suggested typology based on morphological indications of the objects under study reveals "social" status of sacrificial places.

The first type is documented by cultural remains of Eshmess cave. It was a tribal sanctuary and referred to constant places of ancient magic rituals, which were performed in social interests by an elected representative – a shaman of the local group of the aboriginal population of the Pechora Pre-Ural area. Similarity with cultures of Sub-Arctic and Arctic zones of Euro-Asia is observed in the materials of the sanctuary. Especially vividly this similarity is seen in comparison with very rich materials of the completely studied overground inter-tribal Kheibidya-Pedar sacrificial place of the V-XIII/XIV centuries A.D. located in the northern part of the Bolshezemelskaya tundra (Murygin, 1984).

The second type is characterised by materials of Kanin, Unyin and Adak caves. They were intertribal worship places which had existed throughout many centuries and had been known to many generations of different ethnic population of the Pechora Pre-Ural and Ob Trans-Ural areas. Sacred actions here had individual (private) character and might be performed by any person without any shaman, who acted as a mediator between the people and the forces of the other world.

The study of the problem of special attitude of ancient population to such forms of relief development is a very important aspect of archaeological cave deposits analysis, which needs special discussion. This is shown from the cave archaeology of not only the Pechora Pre-Ural, but also of greater area of the Ural Euro-Asia, where high concentration of caves with archaeological sacrificial remains is observed. Thus, outside the Pechora Pre-Ural area archaeological remains of sacrifices of different times, as a rule, of the Middle Ages, are also in most cases associated to karst cavities. Among them are Shaitan, Laksei, Ushmin caves on the eastern slopes of the northern Urals, Gebauer, Chanven, Malo-Vakshur, Kamen Dyrovaty in the Middle Trans-Ural and Pre-Ural area and Temnaya cave in the southern part of the Northern Pre-Urals. I think, a group of Arctic sanctuaries of the Vaigach Island, characterised by the location of sacrificial places near the natural vertical downfalls of the earth-surface, having way out to sea in their lower part, also refers to this category of cult places.

Evidently, the use of caves and other underground cavities not only as short-time camp-sites or refuges, but mainly as specially chosen sacred places which served as a zone of communication between real and unreal upper and lower worlds of the Universe, is rather a specific feature of culture of the tribes that inhabited greater part of the Ural-Timan region, going far back into the ancient times.

Probably, the use of caves for sacrifices stopped in the Ural-Timan region at the end of the Middle Ages, but the worshipping of the former sacrificial caves and the knowledge on them was long kept in the memory of the peoples of the Northern Urals and even later. However, the places where religious heathen rites were performed are not limited here by mystic relation to only underground cavities. Here should be mentioned different sacrificial places and objects of worship associated to natural phenomena and details of overground landscape. These might be precipitous rocky exposures, rocky sheds and rocks cracks, hill-mounds, capes, relic isles of plants and others. Some of them refer not only to archaeological, but also to archaeologo-ethnographic sites, with material implements of relatively recent past included into the composition of material remains.

Author's address

Alexandr MURYGIN
Department of Archaeology
Institute of Language, Literature and History
26, Kommunisticheskaya str.
Syktyvkar 167982
Komi RUSSIA

Bibliography

GOLDINA, R.D., 1985, Lomovatovskaya cultura v Verhnem Prikamye. Irkutsk.

GUSLITSER, B.I. & PAVLOV P.Yu., 1988, Verkhnepaleoliticheskaya stoyanka Medvezhya peshchera (noviye danniye). In Materialy po arkheologii Evropeiskogo Severo-Vostoka 11, 5-18. Syktyvkar: AN SSSR, Komi nauchnyi centr.

KANIVETS, V.I., 1962, Prviye rezultati raskopok v Unyinskoi peshchere. In Materialy po arkheologii Evropeiskogo Severo-Vostoka 1, 103-144. Syktyvkar: AN SSSR, Komi Filial.

KANIVETS, V.I., 1964, Kaninskaya peshchera. Moscow: Nauka.

KANIVETS, V.I., 1971, Otchet o rabotakh I Pechorskogo arkheologicheskogo otryada v 1970 godu. - Arkhiv Komi filiala AN SSSR. - fond 5, opis 2, № 14. - 48 s.; Albom k otchetu. - fond 5, opis 2, № 15; Ego je. 1972, Otchet o rabotakh I Pechorskogo arkheologicheskogo otryada v 1971 godu. - Arkhiv Komi filiala AN SSSR. - fond 5, opis 2, № 47. - 33 s.; Albom k otchetu. - fond 5, opis 2, № 48;

KANIVETS, V.I. & LOGINOVA E.S., 1970, Otchet o rabotakh I Pechorskogo arkheologicheskogo otryada v 1969 godu. - Arkhiv Komi filiala AN SSSR. - fond 1, opis 13, № 198. - 77 s.; Albom k otchetu. - fond 1, opis 13, № 199.

KANNISTO, A., 1858, Materialien zur Mythologie der Wogulen. Memoires de la societe finno-ougrienne 113. Helsinki.

KARJALAINEN, K.F., 1922, Die Religion der Jugra-Volker. Finnisch-ugrische Forschungen 44. Helsinki, Porvoo.

KEREZSI, A., 1990, Arkhaicheskaya simvolika obryadov zhertvoprinosheniya u obskikh ugrov. In Congressus septimus internationalis fenno-ugristarum IV, 18-23. Debrecen.

LEPEKHIN, I.I., 1805, Dnevniye zapiski puteshestviya po raznym provintsiyam Rossiiskogo gosudarstva. Chast IV. Sankt-Peterburg.

MURYGIN, A.M., 1984, Kheibidya-Pedarskoye zhertvennoye mesto. Seria preprintov, Nauchniye doklady 144. Syktyvkar: AN SSSR, Komi Filial.

MURYGIN, A.M., 1987, Drevneye svyatilishche v Eshmesskoi peshchere. In Trudy AN SSSR, Komi filial, Institut yazyka, literatury i istorii 39, 35-42. Syktyvkar: AN SSSR Komi Filial.

MURYGIN, A.M., 1992, Pechorskoye Priural'ye: epoha srednevekov'ya. Moscow: Nauka.

PAVLOV, P. & INDRELID, S., 2000, Human occupation in Northeastern Europe during the period 35.000 - 18.000 bp. In Hanters of the Golden Age, edited by W. Roebroeks, M. Mussi, J. Svoboda & K. Fennema. University of Leiden, p. 165-172.

PAVLOV, P. Yu. & L'ubashkov V., 1998, Pesh'ernoye jertvennoye mesto v nijnem techenii r.Podcherem. In Geologo-arheologicheskiye issledovaniya v Timano-Severo-Ural'skom regione, 83-84. Syktyvkar: RAN, Komi nauchnyi centr.

RYABTSEVA, E.N. & SEMENOV, V.A., 1990, Adakskoye peshchernoye svyatilishche na reke Use i problemy osvoyeniya Poyarnogo Urala. Kratkiye soobshcheniya Instituta arkheologii AN SSSR 200, 66-72. Moscow: Nauka.

SEMENOV, V.A. & RYABTSEVA, E.N., 1986, Raskopki i razvedki v Komi ASSR. In Arkeologicheskiye otkrytiya 1984 goda, 28-29. Moscow: Nauka.

SEMENOV, V.A., 1987, Raskopki v Intinskom raione Komi ASSR. In Arkheologicheskiye otkrytiya 1985 goda, 35. Moscow: Nauka.

THE ETHNIC PICTURE OF THE GREAT HUNGARIAN PLAIN IN THE 6TH–9TH CENTURIES. METHODS AND POSSIBILITIES

Lívia BENDE, Gábor LORINCZY & Csaba SZALONTAI

Résumé : Image de la composition ethnique de la Grande Plaine hongroise dans le VIe– IXe siècle. Méthodes et possibilités d'approche. Dans les dernières décennies plusieurs ouvrages de synthèse modernes ont été publiés sur l'histoire des Avars dans le bassin des Carpates. Dans notre exposé nous voudrions en donner une image plus précise et plus nuancée, en partie pour la modifier et la compléter. Cela apparaît d'autant plus nécessaire que la partie orientale de l'Empire Avar, à l'est du Danube, est assez peu représentée dans ces travaux comme dans les catalogues consultés habituellement par les chercheurs internationaux. Puisqu'il n'existe aucune source écrite originaire de cette période concernant ce territoire, au cours de notre recherche nous avons en partie réévalué les résultats des anciennes fouilles, mais c'est aussi à l'aide de récentes découvertes archéologiques que nous avons essayé d'établir une chronologie différente par rapport à celles qui existaient déjà. En outre nous tentons également de présenter l'histoire ethnique de la Grande Plaine hongroise dans le VIe – IXe siècle en utilisant de façon plus importante les différentes données des rites funéraires (différences dans l'orientation, enterrement partiel des animaux, tombes à niche latérale et frontale).

Abstract: In the recent decades several modern summarizing works have been published on the history of the Avars in the Carpathian Basin. In our presentation we would like to make this picture more precise, partly modify it and add new data to it. This is necessary also because this part of the Avarian Empire (east of the Danube) is less represented in the mentioned works and catalogues used by researchers of different countries. We do not have literary sources on the period and territory in question, so in the course of our work we re-evaluated the old find material and tried to make a chronology, partly differing from the classical one, on the basis of new finds. Our goal was to display the ethnic history of the Great Hungarian Plain in the 6th–9th century using more widely than before the data of the burial rite (differences in orientation, partial animal burials, catacomb and niche graves etc.)

Due to the analysis of the growing archaeological material (GARAM, É., 1995, KISS, A., 1996 etc.) and new interpretations of literary sources (SZÁDECZKY-KARDOSS, S., 1998) and, besides, the examination of the burials rites and the dead cults (Lőrinczy, G., 1992, Lőrinczy, G., 1992a, LŐRINCZY, G., 1994, Némethi, M. & Klima, L., 1992, Tomka, P., 1972, Tomka, P., 1975, Tomka, P., 1978, TOMKA, P., 1992 etc.) make it more and more possible to separate archaeologically peoples and groups of people – among them that of the Avarian Age – who played role in the history of the Migration Period in the Carpathian Basin.

In connection with the Avarian-Byzantine wars literary sources frequently mention beside the Avarians also Slavs, Gepidians, Kutrigurs. If we attempt to define the geographic situation of these peoples inside the Carpathian Basin, the history of their settlement, then, beside the find material, the most significant evidence can be gathered from the examination of different burial customs (taking into consideration that to-date the number of settlement excavations is rather low.)

Concerning the 6th–7th century we can outline the territory occupied by Slavs/Dulebs in the region of the rivers Zala and Mura (SZŐKE, B. M., 1994, SZŐKE, B. M., 1995); the settlement center of the so called Keszthely Culture (a very complex population with Antique roots) at the western part of Lake Balaton (MÜLLER, R., 1987, MÜLLER, R., 1992, MÜLLER, R., 1996, Straub, P., 1999, Straub, P., 1999a); the territory of a relatively compact common communities of Inner Asian origin in the northeastern third of Transdanubia (the territory west of the Danube) (Némethi, M. & Klima, L., 1992, 177) and the territory of their aristocracy between the Danube and Tisza (Kiss, A., 1995, 138–143); the region of the Early Avarian Age Germans/Gepidians at the right bank of the Danube (KISS, A., 1992, 50–58, KISS, A., 1996, 305) and in the central part of Transylvania (Bóna, I., 1978, Kiss, A., 1992, 63, CSEH, J., 1993); the territory of the steppe groups of East European origin. In our presentation we shall deal mainly with this territory east of river Tisza (Lőrinczy, G., 1992, Lőrinczy, G., 1992a, LŐRINCZY, G., 1994).

The group of East European origin settling east of the Tisza can be best characterized archaeologically by the elements of the burial customs. It is customary that they place parts of animals into the graves, that is to say, animals (sheep, cattle, horse) were skinned so that beside the skull feet were left in the skin by cutting the legs. The dead were put into grave oriented to northeast or east with their head. Several types of graves in use served the purpose of the separation of the dead and the sacrificial animal buried together with him or her (so called graves with "ears", graves with shoulders on two sides, niche-graves and catacombs). In most of cases ceramic vessels were placed at the head of the dead.

This ethnic group appeared and settled in the Carpathian Basin after the Gepidian–Langobardian–Avarian war. The territory they occupied corresponded to the agricultural region of the Gepidians along the left bank Tisza valley bordered by the so called Csörsz Ditch from the east.

This occupation is marked by the symmetric belt, shoe and horse-harness decorations with mostly masque patterns of the so called Martynovka type. Burials containing parts of horses, but without iron stirrups also can be dated to the start of this period (Lőrinczy, G., 1996, 185).

The steppe population migrating to the valley of the Tisza started to spread its power: in the first third of the 7th century only slowly, but after the defeat of the Avarians by the Byzantine army in 626, gradually they occupied more and more territories to the east and north. In the first third of the 7th century a new migration wave of a relative ethnic group must have followed.

On the basis of the complex analysis of the archaeological material and that of the burial rite we can determine that the population east of the Tisza is strikingly similar to the archaeological heritage and dead cult known at the ethnic groups of the South Russian steppe in the Bug–Dniepr–Sivash or North Pontic region, and that of the Volga and Kuban region (Somogyi, P., 1987).

At the present stage of the research we are not able to connect our group to this or that above mentioned population of the 6th century, but we can make difference between them and the Avarians, Slavs, Gepidians of the Avarian Age. We must add that Avarians of Khagan Bajan must have swept along with themselves several small ethnic groups from the steppe in 567 to the territory of the Carpathian Basin.

In the middle – last third of the 7th century a new population arrived to the Carpathian Basin, presumably in several waves. This group is characterized by new costume, weapons and several new burial practices not customary before in this region. Judging from the archaeological finds, their leaders settled in the eastern stripe of Transdanubia. At the same time the layer of common people occupied the whole territory of the Carpathian Basin, even those parts that were not or were only temporarily occupied in the Early Avarian Age (BÓNA, I., 1984).

Despite of the characteristic changes of the find material, there are several connecting points between the Early Avarian and later population in certain elements of the burial rites observed east of the Tisza, especially in the territory between rivers Körös, Maros and Tisza. These are such elements as the surviving practice of catacomb graves, the placing of the rump (sacrum and tail vertebra) of the sheep as grave-food and the vessels situated at the head of the dead (BENDE, L., 2000, 250).

However, the quantity of the sacrificed animals became much lower in the Late Avarian Age, which can be the consequence of the decreasing livestock. The background of this phenomenon can be explained by climatic or economic changes, and we must not forget about the role of the new population appearing in the Carpathian Basin in the last third of the 7th century. Due to these changes communities living along the Tisza as a compact block in the Early Avarian Age could have started to split and move leaving the cemeteries used earlier and starting new cemeteries at the relatively distant territories east of the Tisza. This population of the Early Avarian Age with its decreasing livestock, judging from the disappearance of several grave forms (e.g. niche-graves) and the beginning of new burial practices (deepening of the ends or corners of the grave, the appearance of grave constructions), started to mix with the new settlers. It is not easy to trace this process and is hardly possible on the basis of the unified and characteristic find material common in the whole Carpathian Basin of the Late Avarian Age. It is also significant, that in the second half of the Avarian Age, among the people buried in catacomb graves the percentage of the older generations (among them men playing – judging from their grave-goods – important role in the society) was growing. This phenomenon determined by age and sex shows the conservative attitude towards the archaic grave shape amidst the social and ethnic changes (BENDE, L., 2000).

The change between the Early and Late Avarian Age is marked also by the modification of the orientation: in the late cemeteries the western and northwestern orientation starts to dominate (the dead of the early period were oriented to the east).

We have only little information on the ethnic composition, social structure of the Late Avarian population. Titles mentioned in the literary sources of the end of the 8th century (Khagan, Jugurrus, Tudun, Katun, Capcan) show the differentiation of the leading layer of the society. Regional differences of the material culture, known from the earlier periods, disappeared, at the same time we can determine several workshop centres on the basis of the typological analysis of the find material (Bende, L., 1998, Fancsalszky, G., 1999, FANCSALSZKY, G., 2000, Kiss, G., 1991, Kiss, G., 1993, Kiss, G., 1996, Kiss, G., 1998, Szalontai, Cs., 1995, Szalontai, Cs., 1996 etc.). In Transdanubia we certainly meet new ethnic elements: beside the Avarians, Slavic finds material appears more and more characteristically (SZŐKE, B. M., 1994). But in the Avarian cemeteries of Transdanubian peripheries we observe such new burial practices (eastern and southern orientation of the dead, placing of parts of animals into the grave, horse burials) that earlier characterized only the territories east of Tisza (KISS, G., 1996). In the Great Hungarian Plain and especially east of the Tisza we, similarly, find the features referring to a possibly different ethnic background not in the find material. At the same time in the archaeozoological material of the cemeteries there are significant differences in the species and parts of animals used as grave-food. That is to say, in the second half of the Avarian Age, the examination of the burial customs plays an even more significant role than the analysis of other ethnic features, in order to outline the possible moves of populations. Approaching the end of the period we have less and less characteristic elements in the material culture.

After the Frankish wars the Avarian Khaganate split and the ethnocultural development of the Avarian territory followed two directions. Transdanubia became the part of the Frankish Empire under the name of Oriens. Here we have archaeological evidence of a new cultural unit based on several ethnic components, in which beside the surviving Avarians the Slavs played an important role. Also a significant role was played by the elements of

Frankish, Karantanian and Bavarian culture (SZŐKE, B. M., 1992, SZŐKE, B. M., 1994). So, while the culture of Transdanubia was developing under undisputedly western influence, at the same time east of the Danube different tendencies dominated.

Today it became evident that Avarian population did not disappear from the eastern part of the Carpathian Basin as a consequence of wars and most part of the population continued its living at the same place. However, the jewellery centres ceased to function, but the products of the 8th century flourishing metal workshops were still in use until the middle of the 9th century. The material culture becoming poorer and poorer, the total lack of new objects, the use of less and less metal – everything refers to the fact that these populations lived separated from the outside world without exterior impacts (Szalontai, Cs., 1992, Szalontai, Cs., 1995, SZALONTAI, Cs., 1996).

Earlier the research suggested a significant Bulgarian Slavic or Slavic occupation, but today it became certain that there is no archaeological evidence supporting it east of the Danube. That is to say, suggestions on the Bulgarian dominance of the Carpathian Basin and the continuos infiltration of the Slavs cannot be supported. Accordingly, the hypotheses about the absorption of the Avarians by the Slavs lack any evidence (SZŐKE, B. M., 1993, Szalontai, Cs., 2000).

Hungarian conquerors arriving here in the end of the 9th century found this situation. Their appearance fundamentally changed the ethnic picture of the territory and that of the political structure of the Carpathian Basin.

Authors' addresses

Lívia BENDE
Móra Ferenc Múzeum
6701 Szeged
Pf. 474 HUNGARY
E-mail: l_bende@mfm.u-szeged.hu

Gábor LŐRINCZY
Móra Ferenc Múzeum
6701 Szeged
Pf. 474 HUNGARY
E-mail: lorinczy@mfm.u-szeged.hu

Csaba SZALONTAI
Móra Ferenc Múzeum
6701 Szeged
Pf. 474 HUNGARY
E-mail: szalonta@mfm.u-szeged.hu

Bibliography

BENDE, L., 1998, A pitvarosi késő avar kori temető 51. sírja. (Adatok a késő avar kori lószerszámok díszítéséhez.) — Das Grab 51 im spätawarenzeitlichen Gräberfeld von Pitvaros. (Beiträge zur Verzierung des spätawarenzeitlichen Pferdegeschirre.) *A Móra Ferenc Múzeum Évkönyve – Studia Archaeologica* 4, p. 195–230.

BENDE, L., 2000, Fülkesírok a pitvarosi avar kori temetőben. Adatok a fülkés és lószerszámos temetkezések kronológiájához. — Stollengräber im awarenzeitlichen Gräberfeld von Pitvaros. Angaben zur Chronologie der Stollengräber und Bestattungen mit Pferdegeschirr. In *Hadak útján*, edited by L. Bende, G. Lőrinczy & Cs. Szalontai. Szeged, p. 241–279.

BÓNA, I., 1978, Erdélyi gepidák – Tisza menti gepidák. *A Magyar Tudományos Akadémia II. Osztályának Közleményei* 27, p. 123–170.

BÓNA, I., 1984, A népvándorláskor és a korai középkor története Magyarországon. In *Magyarország története I.*, edited by Gy. Székely, Budapest, p. 265–374.

CSEH, J., 1993, Gepida továbbélés. In *Bóna, I., Cseh, J., Nagy, M., Tomka, P. & Tóth, Á.: Hunok–Gepidák–Langobárdok.* Szeged, p. 77–78.

FANCSALSZKY, G., 1999, Avar öv — avar griff — avar társadalom. *Életünk* 1999:2, p. 193–224.

FANCSALSZKY, G., 2000, Állat- és emberábrázolás a késő avar kori öntött bronz övvereteken (1993–1999). — Tier- und Menschendarstellungen auf den spätawarenzeitlichen gegossenen bronzenen Gürtelbeschlägen (1993–1999). In *Hadak útján*, edited by L. Bende, G. Lőrinczy & Cs. Szalontai. Szeged, p. 285–310.

GARAM, É., 1995, *Das awarenzeitliche Gräberfeld von Tiszafüred.* Cemeteries of the Avar Period (567–829) in Hungary. Vol. 3. Budapest.

KISS, G., 1991, A Szombathely-Kőszegi úti avar lovassír (A késő avar négy- és ötkaréjos lószerszámveretek). — Das awarische Reitergrab von Szombathely-Kőszegi út. (Die spätawarenzeitlichen vier- und fünfblättrigen Pferdegeschirrbeschläge). *A Móra Ferenc Múzeum Évkönyve* 1984/85-2, p. 431–462.

KISS, A., 1992, Germanen im awarenzeitlichen Karpetenbecken. In *Awarenforschungen I.*, edited by F. Daim. Wien, p. 35–134.

KISS, G., 1993, A vasasszonyfai avar temető lovassírjai. (A késő avar kori kétkaréjos és lapos rozettás lószerszámveretek). — Die Reiterbestattungen des awarischen Gräberfeldes von Vasasszonyfa (Die spätawarenzeitlichen Pferdegeschirrbeschläge mit Zweiblätterform und flacher Rosettenform). *A Herman Ottó Múzeum Évkönyve* 30–31, p. 197–224.

KISS, A., 1995, Tanulmányok a kora avar kori kunbábonyi vezérsírról. — Studien zum Fürstengrab von Kunbábony aus der Frühawarenzeit. *A Móra Ferenc Múzeum Évkönyve – Studia Archaeologica* 1, p. 131–149.

KISS, A., 1996, *Das awarenzeitlich gepidische Gräberfeld von Kölked-Feketekapu A.* Monographien zur Frühgeschichte und Mittelalterarchäologie 2, Studien zur Archäologie der Awaren 5, Innsbruck.

Kiss, G., 1996, A lukácsházi avar temető 8. számú lovassírja. A késő avar tausírozott vasfalerák. — Reitergrab des 8 des awarenzeitlichen Gräberfeldes Lukácsháza-Hegyalja dűlő. *Savaria Pars Archaeologica* 22/3 (1992–1995) p. 107–143.

KISS, G. 1996, Diesseits und jenseits der Donau. Über etliche Bestattungssitten in W- und N-Avaria. In *Ethnische und kulturelle Verhältnisse an der mittleren Donau vom 6. bis zum 11. Jahrhundert*, edited by D. Bialeková & J. Zábojník. Bratislava, p. 167–178.

KISS, G., 1998, A késő avar kori állatfejes övforgók és akasztóveretek. — Spätawarenzeitliche Gürtel- und Hängebeschläge mit Tierkopfverzierung. *A Móra Ferenc Múzeum Évkönyve – Studia Archaeologica* 4, p. 461–495.

LŐRINCZY, G., 1992, Megjegyzések a kora avar kori temetkezési szokásokhoz. A tájolás. — Anmerkungen zu den frühawarenzeitlichen Bestattungssitten. Die Orientierung. *A*

Jósa András Múzeum Évkönyve 30–32 (1987–1989) p. 161–172.

LŐRINCZY, G., 1992a, Vorläufiger Bericht über die Freilegung des Gräberfeldes aus dem 6–7. Jahrhundert in Szegvár-Oromdűlő. (Weitere Daten zur Interpretierung und Bewertung der partiellen Tierbestattungen in der frühen Awarenzeit.) *Communicationes Archaeologicae Hungariae*, p. 81–124.

LŐRINCZY, G., 1994, Megjegyzések a kora avar kori temetkezési szokásokhoz. (A fülkesíros temetkezés.) — Bemerkungen zu den frühawarenzeitlichen Bestattungssitten. (Die Stollengräber.) In *A kőkortól a középkorig*, edited by G. Lőrinczy, Szeged, p. 311–335.

LŐRINCZY, G., 1996, Kora avar kori sír Szentes-Borbásföldről. — Ein frühawarenzeitliches Grab in Szentes-Borbásföld. *A Móra Ferenc Múzeum Évkönyve – Studia Archaeologica* 2, p. 177–190.

MÜLLER, R., 1987, Die spätrömische Festung Valcumam Plattensee. Fiedhöfe der Keszthely-Kultur. In *Germanen, Hunnen und Awaren*, edited by W. Menghin, T. Springer & E. Wamers. Nünberg, p. 270–284.

MÜLLER, R., 1992, Neue archäologische Funde der Keszthely-Kultur. In *Awarenforschungen I.*, edited by F. Daim. Wien, p. 251–308.

MÜLLER, R., 1996, Keszthely kultúra. In *Évezredek üzenete a láp világából. (Régészeti kutatások a Kis-Balaton területén 1979–1992)*, edited by L. Költő & L. Vándor. Kaposvár–Zalaegerszeg, p. 98–102.

NÉMETHI, M. & Klima, L., 1992, Kora avar kori lovas temetkezések. — Frühawarenzeitliche Reiterbestattungen. *A Jósa András Múzeum Évkönyve* 30–32 (1987–89) p. 173–244.

SOMOGYI, P., 1987, Typologie, Chronologie und Herkunft der Maskenbeschläge. Zu den archäologischen Hinterlassenschaften osteuropäischer Reiterhirten aus der pontischen Steppe im 6. Jahrhundert. *Archaeologica Austriaca* 71, p. 121–154.

STRAUB, P., 1999, Újabb adalék a Keszthely-kultúra eredetéhez egy fenékpusztai sír kapcsán. — Ein neuer Beitrag zum Ursprung der Keszthely-Kultur anhand eines Grabes von Fenékpuszta. *Zalai Múzeum* 9, p. 181–193.

STRAUB, P., 1999a, A Keszthely-kultúra kronológiai és etnikai hátterének újabb alternatívája. — Die neuere Alternative des chronologischen und ethnischen Hintergrundes der Kesthely-Kultur. *Zalai Múzeum* 9, p. 195–224.

SZÁDECZKY-KARDOSS, S., 1998, *Az avar történelem forrásai 557–806-ig.* Magyar Őstörténeti Könyvtár 12, Budapest.

SZALONTAI, Cs., 1992, Megjegyzések az Alföld IX. századi történetéhez II. (Szarvas-Kákapuszta késő avar temetője). — Anmerkungen zur Geschichte der Tiefebene im 9. Jahrhundert II. (Das awarische Gräberfeld von Szarvas-Kákapuszta Kettőshalom). *A Jósa András Múzeum Évkönyve* 30–32 (1987–89), p. 309–347.

SZALONTAI, Cs., 1995, A késő avar kori liliomos övveretek. — Die spätawarenzeitliche mit Lilien verzierte Gürtelbeschläge. *Somogyi Múzeumok Közleményei 11 (A népvándorláskor fiatal kutatói 5. találkozójának előadásai)* p. 127–143.

SZALONTAI, Cs., 1996, Az Alföld a 9. században. In *Honfoglaló magyarság, Árpád-kori magyarság. Antropológia–régészet–történelem*, edited by Gy. Pálfi, Gy. L. Farkas & E. Molnár. Szeged, p. 23–41.

SZALONTAI, Cs., 1996, „Hohenbergtől Záhonyig". Egy késő avar kori övverettípus vizsgálata. — „Von Hohenberg bis Záhony". Untersuchung eines spätawarenzeitlichen Gürtelbeschlagtyps. *Savaria Pars Archaeologica* 22/3 (1992–1995) p. 145–162.

SZALONTAI, Cs., 2000, Kritische Bemerkungen zur Rolle der Bulgaren im 9. Jahrhundert in der Großen Ungarischen Tiefebene und in Siebenbürgen. — Kritikai észrevételek a bolgárok szerepéről a 9. századi Nagyalföldön és Erdélyben. *A Móra Ferenc Múzeum Évkönyve – Studia Archaeologica* 6, p. 263–286.

SZŐKE, B. M., 1992, Die Beziehungen zwischen dem oberen Donautal und Westungarn in der ersten Hälfte des 9. Jahrhunderts (Frauentrachtzubehör und Schmuck). In *Awarenforschungen II.*, edited by F. Daim. Wien, p. 841–968.

SZŐKE, B. M., 1993, A 9. századi Nagyalföld lakosságáról. — Die Bevölkerung der Großen Ungarischen Tiefebene im 9. Jahrhundert. In *Az Alföld a 9. században*, edited by G. Lőrinczy. Szeged, p. 33–43.

SZŐKE, B. M., 1994, A népvándorlás kor és a korai középkor története Nagykanizsán és környékén. — History of the Migration Period and Early Middle Ages in Nagykanizsa and its surroundings. In *Nagykanizsa története*, edited by M. Rózsa. Nagykanizsa, p. 145–214.

SZŐKE, B. M., 1995, Avari e Slavi. In *Gli avari. Un popolo d'Europa*, edited by G. C. Menis. Udine, p. 49–55.

TOMKA, P., 1972, Adatok a Kisalföld avar kori népességének temetkezési szokásaihoz I. Kés a sírban. — Beiträge zu den Bestattungensarten der Bevölkerung von Kisalföld in der Awarenzeit I. Messer im Grab. *Arrabona* 14, p. 27–75.

TOMKA, P., 1975, Adatok a Kisalföld avar kori népességének temetkezési szokásaihoz. II. (Tájolás) — Beiträge zu den Bestattungensarten der Bevölkerung von Kisalföld in der Awarenzeit. II. (Orientierung). *Arrabona* 17, p. 5–90.

TOMKA, P., 1978, Adatok a Kisalföld avar kori népességének temetkezési szokásaihoz. III. Koporsóhasználat a tápi temetőben. — Angaben zum Bestattungstrauchtum der Bevölkerung von Kleine Alföld in der Awarenzeit. III. Sarggebrauch im Gräberfelde von Táp. *Arrabona* 19–20 (1977–78) p. 17–108.

TOMKA, P., 1992, Awarische Grabsitten — Abriss der Forschunggeschichte bis 1963. In *Awarenforschungen II*, edited by F. Daim. Wien, p. 921–1069.

FOR HOTCHPOT AND THE DEVIL THE RITUAL RELEVANCE OF MEDIEVAL BRONZE CAULDRONS

Vincent VAN VILSTEREN

Abstract: This contribution deals with late medieval and early modern bronze cooking pots from the northern part of The Netherlands. Although their name 'Spanish army pots' suggests a Mediterranean origin, they are in fact native products. The cauldrons, dating between the 13th and the 17th/18th century, are to be interpreted as offerings. This conclusion is based on the following arguments:
1. The cauldrons are never found in association with settlement refuse.
2. The number of finds is far too great for them all to have been accidentally lost or casually forgotten.
3. Almost all cauldrons were found in a wet context (i.e. bogs and stream valleys).
4. There is evidence that occasionally the cauldrons were deliberately damaged before deposition.
5. The remaining value of a damaged bronze cauldron was too great simply to throw it away.
6. The cauldrons in all their aspects fit extremely well in the long prehistoric tradition of depositing offerings in wet parts of the landscape.

Thus, the deposition of the cauldrons is a continuation of a pre-Christian habit. The Catholic Church never succeeded in a total banning of what was regarded as superstitious practices. The intentions of the offering (ghosts, the devil, home-made gods?) touch on the world of magic.

Résumé : Cette contribution traite des marmites en bronze de la fin du moyen-age et le début de l'époque moderne trouvées au nord des Pays-Bas. Bien que leur nom 'marmites de l'armée Espagnole' suggère une origine méditerranéenne, ce sont des produits locaux. Les chaudrons qui datent du 13e au 17e/18e siècle doivent interprétés comme des offrandes. Cette conclusion est basée sur les arguments suivants:
1. Les chaudrons n'ont jamais été trouvés en combinaison avec des résidus de foyers d'habitation.
2. Le nombre de trouvailles est trop élevé pour qu'elles aient toutes été perdues accidentellement ou oubliées par hasard.
3. Presque tous les chaudrons ont été trouvés dans des endroits humides (tourbières et vallées des rivières).
4. Il est évident que parfois les chaudrons ont été abîmés de propos délibéré avant d'être déposés.
5. La valeur importante d'un chaudron en bronze, même abîmé, était trop grande pour qu'on le jette.
6. Par leurs différents aspects, les chaudrons s'intègrent parfaitement dans la longue tradition préhistorique du dépôt d'offrandes dans des parties humides de ces régions.

Donc, le dépôt de chaudrons est la continuation d'une habitude pré-chrétienne. L'église catholique n'a jamais réussi à bannir totalement ce qu'elle considérait comme des pratiques superstitieuses. Les intentions d'offrandes (esprits, diable, dieux faits-maison?) touchent au monde de la magie.

INTRODUCTION

At first glance a contribution on late and post-medieval bronze cooking-pots seems rather superfluous. About thirty years ago Drescher in a number of articles thoroughly investigated these cauldrons. He focussed his in-depth study on the subject mainly on Germany, Denmark and the Netherlands. Since then only a limited number of cauldrons have been added to the set of data, but these have not altered any of the conclusions of Drescher with regards to the typology and the dating. They still stand strong.

But Drescher being very much a museum-man with a art-historical background did not pay very much attention to the distribution pattern and the find circumstances of the individual cauldrons. Studying these aspects of bronze pots in the Dutch province of Drenthe reveals a surprising view, which raises many new questions. It also appears that the finds from Drenthe show an exceptionally high degree of damaging, an aspect that slipped Drescher's attention. The nature of the damaging is rather suspect in a number of cases. Both the find circumstances and the damaging justify a new essay on the bronze cooking pots, which will shed a whole new light on the interpretation of these utensils.

BRONZE CAULDRONS

In fact the bronze cauldron is nothing more than a solid piece of medieval cooking utensil. Standing on its three legs it is the less vulnerable equivalent of the earthenware pots. Usually it has two hooked ears, to which an iron handle was attached. This mostly twisted suspension by which the pot could be hanged over the fire, due to corrosion has only seldom survived the lengthy stay in the ground. Different sizes can be encountered, small ones containing only half a litre up to big ones that can hold more than ten litres. Some of the later types have one or two horizontal ridges around the belly that are purely decorative. In contrast, occasionally (the remnant of) a vertical ridge shows where the two halves of the mould joined together. Only very rarely the casting residue is still present at the centre of the bottom of the cauldron. The method of production of the cauldrons is well known from

Figure 1. An old stereophoto shows that in 1873 the Drents Museum already had seven Spanish pots in its collection.

a 12th-century description by the monk Theophilus[1] and by excavation of workshops where bronze pots were cast.[2] The craftsmen sometimes put a sort of signature on their product, the so-called house-mark. In Northern Germany the towns often prescribed this; in Holland this was not the case. If present (in Holland in 30% and in Germany in 60% of the cases) the house-mark is always to be found on the outer rim next to one of the ears.

Dating the cauldrons by typology is a hazardous matter, as the shape of the pots developed only very slowly. The oldest ones, dated to around 1200, still display an almost spherical outline. Their surface seems to be chiselled, the vertical ridge is still lacking and the ears generally are not hooked, but more rounded. From the 14th century onwards all the pots have hooked ears, while in the late 15th and 16th century the pots very gradually widen more and more.[3]

Analysis of the bronze shows that usually the percentage of copper varies from 75 up to 85. The rest is a mixture of lead and tin.[4] In medieval documents in The Netherlands the cauldrons are simply called 'metal pot' or 'copper pot', whereas in the German territories we often find them described as 'Grape'. Old recipe books clearly indicate that the bronze cauldrons served for cooking food.

SPANISH ARMY POTS

In studies on the bronze cauldrons they are - at least in The Netherlands - often called 'Spanish army pots'. This name links the pots with the story of the liberation of the town of Leiden, not far from The Hague. During the night of October 3rd 1574, following a lengthy siege, the Spanish army fled because Dutch freedom fighters had destroyed the dikes, flooding the area. The flight was extremely hasty: an orphan sent out early in the morning to scout the deserted Spanish army camp, found a bronze cauldron filled with hotchpot or stew left hanging over the fire. As a symbol of victory the pot was taken to town and is still kept there in the local museum. To this day, Octobre 3rd is celebrated with, amongst others, the distribution of free hotchpot.[5] Whether the story of Leiden is fact or fiction, since then bronze cooking pots are usually referred to as 'Spanish pots' or 'Spanish army pots'. Contrary to what the name suggests, the pots are certainly not Spanish in origin. When Spanish troops occupied Dutch territories in 1568, the bronze cauldron had already been a standard household utensil in North-western Europe for more than three hundred years.

The publications by Drescher indicate that there must be hundreds of them in Holland, Northern Germany and Denmark. A recent survey in Drenthe alone, one of the twelve Dutch provinces, revealed a total of 45 cauldrons found since 1850. These high numbers are remarkable because, even well into the 17th century, on buying a new cauldron people would hand in the old and broken one. Unlike pottery, broken pots of bronze were not thrown away as rubbish. They were brought to the potmaker to try to fix it. This practice is recorded not only by documents[6], but also by archaeological finds (fig. 2). Even if repair was no longer possible or expected to be too costly, there was no reason to throw the pot away. Every single pot or kettle had considerable scrap value. If the customer wanted a brand-new cauldron, a fair reduction in price could be obtained by handing in an old one. The potmaker would then simply melt it down. In general all copper and bronze

---

[1] Drescher 1982-1983, 158.

[2] Schäfer 1995. More recent discoveries in Rütz 2000.

[3] More details on typology are presented by Drescher 1969 and idem 1982-1983.

[4] Drescher 1982-1983, 158. Although old records sometimes speak of brass pots (Dubbe 1980, 57) none of the analyses gives any evidence that the potmakers used zinc in their products.

[5] Pelinck 1954

[6] Hof 1956, 56 and 115.

Figure 2. This large Spanish pot (H. 24 cm) from Valthe shows that broken bronze cauldrons could be repaired. Photo: JAV Studio's, Assen.

ultimately ended up in the melting pot. It shows that bronze cauldrons were of value. For this very reason, as a rule Medieval inventories of movable property do not refer to the earthenware pots, but do mention the bronze cauldrons.[7] The difference in price of the raw materials was of course an important factor. The evidence for price comparison of cauldrons certainly is not abundant, but we do know that weight was a critical factor in the selling price of a pot.[8] Weights may vary from 500 grams for the small ones up to 8 kilograms for the largest cauldrons.

It will be evident that Spanish army pots, whether intact or broken, had considerable value. There simply was no reason to throw them away. Taking this into account the high number of archaeological finds of bronze cauldrons is all the more noteworthy, not to say suspect. In fact, every single find calls for an explanation as to why did this pot end up in the ground, to be found centuries later.

FOCUS ON DRENTHE

Between 1998 and 2000 a survey was carried out on bronze cauldrons in Drenthe, a province in the northern part of The Netherlands.[9] It started with a study of the collection of the Drents Museum in Assen. This collection has been brought together since the foundation of the museum in 1854 and contains no less than 26 bronze cauldrons. A search through private collections together with documentary evidence on unsalvaged pots further raised the number to a total of 45. For a small province like Drenthe (2700 km^2) this is a fairly high number. Looking at the circumstances in which they were found none of the pots was found in association with settlement refuse. The

---

[7] Dubbe 1980, 57.
[8] Arkenbout 1994, 106; Drescher 1982-1983, 160.
[9] Van Vilsteren 1998; idem 2000.

majority consists of single finds. In four cases though, a bronze pot was accompanied by a second one, in two cases by a copper kettle, in two cases by a pewter jug. Once a bronze cauldron was found with an iron horseshoe, once with a stoneware jug and once with an 'ironing glass'. In all these cases the accompanying items were intact objects, still perfectly fit to be used. What goes for the cauldrons, also applies to the copper kettles and the pewter jugs: their presence in the ground is not at all obvious. They too would normally have been brought back to the melting pot.

A further look at the find circumstances reveals that a small minority (9%) of the finds in Drenthe comes from a dry i.e. sandy context. Of some 33% of the cauldrons too little is known about the origin. The majority (58%) however was found in what can be described as a wet context. This includes both the extensive bog complexes and the little kettlebogs through-out the province, as well as the swampy parts of river- and brook-valleys. Some of the finds with unknown locations of discovery must also have been found in a watery environment, judging from the general state of preservation and the patina. A considerable number of cauldrons turned up during peat-cutting activities. Discoveries made during this large-scale operation could only be taken to the Museum in Assen after the date of 1854, the year the Museum was founded. Peat-cutting however was a major economic activity in Drenthe from the 17th century onwards. Finds from that early period were likely not preserved since there was no museum or logical place to which to take them. It is estimated that at least 30 more cauldrons must have been discovered before 1854, bringing the total to 75. Including the number of pots still buried in the ground, the total will easily exceed a hundred for the province of Drenthe alone. This is far beyond what reasonably can be expected. These kinds of figures on such a small area like the province of Drenthe call for an explanation.

DELIBERATE DAMAGING

Close examination of the cauldrons shows that a considerable number are damaged. Sometimes one of the legs is partly or completely missing, and some of the pots have a hole in the bottom or the belly. In other cases part of the rim is missing or the ears are broken off. At first sight this damage does not seem suspicious: on the contrary one might argue that they explain why the pots have been thrown away. But we have to be cautious with such conclusions because the records show that the cauldrons are never found in association with settlement refuse. One also has to take into account that the bronze pots are very solid items; it takes a lot of force for a leg to break off or the bottom to get pierced. The damage will vary according to the floor it falls on and according to the way it falls on that floor. Loamy or wooden floors, such as the medieval farmsteads usually had, will not affect in any way a cauldron falling on it. The floor rather than the pot would have been damaged. If a bronze pot were to fall on a much harder floor of glazed tiles, bricks or stones, as usual in an urban context, chances of severe damage increase substantially. Of course, a few can may have been

Figure 3. The bottom of a bronze pot from Eelde clearly shows how in two places attempts have been made to deliberately pierce the pot from the inside. Photo: JAV Studio's, Assen.

damaged accidentally, but the number of damaged pots is too great to find this explanation acceptable. A strong suspicion of deliberate damaging is provoked by percentages as high as 53%. In many cases holes in the bottom or the belly are not the result of a weak spot. The thickness of the wall around the hole indicates that great force must have been used to pierce it. Moreover, from at least one of the pots from the province of Drenthe it is certain that the damaging was done on purpose: the bottom of a pot from Eelde shows clear marks of attempts of piercing the pot from the inside in two places (fig. 3). These marks could in no way have been caused by any accidental bump or fall, but must have been the result of a blow with a hammer on a large nail or an awl. The same phenomenon is also encountered on another bronze pot that was buried on the border of a lake in the adjacent province of Groningen[10] along with a second cauldron and two undamaged earthen jugs at the end of the sixteenth century.

INTERPRETATION

Drescher gives several explanations in his studies for the way cauldrons wound up in the ground. These vary from accidental loss[11], disposing of rubbish following the destruction of a village or a castle[12], to (in the case of finds from rivers, harbours and seas) the sinking of ships on which they were being used.[13] These options do not help us to interpret the finds in Drenthe. The number of cauldrons is far too high for accidental loss, especially if the great (scrap-) value of the pot is taken into consideration. None of the finds from Drenthe was found in association with settlement refuse, nor could any find be linked with the destruction of a castle or village. And, finally, shipping never occurred in the bogs of Drenthe. As a fourth option, applicable to the majority of finds, Drescher mentions the deliberate burial of cauldrons in order to hide them during times of war and plunder. The owner would, for some reason, not have had the chance to collect his property. In this respect there is a close link to the communis opinio among numismatists, when they interpret coin-hoards.[14] They too think that threat of war and troops plundering the countryside made people hide their treasure in the ground. After all, there were as yet no banks. An untimely death might have prevented the owner from digging up his money. The fact that coin hoards and cauldrons are similar in this respect is not illogical. For in both cases, the value that was hidden in the ground is quite substantial. It is even not unusual that a coin hoard was buried in a bronze

---

[10] Collection Groninger Museum, inv.nr. 2263, excavated in 1902; cf. Van Vilsteren 2000, 182.

[11] Drescher 1969, 315.

[12] Drescher 1969, 288. Even the extraordinary find of 11 bronze pots in the moat of the castle Heemskerk near Haarlem is interpreted in relation with its destruction in 1351 (Drescher 1969, 302).

[13] Drescher 1969, 288 and 308.

[14] Van Vilsteren 1999.

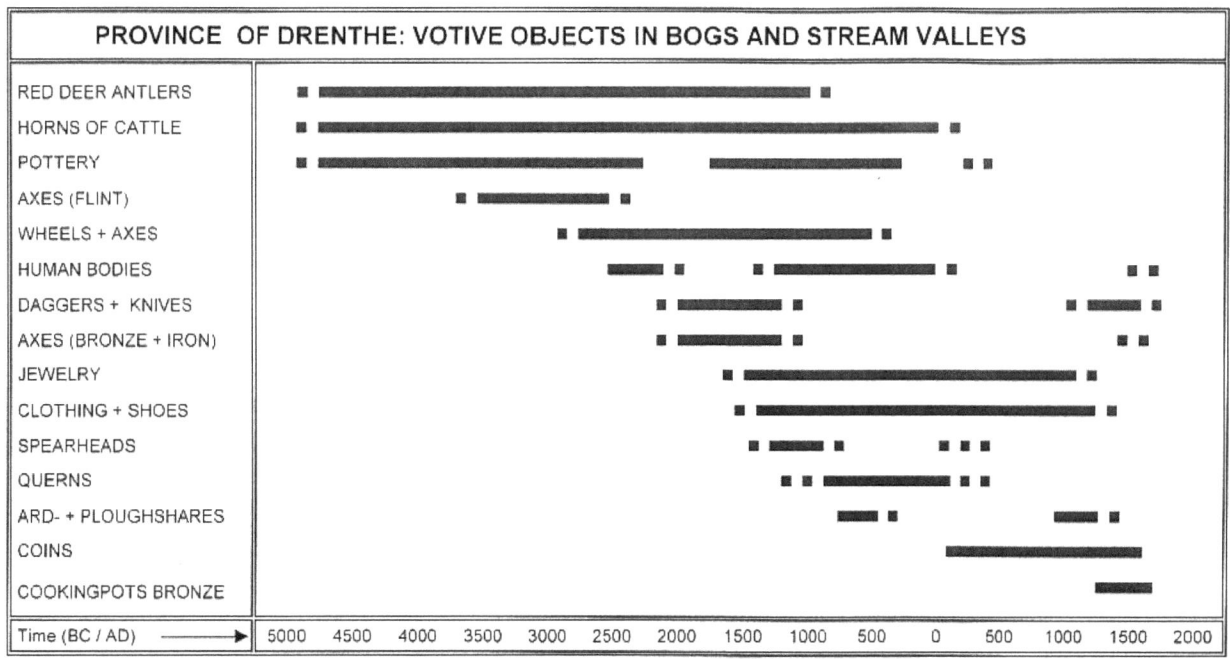

Figure 4. Survey of votive finds from wet context in the province of Drenthe, The Netherlands.

cauldron. In 1931 near Rheinböllen in Germany, a large gold and silver hoard was found which must have been buried in a bronze pot around 1418.[15] Likewise, in 1851 near Huy in Belgium, a bronze cauldron containing a coin hoard from the end of the 14th century was recovered from the bed of the river Maas.[16] In Denmark the combination of cauldron and coin hoard is recorded even more frequently.[17] Occasionally the value of the pot exceeds the value of the coins found in it.

Of course, it is hard to prove that the cauldrons were buried with the intention of later recovery. The former owner has passed away and is unable to tell us his motives. However, a number of arguments can be put forward which support the thesis that it is highly unlikely the pots were meant to be recovered. First of all, a surprisingly high percentage of the pots show signs of damaging, which clearly must have been deliberate in a number of cases. This applies not only to the pots from Drenthe, but also to pots from other parts of the Netherlands. In this respect nothing can be said of the extensive material from other countries, since Drescher has not involved this aspect in his studies. A better study of the foreign cauldrons might well show the same kind of damaging as the Dutch material. A hopeful indication for this, according to the publication, is that the bottom of the above-mentioned pot from Rheinböllen was pierced. If we ignore an interpretation like vandalism, the explanation for this deliberate damaging lies only in making the pot unfit for normal use, thus linking up with the practice, common in prehistoric times, of breaking down offerings before their ritual deposition. As such, it is an extra confirmation of their withdrawal from normal daily use. After all, from the moment they are sacrificed, the offerings are no longer part of the human world, but are owned by some supernatural power. The custom of deliberate damaging of offerings is recorded right up to the Medieval period.[18]

Secondly, we should focus on the specific context in which the cauldrons are found. The fact that the cauldrons are discovered remarkably often in what can be described as a wet context, makes it difficult to retain the view that the owner, when burying his treasure, had the intention of recovering the cauldron. Swamps, (sometimes deep) rivers and lakes certainly are not the most obvious place to hide something. The deposition of objects in these places also links up with a tradition, reaching far back into prehistory, of putting offerings in swamps, kettle-bogs, in rivers and river-valleys (especially at crossings), and in lakes. Fifteen years of research in the province of Drenthe has revealed that in all periods of prehistory many different kinds of objects have been deposited as offerings (fig. 4).[19] This research also shows that the practice of offerings did not end with the spread of Christianity during the early Medieval period. Several kinds of objects from the Middle Ages (kettles, daggers, jewellery, coin-hoards) in their pattern of distribution link up perfectly with the offerings from the pre- and proto-history. The remarkable damages, the absence of settlement refuse, the strange find-spots, the high scrap value and all other questions appear to be easily explained from an offering perspective. Finally, we might mention here a remarkable find that was recorded from Nindorf in Germany in 1938: upside down in a large copper kettle and embedded in heather and moss, a 16th-

---

[15] Hagen 1934.

[16] Haeck 1996, 199-200.

[17] Steen Jensen e.a., nrs. 159, 196, 203, 205, 208, 253, 304.

[18] Schulze 1984; Merrifield 1987, 110-111; Van Vilsteren 1996, 140; Bult, 1999, 8.

[19] Van der Sanden 1999; Bergen, Niekus & Van Vilsteren 2002.

century bronze cauldron was discovered.[20] Under the cauldron a large bone was found, most probably the remains of a large piece of meat. This remarkable find and especially the careful deposition that it shows are very similar to offerings from prehistoric and especially Roman times. Like this find, the other cauldrons -as well as the pewter, stoneware jugs and kettles - might well have occasionally served as containers and therefore have contained something organic that has not survived. If so, the thesis of offering again gives much better explanation than the disposal of rubbish, accidental loss or deliberate hiding during times of war or plunder.

FOR THE DEVIL?

Offerings in bogs and rivers might, in a Medieval context, seem at first sight a bit odd. After all, following the introduction of Christianity many pagan habits were forbidden. Even so, it was seemingly necessary for several centuries to impose a ban on all sorts of pagan traditions. The fact that as late as the 13th century extensive books listing all the penalties for pagan practices were copied over and over, demonstrates the long lasting character of these old habits. It appears it was particularly difficult to ban pagan depositions because the Church did not forbid offerings as such. The only condition was that the offering had to take place in a church, thus benefiting the Church.

Of course, we do not know whether a bronze cauldron, deposited in a swamp, was put there by an individual or by a group of persons, for example by members of a family. The fact that the Church did not approve of these kinds of offerings makes it unlikely to imagine large-scale public gatherings taking place. More likely, a meeting, conducted more or less in secret, was the case. On the other hand, the uniform distribution pattern of the cauldrons indicates that large groups over large areas probably had knowledge at least of these practices. It thus suggests a certain degree of acceptance, if not by the clerics, than at least by society in general.

Neither do we know the intentions of someone who deposited his valuables in a bog or river. We do know however that in the Middle Ages people, in their efforts to bend the march of events to their will, amply practised charms, spells, curses, and other magic rituals. Written evidence[21] as well as archaeological data[22] testify to the long-lasting character of superstition as a phenomenon which, although forbidden by the clerical authorities, paradoxically coexisted surprisingly well and with persistence. The bronze cauldrons in the bogs fit perfectly into this context, although the dedication remains obscure. Maybe the offerings were made to the devil or to spirits. A 13th-century source from central Germany mentions the burial of pots, filled with all sorts of things, in new houses for home-made gods called Stetewaldiu.[23] But it has also been suggested that the pots served as traps for evil spirits, lured into them by the food they might have contained.[24] Taking the pots to the marshes by cart and then throwing them in might have been thought of as a fruitful way of banishing the evil spirits from the village. Requests for salvation, healing, curing or blessing may have been motives for the offering of cauldrons in the bogs, similar to the use of candles, silver or wax in the church. Certainly, this interpretation offers a cogent explanation for the many strange aspects of the Spanish pots. This type of pagan offering, taking place outside a church, would have been a thorn in the flesh of the Spanish, who defended the Catholic religion in the Netherlands between 1568 and 1648. If ever the Spaniards had known that the Spanish pots were being abused for heathen rituals, they would never have permitted their name to be linked to these bronze cauldrons.

Author's address

Vincent VAN VILSTEREN
Drents Museum
Postbus 134
NL-9400 AC Assen
The Netherlands
v.vilsteren@drenthe.nl

Bibliography

ARKENBOUT, A.A., 1994, Frank van Borselen; het dagelijks leven op zijn hoven in Zeeland en het Maasmondgebied, Rotterdam: Stichting Historische Publicaties Roterodamum.

BERGEN, C., NIEKUS, M. & VAN VILSTEREN, V.T. (edited by), 2002, The Mysterious Bog People, Zwolle: Waanders.

BULT, E., 1999, Een schatvondst met een luchtje. Delf; Cultuurhistorisch Bulletin Delft 2 - 1, p. 6-8.

DRESCHER, H., 1968, Mittelalterliche Dreibeintöpfe aus Bronze; Bericht über die Bestandsaufnahme und Versuch einer chronologischen Ordnung. In: Rotterdam Papers, a contribution in medieval archaeology 1, edited by J.G.N. Renaud, Rotterdam, p. 23-33.

DRESCHER, H., 1969, Mittelalterliche Dreibeintöpfe aus Bronze; Bericht über die Bestandsaufnahme und Versuch einer chronologischen Ordnung. Neue Ausgrabungen und Forschungen in Niedersachsen 4, p. 287-315.

DRESCHER, H., 1982-1983, Zu den bronzenen Grapen des 12.-16. Jahrhunderts aus Nordwestdeutschland. In: Aus dem Alltag der mittelalterlichen Stadt, edited by J. Wittstock. Bremen: Focke Museum, p. 157-174.

DRESCHER, H., 2000, Zum dreibeinigen Bronzetopf von der Burg Eberbach am Neckar, Eberbacher Geschichtsblatt 99, p. 54-59.

DRESCHER, H., 1996, Drei Kannen, zwei Grapen und eine Leuchter aus einem mittelalterlichen Schiffswrack in der Trave. Eine Ergänzung zum Baggerfund von 1941. Harburger Jahrbuch 19, p. 39-48.

DUBBE, B., 1980, Kook-, keuken-, eet- en drinkgerei. In: Thuis in de late middeleeuwen; Tentoonstellingscatalogus, Zwolle: Waanders, p. 57-64.

---

[20] Drescher 1982-1983,162.
[21] Thomas 1971; Flint 1991.
[22] Merrifield 1987.
[23] Mostert 1995, 249.
[24] Merrifield 1987, 120.

FLINT, V.I.J., 1991, The rise of magic in early medieval Europe. Princeton: Princeton University Press.

HAECK, A., 1996, Middeleeuwse muntschatten gevonden in België (750-1433). Brussel: Cercle d'Études Numismatiques.

HAGEN, J., 1934, Münzfund aus Rheinböllen (Kreis Simmern) um 1418. Mitteilungen der Bayerischen Numismatischen Gesellschaft 52, p. 31-46.

HOF, J., 1976, Egmondse kloosterrekeningen uit de XIVe eeuw, Zwolle/Groningen: Tjeenk Willink (=Fontes minores medii aevi, 17).

MERRIFIELD, R., 1987, The archaeology of ritual and magic. London: B.T. Batsford Ltd.

MOSTERT, M., 1995, Boerengeloof in de dertiende eeuw. In: De betovering van het middeleeuwse christendom; studies over ritueel en magie in de Middeleeuwen, edited by M. Mostert en A. Demyttenare, Hilversum: Uitgeverij Verloren, p. 217-261.

PELINCK, E., 1954, Overlevering, legende en relieken van het beleg en ontzet van Leiden. Leids Jaarboekje, p. 100-107.

RÜTZ, T., 2000, Die archäologischen Untersuchungen auf dem Gelände des ehemaligen Heilig-Geist-Hospitals in Greifswald, Langestraße 51. (1989-1997), Greifswald: Magisterarbeit Universität Greifswald.

SCHÄFER, H., 1995, Eine Greifswalder Grapengießerwerkstatt des 14. Jahrhunderts in der Brüggestraße 25a. Bodendenkmalpflege in Mecklenburg-Vorpommern, Jahrbuch 1994, 42, p. 151-169.

SCHULZE, M., 1984, Diskussionsbeitrag zur Interpretation früh- und hochmittelalterlicher Flußfunde. In: Frühmittelalterliche Studien, edited by K. Hauck, Berlijn/New York: Walter de Gruyter, p. 222-248.

STEEN JENSEN, J., K. BENDIXEN, N.-K. LIEBGOTT & F. LINDAHL, 1992, Danmarks middelalderlige skattefund c. 1050 - c. 1550. Det Kongelige Nordiske Odlskriftselskab: København (=Nordiske Fortidsminder, Serie B, Bind 12,1).

THOMAS, K., 1971, Religion and the decline of magic. New York: Oxford University Press.

VAN BEEK, R. & VAN VILSTEREN, V.T., 1994, Van vóór de Voorst; enkele 12de- en vroeg 13de-eeuwse vondsten en hun betekenis. Archeologie en Bouwhistorie in Zwolle 2, p. 142-153.

VAN DER SANDEN, W.A.B., 1999, Wetland archaeology in the province of Drenthe, the Netherlands. In: Bog bodies, sacred sites and wetland archaeology; proceedings of a conference held by WARP and the National Museum of Denmark, in conjunction with Silkeborg Museum, Jutland, September 1996, edited by B. Coles, J. Coles en M. Schou Jørgensen, Exeter: University of Exeter, p. 217-225.

VAN DER SANDEN, W.A.B., 2001, From stone pavement to temple – Ritual structures from wet contexts in the province of Drenthe, The Netherlands. In: Enduring Records; the environmental and cultural heritage of wetlands. Papers of the Wetlands Archaeology Conference (WARP in Florida), dec. 1-5 1999, edited by B.A. Purdey, Oxford: Oxbow Books, p. 132-147.

VAN VILSTEREN, V.T., 1992, De 14de-eeuwse schatvondst van Coevorden. Paleo-aktueel 3, p. 123-126.

VAN VILSTEREN, V.T., 1996, Pars pro toto; over wagenwielen, haarvlechten en nog zo wat. Nieuwe Drentse Volks-almanak 113, p. 130-147.

VAN VILSTEREN, V.T., 1998, Voor hutspot en de duivel - over de betekenis der 'zoogenaamde Spaansche legerpotten'. Nieuwe Drentse Volksalmanak 115, p. 142-170.

VAN VILSTEREN, V.T., 2000, Hidden, but not intended to be recovered; an alternative approach to hoards of medieval coins. Jaarboek voor Munt- en Penningkunde 87, (in press).

VAN VILSTEREN, V.T., 2000, 'Die potten in deze ruwe veenen' – aanvullende vondsten van zgn. Spaansche legerpotten. Nieuwe Drentse Volksalmanak 117, p. 169-187.

VAN VILSTEREN, V.T., 2001, Een Spaanse pot avant-la-lettre. Terra Nigra 152, p. 10-16.

SOME ASPECTS OF THE MEDIEVAL FOUNTAINS IN VITERBO

Chiara DE SANTIS

Résumé : QUELQUES ASPECTS DES FONTAINES MÉDIÉVALES A VITERBO. Les fontaines de Viterbo eurent grande importance au Moyen Âge. Nées en premier pour satisfaire le besoin d'eau de la ville, elles se placent par conséquent à l'intérieur de la triade place/paroisse/fontaine où la vie de la "contrada" était attirée. Il est donc évident que en ayant un rôle tant essentiel soit comme point de rencontre soit comme moyen de distribution hydrique, ces structures devaient avoir des considérations et des soins particuliers. En effet, les statuts de l'époque suivent tout près la réalisation et la fonctionnalité de ces exemplaires qui sont sauvegardés contre éventuels abus et sont l'objet d'un régulier nettoyage. Les fontaines publiques médiévales par nous prises en examen sont stylistiquement à reconduire à deux typologies: celle qui est constituée par les particulières fontaines "à fuseau" et celle qui se caractérise par une installation "à coupes superposées". C'est incontestable que l'aspect fonctionnel des sources, représenté par l'offrande d'un service publique nécessaire fût associé à un aspect architectonique de style appréciable, tous les deux destinés à exalter soit l'efficacité des institutions soit l'organisation et le zèle des communautés.

Abstract: The fountains of Viterbo were of great importance in medieval times. They were originally built to satisfy the city's water supply, so they were located within the triad square-parish-fountain where the life of the "contrada" was concentrated. As these fountains became more and more important, because of the way they were assembled and for their functional use, they took great care of them. The medieval law was very accurate in passing regulations to safeguard the fountains from any kind of vandalism and to govern their maintenance. We have taken into consideration two types of public fountains: the typical "spindle shaped" fountain and the "overlapping cups" structure. The functional aspect of the fountains, a necessary public water supply, was closely linked to the architectural aspect, both to magnify the efficiency of the institutions and, the organization and commitment of the community.

INTRODUCTION

The structure of medieval Viterbo, which in many places follows the same road pattern of the Etruscan Viterbo of which there are many interesting traces, is often characterised by the coexistence of a church and a fountain within the same square.

The link between these three elements, square/church/fountain is surely significant of the intention of creating a centre where in the past the local life developed and was organized.

It is a fact that the fountains of Viterbo are a vast architectural complex which cannot be found in other parts of Italy and it is also possible to see its development through the centuries up to the present day. Unfortunately, we have not yet found in a fountain in this area that dates back to the Etruscan period. The public and private fountains date back to 1200 even if many of them were rebuilt in later centuries. Because of these reconstructions the fountains we see now are often totally different from the original ones. Speaking of these restorations, which were more or less drastic, we should mention the public fountains of Piazza delle Erbe, Piazza della Rocca and Piazza del Gesù. To give a more complete view of the fountains in Viterbo we should not forget the monumental and 'plain' fountains which were moved from their original location or destroyed as a consequence of certain events.

Some of these were the fountain of Cranisi, of St. Simeone, of Cunicchio and of St. Matteo's Gate. Also the fountain located in Piazza Nova[1] in 1206, which was later destroyed, was removed in 1243[2] and, as mentioned in the statute of 1251-52, rebuilt in that same year[3].

In the XIII century the building and restoration of the fountains were supervised and taken care of by the local magistrates, as certified in the statutes of that time. I will deal with this matter in more detail later on. The value of these fountains, both public and private, is not only for the architectural typology shaping them but also for their particular historical, legendary, political function and connection to a community or a guild.

The fountain of Crocetta, for instance, is linked to the patron saint of Viterbo, St. Rosa who went to get water from that fountain and miraculously mended a jug which had been shattered to pieces.

The fountain of piazza del Comune, of which there are no more traces, is proof of the consolidation of the communal political life and the strengthening of the institutions and the local magistrates[4]. It was built presumably in 1268[5] and destroyed in 1466 because it seemed that its location obstructed or somehow limited the overall view of the square[6]. It was rebuilt later on but completely different from the original one.

---

[1] CRISTOFORI, F., 1890, 1973, *Cronica di Anzillotto Viterbese dall'anno MCLXIX all'anno MCCLV. Continuata da Nicola di Bartolomeo della Tuccia sino all'anno MCCCCLXXIII*, Roma, Viterbo, p.27.

[2] CRISTOFORI, F., 1890, 1973, *Cronica di Anzillotto Viterbese dall'anno MCLXIX all'anno MCCLV. Continuata da Nicola di Bartolomeo della Tuccia sino all'anno MCCCCLXXIII*, Roma, Viterbo, p. 43.

[3] Statuto di Viterbo 1251, III, 55.

[4] PIANA AGOSTINETTI, C., 1985, *Fontane a Viterbo*, Roma, p.19.

[5] CIAMPI, I.,1872, *Cronache e Statuti della Città di Viterbo*, Firenze, p. 30.

[6] CIAMPI, I., 1872, *Cronache e Statuti della Città di Viterbo*, Firenze, p. 90.

Ciampi writes "In that year (1470) they started to build a beautiful fountain in Piazza del Comune in Viterbo with six callipers and six small pipes from which gushed water. At the top there was a badly made statue of Hercules, shaped like a woman. The masters were from Florence and in my opinion they did not do their work very well"[7].

The fountain inside the loggia of the Palazzo Papale, the *fons papalis*, is a reminder of when the town was the popes' favourite seat and at the same time it shows the close relation with Rome especially for the classical shape of the basin[8].

Unfortunately the fountain of Pianoscarano was the victim of an unfortunate event in 1367 when there was a local uproar caused by the local people because a servant of the pope's court on returning from Avignon, had washed his dog in the fountain's basin. In this case the main "character" or "co-star", the fountain, was associated to this dramatic event as one of its causes and for this reason its punishment was its destruction[9].

Many public fountains bore the coats of arms of aristocratic families of Viterbo who in the Middle Ages took an important part in the political and social life of the town. These families, probably, having given generous donations to build or restore some of these fountains, were remembered by engraving their coat of arms on them.

So, for instance, the fountain of Sepale with the coats of arms of the Gatti and Orsini families reminds us of them. The plain XIII century rectangular fountain, located in piazza S. Carluccio, shows the engraved emblems of the Gatti and the Anguillara families[10]. On the contrary the coats of arms that decorate the pyramidal part of the fountain of St. Faustino are still unknown.

The "monumental" public fountains can be divided into two types: those characterised by the peculiar "spindle" shape and those characterised by the "superimposed basins" ones. The characteristic of these two types of fountains is that they are not only functional but have also an aesthetic appearance, which makes them real works of art. It is clear that the functional side of the fountains, which was to offer a necessary public service, was combined with its remarkable architectural appearance. They were to enhance both the efficiency of the institutions and the organisation and commitment of the local communities.

---

[7] CIAMPI, I., 1872, *Cronache e Statuti della Città di Viterbo*, Firenze, p. 98.

[8] PIANA AGOSTINETTI, C., 1985, *Fontane a Viterbo*, Roma, p.19.

[9] CRISTOFORI, F., 1890, 1973, *Cronica di Anzillotto Viterbese dall'anno MCLXIX all'anno MCCLV. Continuata da Nicola di Bartolomeo della Tuccia sino all'anno MCCCCLXXIII*, Roma, Viterbo, pp.58-59; SIGNORELLI, G., 1907, 1969, *Viterbo nella Storia della Chiesa*, Viterbo, vol. I, p.411, pp. 414-415; PINZI, C., 1887, 1913, *Storia della città di Viterbo*, Viterbo, vol. III, p. 347; EGIDI, P., 1901, *Le Croniche di Viterbo scritte da frate Francesco D'Andrea*, Roma, p.98.

[10] SCRIATTOLI, A., 1920, *Viterbo nei suoi monumenti*, Roma, pp. 183, 197; PIANA AGOSTINETTI, C., 1985, *Fontane a Viterbo*, Roma, p. 74.

SYMBOLOGY AND COMMUNITY USE OF THE MEDIEVAL FOUNTAINS

The widespread water distribution for the community was certainly the first function the fountains had to perform. We should remember that only a few aristocratic families, besides certain ecclesiastic institutions, benefited from a private water provision which supplied water directly to their homes.

The fact that the fountains were important mainly for their utility, because they supplied a vital element, justifies not only the requests the citizens made for fountains to the local magistrates but obviously also the great number of examples in the town.

The medieval statutes of Viterbo report the many requests made and show how these fountains were dear to the local authorities as we will see in greater detail further on.

For instance the Statute of 1237-38 states:

"De licentiam dando hominibus de contrada S. Stephani, S. Crucis, S. Simeonis facere fontem.

(Statuimus quod) liceat hominbus contradarum S.) Stephani, S. Crucis, S. Simeonis, cum (velint facere f)ontem in loco de quo convenerint, de aqua (ducere font)is Sepalis, que fuit ob hoc dismissa."[11]

In the same years they decreed the building of the fountain called 'of the roses':

"De aptando fontem rosarum, manentem extra portam ecclesie S.Xisti.

Teneatur potestas vel consules cogere homines de hora S. Xisti et homines de h(ora S. Leonardi) et de hora S. Mathei fecere fieri et aptari, expensis dictorum hominum, fontem pulc(herrimum et bene) muratum cum uno lavatorio in loco extra portam ecclesie S. Xisti, qui dicitur f(ons Rosarum), si de dictarum horarum hominum proceserit voluntate".[12]

The Statute of 1251-52 repeats nearly word for word the previous decree, the reason why is not clear, perhaps because that fountain was not actually built:

"Quod potestas faciat fieri fontem rose cum abbeveratorio.

Teneatur potestas, vel consules cogere homines contrate sancti Xisti, de ora sancti Leonardi et de ora sancti Mathei facere fieri et aptari expensis dictorum cum abbeveratorio extra portam sancti Xisti in loco, qui dicitur fons Rosarum, et hoc facere teneatur infra spatium IIII mensium si de dictarum contratarum hominum proceserit voluntate".[13]

Some of the decrees plainly show that the building of the fountains and their relative maintenance were up to the

---

[11] *Statuto di Viterbo* 1237-38, CCCLXXXXV.

[12] *Statuto di Viterbo* 1237-38, CCCCXXXXIIII.

[13] *Statuto di Viterbo* 1251-52, III, 200.

inhabitants of the "contrada" (though in some cases the aristocratic families of Viterbo very likely contributed with generous sums of money).

This is the unequivocal case of the fountain known as of the Roses (Statuto di Viterbo 1237-38, 444; Statuto di Viterbo 1251-52, III, 200), the one of St. Faustino (Statuto di Viterbo 1251-52, I, 65), the one of Pianoscarano (Statuto di Viterbo 1251-52, III,1) and the one of St. Luca (Statuto di Viterbo 1251-52, III, 237).

So it is possible to assert that the expenses for the building and maintenance of the fountains were on behalf of those who used them. This fact emphasises the social character of the fountains.

Furthermore the fact that, in most cases, the users, that is the citizens of a certain area in particular, had to pay for the expenses and duties, underlines how these fountains were really considered not so much as a communal public property but a form of property, if it can be called as such, of the "neighbourhood".

However we cannot certainly deny that the fountains together with the local church were the symbol of the medieval community. Even the town development is emblematic of this type of situation. Each "contrada" focuses its life around the square characterised by a church and a fountain.

This need to create a centre around which the community life could develop follows at the same rate of expansion of the town itself. So the last medieval quarters, created in Viterbo and included at a later stage within the city walls, did nothing else but create the same conditions which were characteristic of the older "contrade".

This reference to the expansion of the town through the development and absorption of new quarters such as St. Faustino and Pianoscarano which developed later on because they were built according to a precise town plan which was subordinate to a regular town lay-out.

Even in these cases the three elements, square, church, fountain, are closely linked. The Statute of 1251-52, III, 27, that repeats nearly word for word the one of 1237-38, CCCV, gives us in depth detail of the division of the town in four zones, each made up of various "contrade", giving us an overall picture of the urban topography.

In the many quarters it is possible to determine a close connection between the parish church and the public fountain. This kind of link between church and fountain, naturally considering also the fountains which have now disappeared but are well attested in accurate documentation, is a peculiar characteristic of each district which makes us suppose that this combination was a kind of town planning regulation.

C. Piana Agonistinetti has already identified an existing link, according to the above mentioned statute, between quarter-church-fountain in the following cases:

"The quarter of Porta S. Lorenzo: the castle of St. Lorenzo (fountain), 'contrade' of St. Tommaso (fountain), of St. Salvatore (fountain), of Pianoscarano (fountain).

The quarter of Porta S. Pietro: 'contrade' of St. Silvestro (fountain), of St. Maria Nuova, of St. Vito, of St. Antonino, of St. Giovanni in Pietra, of St. Leonardo (fountain), of St. Bartolomeo (fountain), of St. Fortunato, of St. Erasmo (fountain), of St. Pellegrino (fountain).

The quarter of Porta S. Sisto: 'contrade' of St. Sisto (fountain), of St. Matteo dell'Abate, of St. Nicola (fountain), of St. Giovanni in Zoccoli (fountain), of St. Simeone (fountain), of St. Biagio, of St. Martino of St. Giacomo, of St. Croce.

The quarter of Porta S. Matteo in Sonsa: 'contrade' of St. Marco, of St. Luca (fountain), of St. Pietro alla Rocca (fountain), of St. Angelo (fountain), of St. Faustino (fountain), of St. Stefano (fountain), of St. Maria in Poggio (fountain), of St. Quirico (fountain), of St. Egidio".[14]

It must be taken into consideration that lots of fountains have, or had, a very simple shape.

These are the ones having a plain rectangular shaped basin and were used also as drinking-troughs.

In this case they were very often located near the gates that led to the town but it was not also unusual to find them in the city centre. For instance there is the XIII century one called of St. Moccichello which can still be seen against the outside wall of Palazzo Gatti in Via C. La Fontaine[15].

They were often located against a wall and in many cases near a washing trough such as the remaining ones of St. Carluccio, of St. Pellegrino (a reproduction of the original medieval one) and of Capone. Speaking of these, we should remember the medieval origin of the washing troughs and their purpose and their role which is clearly explained in the statutes[16].

In connection with the non monumental fountains, we should also mention the fountain of St. Lorenzo, which dates back to the XII or XIII century[17], with its hemispheric basin. Now it is located on the left side of the staircase of the Duomo (though originally it was leaning against the bell tower).

Monumental fountains were preferred in the squares and were generally characterised by the "spindle" shaped type or by the "superimposed basin" type.

The first type includes the fountain of Morte, the fountain of St. Giovanni in Zoccoli, the fountain of Crocetta, the

---

[14] PIANA AGOSTINETTI, C., 1985, *Fontane a Viterbo*, Roma, p.22, nota 4.

[15] PIANA AGOSTINETTI, C., 1985, *Fontane a Viterbo*, Roma, p. 76.

[16] *Statuto di Viterbo* 1237-38, CCCCXXXXIIII; 1251-52, III, 59.

[17] PIANA AGOSTINETTI, C., 1985, *Fontane a Viterbo*, Roma, p. 32, p.124.

one of St. Faustino and the one of Pianoscarano which can still be found in their original positions.

Belonging to the second type the only fountain of Sepale maintains, more or less, its original shape.

Indeed the fountain of St. Pietro alla Rocca, which replaces the medieval structure, dates back to the XVI[18] century; the fountain of St. Stefano, known as the fountain of Erbe, substitutes the medieval one which originally was near the homonymous parish church and very likely it was a "spindle" shaped one[19].

The fountain of Piazza del Gesù is a XX century reproduction replacing another one the origins of which date back to the middle of the XVI century[20].

It must be noted that a monumental fountain had to be placed next to a drinking-trough as the statutes of those times state[21].

The peculiar position of the monumental fountains has already been noted in relation to the square and the parish church. This lay-out has to be studied in great detail so as to determine the specific location of these fountains within their respective squares.

These were places where people met, fought, where they had civil demonstrations, trade exchanges, religious celebrations, political meetings and in brief where the heart of quarter's life took place.

The lay-out of the fountain must be studied in detail so as to answer and to perform particular needs.

Regarding this matter C. Piana Agostinetti writes: "They seem to be located on the border line between the area of the parish or 'contrada', and the road, to which they are in a rear position, so they could offer refreshment without occupying precious walking space"[22].

So the fountains of St. Giovanni in Zoccoli and the one of Crocetta are tangent to Via Mazzini (the former was slightly moved in the eighteenth century because it was blocking the way of the building opposite).

The fountains in Piazza delle Erbe and Piazza della Morte were in a similar position (the latter was also moved, even if only slightly, from its original position in the nineteenth century). They are located along the route of Corso Italia, Via Roma, Via St. Lorenzo (this road follows the same pattern as the original); this route opens onto Piazza del Comune where there was a fountain but which is no longer there, and onto Piazza del Gesù now embellished with a reproduction of the old fountain.

The fountain of Pianoscarano is tangent to the homonymous street; the fountain of St. Faustino is tangent to St. Maria Liberatrice and via Cairoli; the fountain of Rocca is located at the end of Via Matteotti towards Porta Fiorentina; lastly the fountain of Sepale is placed along the road axis formed by the point of contact of Via Garibaldi which starts from Porta Romana and Via Cavour that leads to Piazza del Plebiscito.

MEDIEVAL LEGISLATION FOR THE MAINTENANCE AND PROTECTION OF THE FOUNTAINS

We have seen how important the medieval fountains of Viterbo were.

Originally they were built for the need of the town, and as we have already seen, they were located within the triad square-parish-fountain where the life of the "contrada" was centred.

So since the fountains achieved such an important role for both their position and their water supply function, these structures were respected and looked after with particular care.

Indeed the building, the maintenance and the protection of the fountains were highly taken into consideration by the local authorities of the town.

The statutes of that period closely follow up the construction and function of these fountains that were protected from possible abuses and were cleaned once a month[23]. The punishment for polluting the water in the fountains and in the drinking-troughs, and probably also in the surrounding areas, was quite severe. In fact the offender was obliged to pay a fine from II to X solids in addition to being banished.

The statutes state the following regarding this matter:

"De non faciendo turpitudinem in fonte vel abeveratorio.

Item quicumque in fonte vel abeveratorio aliquid turpitudinis studiose fecerit,.II. soll. det (pro b)anno, quod habeant balivi viarum et fontium, si vero forenses fuerint turpitudinem facientes, (quia sta)tuta nostre nesciunt Civitatis, nullam penam exinde solvat".[24]

"Quod nullus faciat turpitudinem in abbeveratorio.

Qui in abbeveratorio fontis turpitudinem fecerit studiose, II solidos balivis fontium et viarum persolvat, nisi esset forensis qui statum civitatis ignoret."[25]

---

[18] EGIDI, P., 1901, *Le Croniche di Viterbo scritte da frate Francesco D'Andrea*, Roma, p.88; PINZI C., 1916, *I principali monumenti di Viterbo*, Viterbo, pp. 132-133.

[19] SCRIATTOLI, A., 1920, *Viterbo nei suoi monumenti* Viterbo, pp. 274-275; PIANA AGOSTINETTI, C., 1985, *Fontane a Viterbo*, Roma, p. 72.

[20] PIANA AGOSTINETTI, C., 1985, *Fontane a Viterbo*, Roma, p. 62.

[21] *Statuto di Viterbo* 1237-38, CCLIII; 1251-52, III,55; 1251-52, III,200: 1251-52 ,III, 237; 1251-52, IV, 83.

[22] PIANA AGOSTINETTI, C., 1985, *Fontane a Viterbo*, Roma, p. 20.

[23] *Statuto di Viterbo* 1251-52, I, 47.

[24] *Statuto di Viterbo* 1237-38, CCLIII.

[25] *Statuto di Viterbo* 1251-52, I, 57.

"*Quod nullus faciat turpitudinem circa fontes.*

Statuimus quod nullus turpitudinem faciat circa fontes, et qui contra fecerit puniatur in X solidis et bandiatur."[26]

"*De pena facientis turpitudinem circa fontes.*

Statuimus quod nullus faciat turpitudinem circa fontes: et qui contra fecerit puniatur in X solidis: et bandiatur hoc capitulum."[27]

These were the general laws but there were more detailed ones, in particular those concerning the fountain of Sepale which probably had a special importance compared to the others not only for its architectural relevance but also for the great number of people who used it. The last statement is confirmed by the fact that while the other fountains were cleaned once a month, this fountain and its drinking-trough were cleaned twice a month. Regarding this matter the Statute of 1251-52 reports the following decree:

"*De purgatione fontis Sepalis.*

Ordinamus quod unus de balivis viarum vel alius ab eis positus fontem Sepalis et abbeveratorium purgari faciat bis in mense, et eligatur talis ab eis qui inhabitet iuxta fontem. Et si quis in dicto fonte fecerit aliquam turpitudinem, dictus balivus aut a balivis positus habeat licentiam pignorandi eum in II solidis."[28]

In the Statute of the same year they also mention the fine they would give to those unblocking or polluting the fountain watering the horses or any other kind of animal:

"*De pena sturantis fontem Sepalis.*

Statuimus quod si quis sturaverit fontem Sepalis, vel abbeveratorium sine licentia balivi ad idem electi, solvat curie X solidos: et quicumque in eodem fonte adaquaverit equum, vel aliquod aliud animale abeveraverit, in eadem pena incurrat."[29]

To give a more complete view I will briefly refer to the fact that the fines concerning the damaging of the aqueducts and the channels or the unlawful water supplying were even more severe and in some cases they imposed fines even to the personnel, as is later mentioned, who did not do their duty properly.

I have already underlined that the building and maintenance of the fountains was generally financed by the "contrade" who benefited from this service and whose efficiency obviously had to be fully guaranteed.

The supervision of its function, cleaning and respecting the legislation concerning the fountains and water mains, was given to an institution whose members had the general qualification of *balivi viarum* or the more specific one of *balivi viarum et fontium*.

Their job is described in the Statute of 1251-52:

"*De officio balivorum viarum.*

Balivi fontium et viarum iurent bona fide et sine fraude eorum officium portare et facere, et vias, quas infra civitatem et extra scient, etiam nullo denuntiante, vel ab aliis diceretur eisdem esse destructas, facient ab omnibus ibidem adiacentibus reaptari ita quod habeant omnes balivi pro qualibet die XII denarios donec opus finietur et non plus. Si autem questio fuerit de via vel quolibet alio in suis locis vel aliquo ipsorum locorum posito vel statuto, turca (?) torcularibus, lapidibus, disco, porticis, stillicidiis, carbonariis, grondariis, terminis vel fossato, facta estimatione res unde lix (sic) est, post litis sedationem VI denarios per libram accipiant inter ambas parte et non plus.

Fontes etiam et abbeveratoria infra civitatem mundari omni mense facere teneantur. Si vero contra fecerint, puniantur in X libris, quoquo denuntiante. Qui vero ab illis fuerit gravatus, ad potestatem vel consules licentiam habeat recurrendi. Pro quolibet termino, quem miserint partium voluntate, habeant XII denarios et non plus inter ambas partes. Pro viatico nichil accipiant".[30]

Many other decrees[31], besides the ones already quoted concerning the general regulations, mention the duties of the personnel who for many aspects can be definitely compared to the ancient Roman executive staff (*familia aquaria*).

It must be remembered that between the XV and the XVI century the *Balivi* were replaced by the *Antepositi*, appointed by the inhabitants of the quarter, who also took care of the administration of the parish endowments[32] as *Santesi*.

Author's address

Chiara DE SANTIS
Via Vicenza, 58
01100 Viterbo ITALY

Bibliography

CIAMPI, I., 1872, *Cronache e Statuti della Città di Viterbo*, Firenze.

CRISTOFORI, F., 1890, 1973, *Cronica di Anzillotto Viterbese dall'anno MCLXIX all'anno MCCLV. Continuata da Nicola di Bartolomeo della Tuccia sino all'anno MCCCCLXXIII*, Roma, Viterbo.

EGIDI, P., 1901, *Le Croniche di Viterbo scritte da frate Francesco D'Andrea*, Roma.

---

[26] *Statuto di Viterbo* 1251-52, III, 145.

[27] *Statuto di Viterbo* 1251-52, IV, 184.

[28] *Statuto di Viterbo* 1251-52, I, 61.

[29] *Statuto di Viterbo* 1251-52, IV, 83.

[30] *Statuto di Viterbo* 1251-52, I, 47.

[31] *Statuto di Viterbo* 1237-38 CCCCL; CCLI; CCLVIII; CCCLXXXXVI; CCCLXXXV; *Statuto di Viterbo* 1251-52, I, 49; I, 50; I, 61; III, 187; I, 53; I, 56; I, 98; I, 99; IV, 83.

[32] SIGNORELLI, G., 1907, 1969, *Viterbo nella Storia della Chiesa*, Viterbo, vol. II, p. 241.

PIANA AGOSTINETTI, C., 1985, *Fontane a Viterbo*, Roma.

PINZI, C., 1916, *I principali monumenti di Viterbo*, Viterbo.

SCRIATTOLI, A., 1920, *Viterbo nei suoi monumenti*, Roma.

SIGNORELLI, G., 1907, 1969, *Viterbo nella Storia della Chiesa*, Viterbo.

Statuti della Provincia Romana, 1930, a cura di Federici, V., Roma.

Statuto di Viterbo 1237-38 (Biblioteca Comunale degli Ardenti di Viterbo).

Statuto di Viterbo 1251-52 (Biblioteca Comunale degli Ardenti di Viterbo).

THE MIDDLE AGES IN THE VITERBESE TUSCIA REGION: THE CASE STUDY OF CASTEL D'ASSO (VITERBO)

Lucilla VENTURI

Résumé : LE MOYEN ÂGE DANS LA TUSCIA VITERBIENNE: LE CAS DE CASTEL D'ASSO (VITERBO). Dans une cause de droit civil (Pro Caecina) Cicéron mentionne le toponyme de Axia (l'actuel Castel d'Asso) en le situant "in agro Tarquiniensi", dans une zone qui se trouve au Sud de Viterbo (l'ancienne Sorrina), à environ 50 milles de Rome. Le site est connu pour la monumentale nécropole rupestre qui se développa pendant la période hellénistique étrusque (IV-II siècle a. J. C.) et pour les ruines du château du XII ème siècle qui se détachent sur le plateau où s'élevait l'ancienne agglomération. Ici on présente les résultats des recherches qui concernent Castel d'Asso pendant le Moyen Âge, une période historique très délicate qui traverse et change une grande partie des sites archéologiques viterbiens. Une grande quantité de grottes disséminées dans le territoire de l'ancienne Axia, en témoignant le typique établissement médiéval à caractère éparpillé, stimule l'analyse historique et archéologique relative aux modifications de l'aire funéraire spécifiquement aux fins des habitations. Dans le texte on illustre les résultats des recherches qui intéressent ces monuments caractérisés par un changement de destination d'usage de tombes étrusques à étables, refuges ou habitations. Il s'agit de transformations dues aux interventions réalisées sur leurs structures, comme cheminées et foyers tirés de la roche ou l'adjonction des portes ou palissades en bois sur les seuils des ouvertures mêmes. Les résultats montrent un profil économique et historique de la socialité de cette zone située à l'abri de Viterbe, une ville très forte, née le long d'anciens cheminements et routes commerciales qui, de la côte tyrrhénienne, pénétraient dans l'intérieur.

Abstract: In a civil law case (Pro Caecina) Cicero mentions the toponym AXIA, the present name for Castel d' Asso for the first time, locating it "in agro tarquiniensi" in an area situated in south Viterbo, ancient Murrina, approximately 50 miles from Rome. Its location is famous for the monumental rocky necropolis, which developed during the Etruscan Hellenism (IV-II cent. B.C.) and for its castle ruins, built in the XII century. In this brief study the results of a research carried out on the rocky settlements of Castel d'Asso during the Middle Ages will be shown. It was a delicate historical period that changed in form rather than in substance a large number of archaeological sites in the Viterbese Tuscia region. A certain number of caves widespread throughout the territory of ancient AXIA prove the intervention of man towards nature in this area, thus adapting it to fit his needs during the medieval period. This was characterised by reusing and partially modifying the funeral architecture that made up the Etruscan necropolis into dwelling places. In particular, the research was carried out to outline the peculiar features of medieval dwellings " in caves" which shows the transformation of funeral environments into dwelling places, stables, shelters, fireplaces and hearths obtained from inside the tufaceous mass, or by adding doors or wooden palisades for animals, as the holes in the rock walls prove. The results show the social and economic split within a minor centre, but proved significant for the Viterbese territory, so much so that AXIA, situated far from the most important commercial and military routes such as the Via Cassia, experienced nonetheless a true sheep farming economy establishing its settlement.

The ancient Etruscan site of AXIA, the ancient onomastics known by Cicerone (*Pro Caecina oratio*), rises in south west Viterbo (Lazio), the ancient Sorrina which was part of the Etruscan centre, is situated along the Via della Dogana, that from Sorrina heads towards the Tolfa Mountains and then towards the Tyrrheanian Sea.

The rocky necropolis of the Etruscan settlement has been well preserved. The tombs belonging to the nobles have provided useful information, mainly epigraphical, concerning the wealthy (*gentes*) who lived during the Hellenistic period at the decline of the Etruscan civilization.

The fertile land, water in abundance and the presence of a rich system of internal roads classified it as a settlement, together with the ever increasing quantities of land concentration in the solid hands of the landowners.

By the end of the Imperial Roman Age, the land surrounding Sorrina was divided into a series of *latifundia*. Such a system lasted quite some time and required a social organisation characterized by a few rich families that possessed the land, while the poor farmed it: in fact the toponym "AXIA" lasted a long time almost as if to underline the continuity in the use of the land.

From 1100 the toponym "AXIA", was connected to the erection of the castle (from which today's name Castel d'Asso), an abrupt construction of tufa blocks, situated on the plain facing the rocky necropolis, in the confluence of two waterways (Riosecco and Freddano) in defence of the road network from the coast towards the hinterland.

The reasons for this construction are not clear. The construction dates back to the second half of the XII century (Colonna & Colonna Di Paolo 1970), but it is clear that from the moment of its construction, the castle became the nodal point of the surrounding land.

Due to its construction, work on the defensive Etruscan moat at the beginning of the plain was reinstated and it was made deeper. The castle shows a very simple planimetric structure, a courtyard closed by a high boundary wall, a tower at the entrance and external protuberances according to a medieval architectural typology found in other castles in the Tuscia region.

What deeply distinguishes from these is the fact it was AXIA's castle planned and built as an autonomous structure, in defence of itself, with evident strategic intentions to control the road and water networks of the surrounding land; control but not defence.

Norchia, another ancient centre in the Tuscia region, has the same geomorphological land characteristics and the same historical formation of the site.

The castle was built on the most exposed point of the plain, controlling the road that gains access to it, defending the structure which was undoubtedly of a certain extent, due to two evident churches on the rise.

In Castel d'Asso, on the contrary, the castle is situated on the farthest and safest point of the plain, practically on the boundary of it.

It did not defend any road and it did not protect any structure, but itself.

Such a characteristic reveals a total detachment between castle and home, which had been already established and was thriving too, as the numerous citations from AXIA in medieval documents show, proving the existence of a built up urban area relating to the castle. However, there is no trace of a built up area on the plain around the castle, while there is plenty of evidence of homes in caves obtained from the inside of the rocky architecture of Etruscan tombs.

The houses are troglodytic, according to the widespread medieval use present here as in Norchia; they mainly used the tombs which teemed the west-south west rocky slopes, a favourable position for the sun's exposure. There are areas, adapted from burial chambers or the under façade tomb chambers, for families and livestock, many sheep, pigs and chickens.

The tombs were gradually occupied in the early Middle Ages, and even more so following the destruction of the castle, proving the existence of a stable form of human settlement. This was also favoured by the presence of minor road beds, in close proximity to the Etruscan burial ground.

Several tombs from the Hellenistic necropolis of Castel d'Asso were examined and the structural modifications clearly underline the *modus vivendi* of the inhabitants of this internal zone in northern Lazio.

The Tombs 37, 56, 60, 61, 66, 67, 71, 77 (Colonna & Colonna Di Paolo 1970) are 'cubic' tombs generally made up of a parallelepiped (a cube), of an under façade and a hypogean burial chamber used as a *dromos* access: the only cube, that does not appear to have been used as a home, not having undergone any changes during the Middle Ages.

The examinations carried out on the tombs show how the structural modifications, in accordance with specific problems of optimization regarding the internal spaces, prove to have common characteristics:

1. The *dromos* was extended as far as the road bed (T. 77) widening the internal walking ground (T. 37). The *dromos* floor was modified to increase the inclination towards the road bed and to facilitate the flow of meteoric water toward the eternal part of chamber.

2. The entrance to the burial chamber, which in Etruscan tombs has reduced measurements to facilitate its closure whit a stone, was widened by chiselling the doors jambs, of which there were often traces on the floor (T. 60). Sometimes the entrance was widened through the ceiling, thus involving a part of the head of the *dromos* (T. 60).

The height of the entrance to the burial chambers was often lowered to the level of the floor of the *dromos*, and at times over the level to allow the free circulation of men and animals to and from the area (T. 60). If the internal height of the room was already at a lower level than the *dromos* it was ideal from reoccupation.

3. The internal walls of the chambers, such as the platforms of the under façade rooms, are structural parts that have mainly undergone modifications. Holes were almost always chiselled at the sides of the door, generally in pairs, 6 – 10 cm in diameter. These holes were used to insert planks of wood in an oblique position, or there were holes that were in a specular position in which support poles for the door were inserted to prevent the animals from escaping (TT. 61, 71).

Such evidence leads us to believe that certain rooms which did not have great depth were shared with the animals, given that this was the only area available.

On the walls, still on long vertical levels are pairs of loop holes in the rock, which were no doubt used for ropes to tie up the livestock (T. 60). Sometimes the thin partition walls between the tombs were either completely or partially knocked down to facilitate access from one room to another (T. 61); from the marks in the grooves and the holes it can be seen that the spacing inside was organized, especially for the livestock (T. 74), which were settled in the smaller areas.

The walls and ceilings of some of the reused burial chambers, as those rooms pertaining to the under facade, are covered in lampblack.

4. The under facade rooms of the tombs, furnished with platforms obtained from the tufaceous mass were generally lowered by 30 – 40 cm. or more (T. 74) to create necessary floors. Sometimes the Etruscan graves were partially removed as traces show, or they were totally eliminated to gain greater space inside. The marks on the floors and ceilings of the rooms of the under facade reveal unmistakeable evidence of internal partitions, achieved through wooden divisions supported by fixed beams on the horizontal levels, strengthening its endurance (TT. 66, 67).

On the floors obtained by lowering the platform the necessary domestic instruments were obtained:

- the hearth, often obtained by a canal passing through the rock that had an external connection, serving as a draught for kitchen fumes (T. 61). In the under façade room the hearth was situated in a more central position not far from the door to the room (T. 61).
- Small basins, single or double, for liquids, some with draining holes on the lower floor level (T. 74) and others were completely closed (T. 56)
- The stove was built in the platforms (TT. 75, 110), unlike the heart because of its semi-circular niche shape, with a worktop connected to a vertical duct created in the rock, that reached down to the floor.

Therefore, regarding medieval dwellings in Castel d'Asso, pre-existent caves (tombs) were privileged indifferently during the post-ancient period and in the XII and XIII centuries when the area was presided over by the castle.

For humans and animals to adapt in the rocky tombs, at first less work was carried out on a tufa, thus choosing as far as it was possible, areas that had better living characteristics, such as the height of the room and the under façade room comparated to the height of the road and a better sun exposure.

Subsequently certain internal areas were widened, doubling the size of the rooms of the under façade along the longitudinal axis or subdividing the internal space with mobile wooden structures.

Undoubtedly the position of the 'facilities' (heart, basins, etc.) were primarily positioned in the foreground and near the door leading us to believe that this part was used for human activity the far end of the room for the animals.

Author's address

Lucilla VENTURI
Via Aldo Moro, 12
01013 Cura di Vetralla (VT) ITALY

Bibliography

COLONNA, G., & COLONNA DI PAOLO, E., 1970, *Castel d'Asso*, vol.I, II, Roma.

ETUDE ANTHROPOLOGIQUE DU CIMETIERE MEDIEVAL DE SAINT-ESTEVE-LE-PONT (BERRE L'ETANG, BOUCHES-DU-RHONE)

Aminte THOMANN, Silvia BELLO, Loïc LALYS, Pascal ADALIAN,
Yann ARDAGNA, William DEVRIENDT, Morgane GIBERT, Alain GENOT,
Olivier DUTOUR & Michel SIGNOLI

Résumé : L'étude de la collection ostéoarchéologique du site médiéval de Saint-Estève-le-Pont concerne les aspects d'anthropologie funéraire (modalités d'inhumation, analyse spatiale) et d'anthropologie biologique (résultats paléodémographiques, biométriques, paléopathologiques et paléoépidémiologiques). Elle présente l'avantage d'un suivi anthropologique du terrain au laboratoire et se révèle primordiale pour l'étude de ce site, notamment en raison de la rareté de matériel archéologique dans les tombes. Le site de Saint-Estève-le-Pont, situé dans la commune de Berre l'Etang (Bouches-du-Rhône), présente deux ensembles funéraires. Le premier concerne des tombes de typologie diversifiée (sarcophages monolithiques, tombes sous bâtière de tuiles, tombes anthropomorphes sous dallage de pierre, tombes en cercueil, etc.), datées entre le VIème et le XIème siècles et situées autour d'un édifice orienté (probablement une chapelle), ayant subi plusieurs remaniements et destructions. Le second ensemble est situé à environ 50 mètres au Nord de l'édifice et se compose de tombes anthropomorphes, sous dallage de pierre, orientées Est-Ouest et Nord-Sud. Il s'agit d'un ensemble plus homogène, sans chevauchement de tombes, correspondant à l'établissement d'un cimetière de type « village » à une époque comprise entre le VIIème et le XIème siècles. L'échantillon paléodémographique de ce site, qui reste en cours de fouille, représente un document exceptionnel pour l'étude des populations provençales du haut Moyen Age encore mal connues.

Abstract: Saint-Estève-le-Pont (Berre l'Etang, Bouches-du-Rhône) medieval cemetery anthropological study. The osteoarchaeological collection study of Saint Estève le Pont medieval site concerns both the funeral anthropological (burial mode, spatial analysis) and the biological anthropological (paleodemographic, biometrical, paleopathological and paleoepidemiological results) aspects. The collection has the advantage of providing an anthropological monitoring from the actual outdoor site to the laboratory, and turns out to be essential to the study of this site, particularly because of the scarcity of the archaeological material in the graves. The site of Saint Estève le Pont, located in the district of Berre l'Etang (Bouches-du-Rhône) consists of two funeral units. The first one concerns graves of varied typologies (monolithic sarcophagus, graves under saddleback tiles, anthropomorphic graves under pavement from stones, coffins, etc.), dated between the 6th and 11th century and located around an edifice facing East (probably a chapel), which has been subject to modifications and destructions. The second unit is located 50 meters north of the edifice and is composed of anthropomorphical graves under pavement from stones oriented East/West and North/South. It's a more homogeneous unit, without overlapping graves, corresponding to the establishment of a « village » type cemetery between the 7th and 11th century. The paleodemographic sample of this site, still under excavation, is an exceptional document for the study of the early Middle Age Provençal populations, which are still ill-known today.

1. INTRODUCTION

Le site de Saint-Estève-le-Pont a été découvert fortuitement lors d'un labour profond effectué par le propriétaire du terrain en décembre 1998. Ce dernier, ayant trouvé des dalles de calcaire et des os humains, en a averti les autorités compétentes.

A partir de février 1999, plusieurs fouilles se sont succédées :

I : fouille préventive, 01.02 – 19.02.1999. (responsable des opérations de terrain A. Genot, responsable anthropologique M. Signoli). Elle a permis de mettre au jour 27 tombes et 25 squelettes (fouille de la zone Nord-Est de la zone Nord; Genot *et al.*, 1999, Bello *et al.*, 1999)

II : fouille préventive, 26.02. – 25.03.1999. Cette opération de terrain, sous la responsabilité d'A. Genot, responsable de secteur A. Thomann, a permis de mettre au jour 4 tombes délivrant 4 squelettes (Genot *et al.*, 1999 ; Thomann *et al.*, 1999) ;

III : fouille préventive, 21.06 – 16.07.1999 (Responsable des opérations de terrain A. Genot, responsable de secteur S. Bello et G. Dagnas) ; fouille d'évaluation archéologique, 06. 09 – 10.09.1999 (responsable des opérations de terrain A. Genot, responsable anthropologique S. Bello). L'ensemble des deux opérations a permis de mettre au jour 57 tombes délivrant 55 squelettes (Genot, 2000 ; Bello *et al.*, 2000) ;

IV : fouille programmée, 15.04 – 30.10.2000 (responsable des opérations de terrain A. Genot, responsable anthropologique A. Thomann). Fouille des zones Nord et Sud (Genot, 2000) ;

V : fouille programmée, 01.06 – 30.10.2001 (responsable des opérations de terrain A. Genot, responsable anthropologique A. Thomann). Fouille des zones Nord et Sud (étude en cours) ;

Le complexe de Saint-Estève-le-Pont se présente sous la forme de deux ensembles distincts. Au sud du site, s'étend un premier ensemble très homogène dont la première occupation des structures remonte au IIIème siècle après J.C. et la dernière aux environs du XVIIIème siècle. Au nord, un deuxième ensemble est constitué d'une nécropole où les tombes anthropomorphes sous dallage de pierre ont été datées entre le VIIème et le XIème siècles.

Nous présenterons le site selon une succession chronologique. Tout d'abord, donc, nous décrirons la zone Sud du site qui constitue la partie plus ancienne du complexe et, peut-être, la plus intéressante d'un point de vue archéologique. Nous aborderons, par la suite, la description de la nécropole située au nord du site, pour laquelle nous disposons aussi de l'étude anthropologique des 85 individus qu'y ont été retrouvés (Thomann *et al.*, 1999 ; Lalys, 2000).

2. METHODES

2.1. Méthodes archéologiques

Sur le terrain, nous avons utilisé la méthodologie de traitement des données employée sur les chantiers AFAN (Association pour les Fouilles Archéologiques Nationales), méthodologie développée par M. Py sur le site de Lattes (Py, 1993).

Cette méthodologie est un découpage diachronique et synchronique de la fouille en Unités Stratigraphiques (US) et en Faits. En ce qui concernent les sépultures, nous avons utilisé deux types de fiche :

La fiche archéologique sur laquelle sont notés les US composantes, les altitudes et des croquis de la couverture, du squelette et de la fosse (ou coffrage), ainsi que des indications concernant le matériel ;

La fiche anthropologique comprenant une fiche avec des renseignements de terrain (position d'inhumation, liaisons articulaires, perturbations, etc.) et des renseignements anthropologiques (sexe, âge, pathologies), et une fiche de conservation pour évaluer l'état de conservation des os du squelette.

2.2. Méthodes anthropologiques

La **diagnose sexuelle** a été effectuée à partir de l'étude macroscopique de l'os coxal. La détermination a été basée sur les éléments morphologiques de la grande échancrure sacro-sciatique et de la face sacro-pelvienne du pubis (Ferembach *et al.*, 1979; Bruzek, 1992, 2002). Lorsque les os coxaux étaient mal conservés ou totalement absents, nous avons pratiqué une diagnose à partir de la gracilisation ou de la robustesse des autres éléments du squelette. Enfin, quand le seul élément présent était le crâne, nous avons étendu à celui-ci l'étude de la diagnose sexuelle (Ferembach *et al.*, 1979, Buikstra et Ubelaker, 1989).

L'**estimation de l'âge** est une diagnose plus délicate à effectuer sur le terrain car l'observation correcte de certains critères requiert l'absence totale de sédiment autour de l'os, surtout en ce qui concerne les individus adultes. Sa réalisation doit donc être très minutieuse en laboratoire.

L'estimation de l'âge au décès des individus immatures a pris en compte plusieurs paramètres. Le plus utilisé au sein du site de Saint-Estève-le-Pont est l'étude des stades d'éruption dentaire par comparaison avec les tables de références établies par D.H. Ubelaker sur des populations archéologiques (Ubelaker, 1978, 1989). Cette méthode, comportant des problèmes liés aux référentiels, est d'une utilisation simple et directe sur le terrain et en laboratoire. Cette méthode a été préférée à d'autres du fait de la très mauvaise conservation des ossements dans la zone nécropole, notamment ceux des plus jeunes. Lorsque la conservation des os l'a permis, nous avons observé la maturation osseuse ou les différents stades de fusion épiphysaire du squelette post-crânien en utilisant les planches de Brothwell (1981), ainsi que la longueur des os longs selon les références de M. Stoukal et H. Hanakova (1978). Par ces méthodes, la répartition des individus immatures a été faite selon les cinq classes d'âge suivantes : fœtus (Fazekas et Kosa, 1978) ; 0-4 ans ; 5-9 ans ; 10-14 ans ; 15-19 ans (adolescents).

L'estimation de l'âge des adultes reste plus délicate et moins précise ; nous avons choisi de prendre en compte des indicateurs dentaires (Lamandin, 1978 ; Miles, 1963 ; Brothwell, 1981) et squelettiques en relation avec des pathoplogies liées au vieillissement (Stewart, 1957). Ainsi, nous avons pu séparer les adultes en trois classes d'âge (Jeunes, Matures, Agés) et deux classes intermédiaires (Jeunes-Matures et Matures-Agés).

L'**évaluation de la stature** a été réalisée à partir des droites de régression établies sur la longueur des os longs en utilisant les formules de Olivier (Olivier *et al.*, 1978).

Enfin, la **classification des lésions osseuses d'origine pathologique** relevées sur les restes osseux a été réalisée sur la base de l'examen macroscopique à l'aide des modèles paléopathologiques classiques (Ortner et Putschar, 1981; Thillaud, 1996; Roberts et Manchester, 1995). Les altérations paléopathologiques ont été relevées et classées dans quatre groupes nosologiques : pathologies dégénératives, traumatiques, infectieuses et tumorales.

3. RESULTATS

3.1. La zone Sud[1]

La première occupation du site est actuellement matérialisée par deux sols de béton de tuileau situés à l'extrême sud du site. Ces sols sont datés entre le IIIème et le Vème siècles après J.C. par le matériel associé (notamment amphore africaine, Py, 1993). A certains endroits, les fondations de murs ainsi que des restes de la paroi en élévation ont été conservés sur quelques centimètres de hauteur ce qui montre que ces sols représentent trois pièces distinctes d'un édifice tardo antique. Ces structures peuvent appartenir à une **villa agricole gallo romaine** liée à l'exploitation d'un vignoble (dont des traces ont été largement observées dans la zone Nord). L'hypothèse de la présence d'une villa associée à

---

[1] La fouille de la zone Sud n'étant pas terminée, cet article présente les premiers résultats issus des données de terrain. Les hypothèses émises pourront évoluer en fonction des découvertes de l'éventuelle prochaine campagne ainsi que de l'approfondissement du travail de post-fouille.

l'exploitation d'un vignoble est très largement probable, mais il restera difficile de la certifier par des faits archéologiques à cause du hiatus stratigraphique existant entre les sols de béton de tuileau (zone Sud) et les traces agraires (zone Nord). Néanmoins, la présence d'un édifice antique sur le site de Saint-Estève est archéologiquement attestée par les sols, mais aussi par l'important matériel dans les couches archéologiques (céramique antique, enduits peints, tessselles de mosaïque, tuiles romaines).

La chapelle constitue le complexe majeur de cette zone dont la première occupation semble remonter aux $V^{ème}/VI^{ème}$ siècles. Les vestiges apparentés à cet état sont les murs sud constitués de moellons de moyen appareil liés par du mortier. Ce premier bâtiment, daté par l'apposition de sarcophages à acrotères utilisés à partir du Vème siècle après J.C., présente une forme en Tau.

Le deuxième état de la chapelle réside en la construction d'une nef unique. La construction de cette nef se compose d'un mur externe en moellons de moyen appareil liés entre eux par du mortier, et d'un plaquage interne de blocs antiques de grand appareil provenant de bâtiments publics et de stèles funéraires antiques utilisés en remploi.

Ce deuxième état de la chapelle n'est pas encore daté précisément. La datation est rendue très difficile, d'une part à cause de l'importante activité sépulcrale dans le temps et dans l'espace qui a perturbé les couches archéologiques associées à la construction et à l'activité de la chapelle et, d'autre part, à cause de l'utilisation de ce site comme carrière de pierres autour du XVIIème siècle. La conséquence de cette dernière activité a été l'épierrement total des murs dans la partie ouest de la chapelle et de l'élévation dans sa partie est, mais aussi la vidange de la quasi totalité de l'espace interne de la chapelle. Il en résulte l'absence totale de vestiges et de niveaux de fonctionnement en place associés aux murs. L'actuelle datation proposée vient des faits historiques qui indiquent que, selon l'usage, les restaurations d'édifices religieux, et notamment les plaquages, sont fréquentes autour de l'An Mil. A Saint-Estève, ce plaquage serait d'origine structurelle : en effet, certains blocs remaniés du site présentaient une face concave, indiquant qu'ils appartenaient initialement à une voûte de pierre. L'important poids de cette voûte semble être à l'origine du choix de sa position interne, ceci aux vues d'en assurer un meilleur soutien. En revanche, il est nécessaire de rester prudent sur ces hypothèses car les observations n'ont pu être effectuées qu'en fondation en raison de la très faible hauteur des structures conservées (deux assises de grand appareil au maximum).

L'activité sépulcrale est intense tout autour de la chapelle. Ce complexe présente un répertoire typologique large qui nous permet de placer l'occupation entre le VIème et le Xème siècles après J.C. La typo-chronologie des tombes provençales souffre actuellement du faible nombre de travaux de synthèse. Citons celui de S. Gagnière pour la basse vallée du Rhône (Gagnière, 1965) et la synthèse collective rapportée par M. Collardelle pour les sépultures du Sud-Est de la Gaule (Collardelle et al., 1996). La poursuite de l'étude et l'apport des datations radiocarbones permettront de compléter les travaux typo-chronologiques antérieurs. Le complexe sépulcral autour de la chapelle est composé de tombes orientées Est-Ouest et Nord-Sud. Plusieurs typologies sont observables : les tombes à coffrage de section triangulaire en tuile (très repandues aux VIème et VIIème siècles), les sarcophages monolithiques (fin Vème jusqu'au VIIème siècles), les tombes à contenant en bois non cloué ($VI^{ème} - VII^{ème}$ siècles), les tombes en coffrage mixte ($VIII^{ème} - X^{ème}$ siècles), les tombes à coffrage ovales de moellons (autour de l'An Mil) et les tombes rupestres à fosse anthropomorphe ($X^{ème} - XIII^{ème}$ siècles). Ces datations proviennent des travaux de Collardelle et al., (1996) et seront précisées pour le site de Saint-Estève grâce à des datations radiocarbone. Au sein du complexe, l'orientation des tombes est double : Est/Ouest avec la tête à l'Ouest et Nord/Sud avec la tête au Nord, cas classiques pour cette période.

L'occupation s'est développée en plusieurs phases, comme le montrent les réutilisations de tombes (réouverture des sarcophages, réduction de corps, tombes multiples, couvercles déplacés), ainsi que les cas de recoupement des fosses, ce qui prouve (pour une période indéterminée) l'absence de marquage au sol de l'emplacement de plusieurs tombes.

Le matériel à l'intérieur des tombes est très rare : quelques cas d'agrafes en bronze à double crochet (« de linceul ») et deux anneaux. Cette absence d'objets dans les tombes est en conformité avec les autres exemples des mêmes époques.

Cette très forte concentration de tombes autour de la chapelle, ainsi que leur réutilisation montre que cet endroit était un emplacement extrêmement recherché. Il s'agit d'un phénomène fréquemment observé : à cette époque, il existe une volonté de se faire inhumer au plus proche d'un lieu sacré (et notamment près de reliques saintes), afin de bénéficier de la grâce du Saint protecteur de l'édifice religieux. Nous serions donc en présence, du moins en ce qui concerne les sépultures intensément réoccupées, d'inhumations privilégiées.

Dans la partie ouest du site, un réseau de silos a été découvert. **Ces silos**, creusés en partie dans le substrat géologique, ne sont pas précisément datés mais sont postérieurs aux inhumations ; en effet, l'installation d'un silo perturbait une sépulture d'immature en fosse qui appartient typologiquement aux tombes les plus récentes du site ($VII^{ème}-XI^{ème}$ siècles). L'installation de la dizaine de silos mis au jour est donc postérieure à l'utilisation de l'espace pour l'inhumation et marque certainement la fin de l'occupation sépulcrale. Ainsi, on assiste probablement à un changement de vocation de l'espace aux alentours de la chapelle.

La présence des silos est actuellement rattachée à celle de **fours alimentaires** au nord de la zone. Ils sont actuellement datés par un tesson de céramique du VIIIème siècle. Ces deux ensembles (non encore reliés stratigraphiquement) peuvent être mis en relation avec les banalités. Le développement de la fouille de la zone située entre la zone d'ensilage et celle des fours, encore trop

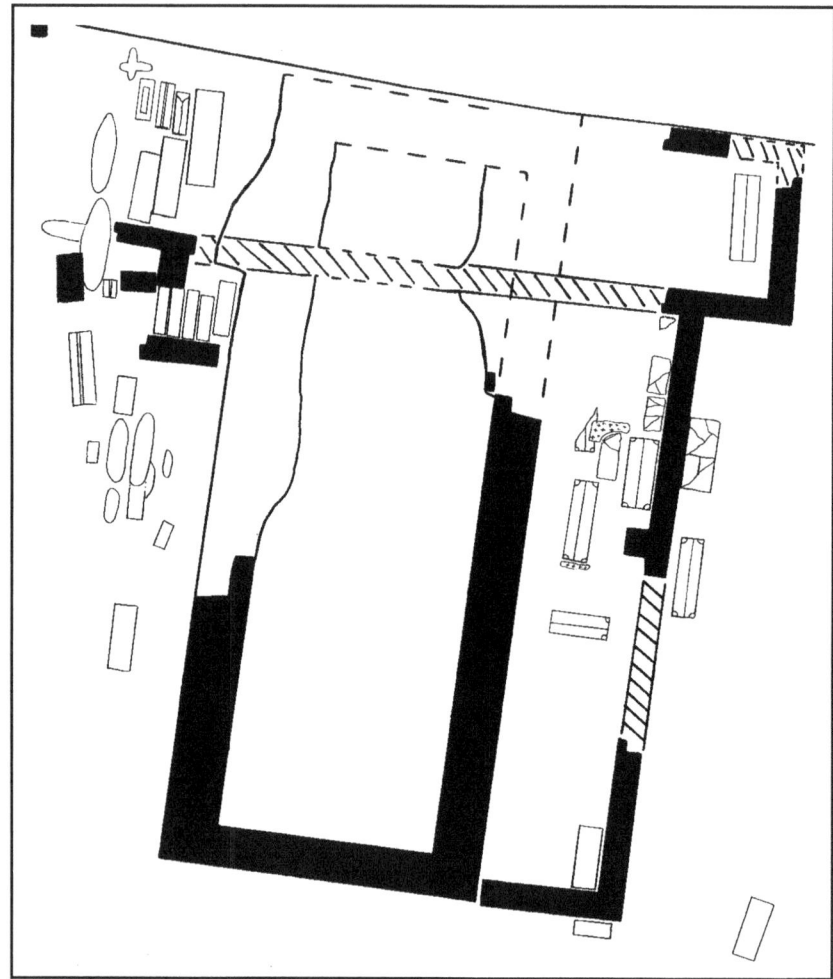

Figure 1. Plan de la chapelle orientée et des sépultures dans la zone Sud du site de Saint-Estève-le-Pont.

sommaire, permettra certainement d'apporter des informations complémentaires pour confirmer ou infirmer cette hypothèse.

Il reste à déterminer la cause initiale du changement de vocation de l'espace, à savoir si les silos ont été installés pour cause d'abandon de l'espace funéraire ou si c'est l'installation de ces silos qui a engendré le déplacement des inhumations de la chapelle vers la zone nécropole.

3.2. La zone Nord

A une cinquantaine de mètres au nord de la chapelle, la nécropole présente un espace sépulcral homogène et beaucoup plus simple spatialement et stratigraphiquement. Toutes les tombes appartiennent au même répertoire typologique (tombes anthropomorphes, figure 2).

L'organisation spatiale de la zone de la nécropole diffère nettement de celle de la zone Sud (cf figure 2). En effet, aucune réoccupation ni réutilisation de tombes n'a été observée et le plan général de cette partie du site montre clairement une organisation homogène avec une double orientation des sépultures (Nord-Sud, Est-Ouest), un alignement de tombes par rangées dans certaines parties et, enfin, la présence d'un axe de circulation. De même, nous pouvons remarquer sur le plan d'éventuelles zones de regroupement de tombes d'immatures. Par ailleurs, la présence de trois petites tombes orientées différemment et intercalées entre deux tombes d'adultes permet d'émettre l'hypothèse d'un système de concessions familiales : en effet, juste au nord de cette concentration de tombes, nous remarquons un espace vierge d'aménagement sépulcral ; cette observation, en plus de la disposition en rangées des tombes au Nord-Est de la zone, montre l'existence probable d'une organisation familiale et/ou sociale qu'il est encore difficile de cerner.

L'absence de recoupement de sépultures plaide en faveur d'une occupation relativement brève du cimetière. En effet, le non recoupement signifie que les tombes étaient toutes visibles grâce à un marquage au sol en matériaux périssables (aucune trace n'a été retrouvée sur le site) pendant toute la durée de l'occupation et qu'il n'y a pas eu d'abandon, ni d'oubli de la mémoire des défunts. Ce n'est pas le cas, comme nous l'avons vu précédemment, dans certaines zones autour de la chapelle. La zone fouillée de la nécropole a probablement été en activité un ou deux siècles tout au plus.

Les sépultures de cette zone sont toutes individuelles (notons le cas d'une femme enceinte) et toutes creusées dans le substrat. La plupart présente un dallage en calcaire, complet ou partiel, quelques tombes ont un dallage mixte

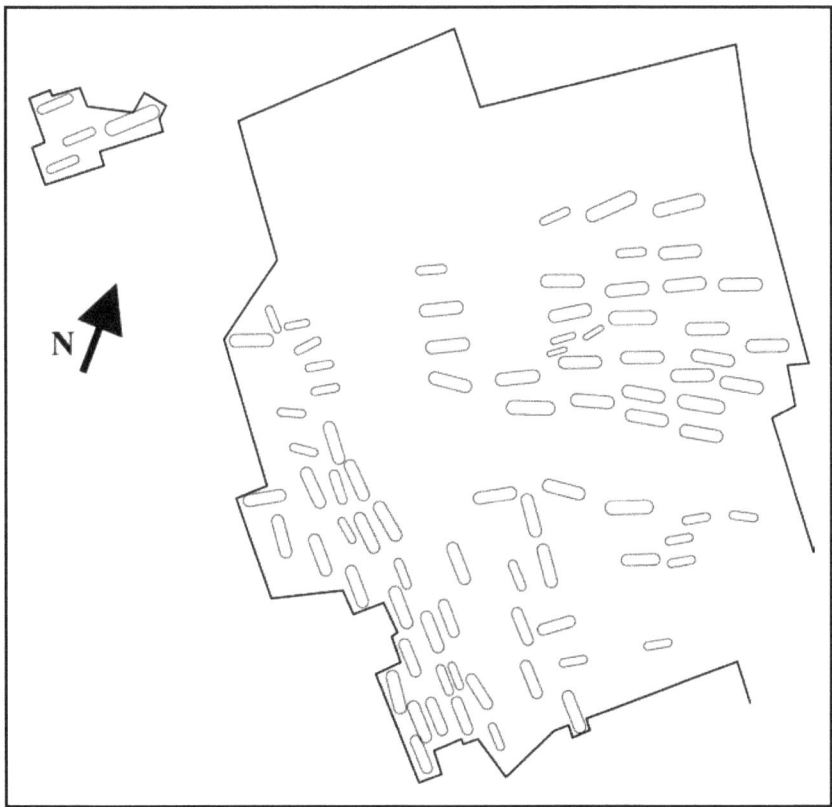

Figure 2. Plan de la nécropole située dans la zone Nord du site de Saint-Estève-le-Pont.

formé de dalles et de tuiles et les autres n'ont pas de couvertures mais présentent un liseré de galet sur le méplat entre les deux creusements (creusement sub-rectangulaire externe et creusement anthropomorphe interne). L'observation de l'espace de décomposition des individus inhumés (espace libre) indique que ces sépultures sans dallage présentaient néanmoins une couverture en matériaux périssables qui ne se serait pas conservée dans le sédiment. Les individus sont en position de décubitus dorsal avec les membres inférieurs en extension et diverses positions concernant les membres supérieurs : mains posées sur le bassin, sur la poitrine, bras le long du corps ou repliés sur eux-mêmes. La tête de certains individus reposait sur un coussin céphalique, toujours en matériaux périssables non conservés et des indices sur la position de certaines régions anatomiques (notamment la constriction au niveau des genoux et des chevilles) dénote la présence ancienne de linceuls non conservés.

Les 89 sépultures fouillées dans la zone Nord de la nécropole ont livré 85 individus.

La diagnose sexuelle effectuée sur les 51 individus adultes donne la répartition suivante :

29 individus de sexe féminin, soit 56,8 % de l'effectif total,
22 individus de sexe masculin, soit 43,2 % de l'effectif total.

Ces résultats montrent que le *sex ratio* de l'échantillon étudié est relativement équilibré avec une part légèrement supérieure de l'effectif féminin qui doit être pondérée par le faible nombre d'individus étudiés.

La répartition par âge des 85 individus exhumés est la suivante :

33 immatures, soit 38,8 % de l'effectif total,
52 adultes, soit 61,2 % de l'effectif total.

Nous remarquons que la part des sujets immatures est peu importante comparée aux référentiels des populations préjenneriennes où la mortalité infantile (entre 0 et 1 an) va de 200 ‰ à 400 ‰ (Ledermann, 1969) et dans quelques cas, la mortalité entre 0 et 5 ans atteint presque les 500 ‰ (Guy et Masset, 1997), ce qui signifie que, dans un cimetière datant d'une époque antérieure à 1798 et dont le recrutement n'a subi aucune sélection ni exclusion, l'effectif des immatures avoisine régulièrement les 50 % (cas fréquemment observé dans les cimetières historiques). L'effectif des immatures du cimetière de Saint-Estève est en deçà des cas « classiques » de populations préjenneriennes. Cette sous-représentation des sujets immatures pourrait être la conséquence d'un bon état sanitaire de la population. En effet, la nécropole ne semble pas avoir perduré plus de deux siècles et l'effectif paléodémographique exhumé pourrait hypothétiquement avoir bénéficié d'une période clémente. Néanmoins, la petitesse de l'effectif ne permet pas de garder ces taux comme définitifs car les limites de la nécropole n'ont pas encore définies et le cimetière semble être vaste (peut-être plusieurs centaines de tombes).

Par ailleurs, le plan de la nécropole présente quelques indices de regroupements de tombes d'immatures. Nous remarquons, en effet, la présence de deux regroupements de petites fosses sur le plan (7 tombes au Nord-Ouest et 3

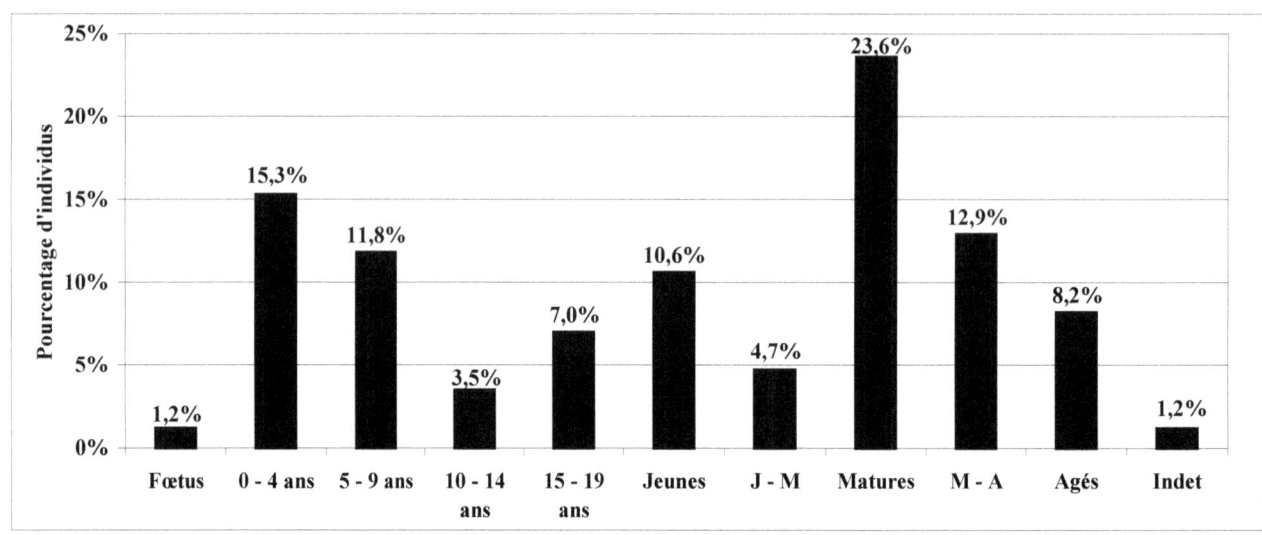

Figure 3. répartition par catégorie d'âge des 85 individus de la zone Nord.

tombes légèrement désorientées vers le centre du plan). Etant donné que la fouille de la nécropole n'est que partielle et seule la limite sud du complexe cimetérial est connue, nous pouvons imaginer que des regroupements spécifiques de tombes d'immatures se trouveraient dans des zones non fouillées. Cette hypothèse nécessiterait néanmoins une fouille exhaustive de la nécropole pour être vérifiée.

Enfin, dans notre cas, la conservation des ossements crée une fois de plus un biais non négligeable dans la reconstruction paléodémographique du cimetière. Les résultats énoncés plus haut sont des résultats issus du laboratoire. Or, sur le terrain, nous avons observé 4 fosses (SP 1002, SP 1005, SP 3084 et SP 3092) de petite dimension totalement vides d'ossements humains. Par comparaison avec les dimensions des autres fosses d'individus immatures (dont l'état de conservation est très faible), ces fosses pouvaient accueillir des sujets d'un âge inférieur à 2 ans (Bello et al, 2000 et 2001) et dont les ossements ne se seraient pas conservés. La fragilité des ossements d'enfants aux agents taphonomiques est un phénomène déjà bien attesté (Walker et al., 1988, Guy et Masset, 1997, Dutour, 1989). D'autres cas de cimetières connaissent ces problèmes de conservation différentielle, notamment le site d'Elko Switch en Alabama, cimetière de noirs américains utilisé entre 1850 et 1920 (Shogren et al., 1989) : sur 52 tombes, 15 étaient vides d'ossements humains et correspondaient à des enfants d'âge inférieur à 5 ans. Certains auteurs (Guy et Masset, 1997) avancent l'hypothèse d'un effet de seuil entre un type « nourrisson » et un type « adulte » qui se mettrait en place quelque part entre 1 et 5 ans. Ce problème de conservation des ossements des plus jeunes montre à quel point il est essentiel d'observer les données archéologiques afin de nuancer ou de compléter les résultats paléodémographiques et de restituer le plus correctement possible le recrutement du cimetière.

En ce qui concerne l'âge des individus adultes, le quotient de mortalité baisse pour la catégorie d'âge 20-49 ans et augmente successivement pour la catégorie d'âge de plus de 60 ans (Ledermann, 1969). Les résultats de l'échantillon paléodémographique de Saint-Estève-le-Pont montre un quotient de mortalité de 98,77 ‰ pour les individus Jeunes (20-29 ans) et quotient de mortalité de 86,42 ‰ pour les individus de plus de plus de 60 ans.

Ainsi, la répartition par âge de la population adulte de Saint-Estève-le-Pont est compatible avec une mortalité archaïque, avec une anomalie résidant dans la sous-représentation de la classe d'âge de plus de 60 ans. Comme dans le cas des individus immatures, la sous-représentation de cette catégorie d'âge pourrait être mise en relation avec un processus de conservation différentielle : le processus de vieillissement de l'os, qui se manifeste par sa déminéralisation généralisée, devrait alors induire une sous-conservation des individus plus âgés (Bello, 2001). Il est toutefois difficile d'affirmer dans quelle mesure cette sous-conservation osseuse ait pu déterminer la sous-représentation de cette catégorie d'individus.

Inversement, nous notons sur la figure 3 la prédominance de la classe d'âge Matures. Même si certaines études (Baud et Gossi, 1980) montrent que la meilleure corrélation entre l'âge au décès et la conservation des os dans la terre avoisine les 40 ans, ce cas ne peut expliquer nos résultats. Il s'agirait davantage de ce que C. Masset (1990) appelle l'« attraction de la moyenne », c'est-à-dire la croissance abusive des classes moyennes aux dépends des classes extrêmes, qui doit être accentuée par une observation limitée des critères d'estimation de l'âge liée à la mauvaise conservation des surfaces corticales. En effet, la catégorie d'âge Matures pourrait avoir bénéficié de quelques cas appartenant aux classes d'âge Jeunes-Matures et/ou Matures-Agés, la disproportion étant, par ailleurs, gonflée par le faible nombre d'individus contenus dans l'effectif paléodémographique étudié. La suite de l'étude permettra probablement de donner d'autres éléments de réponses.

La stature a pu être calculée sur 15 individus masculins et 15 féminins. Pour les sujets masculins, les statures se

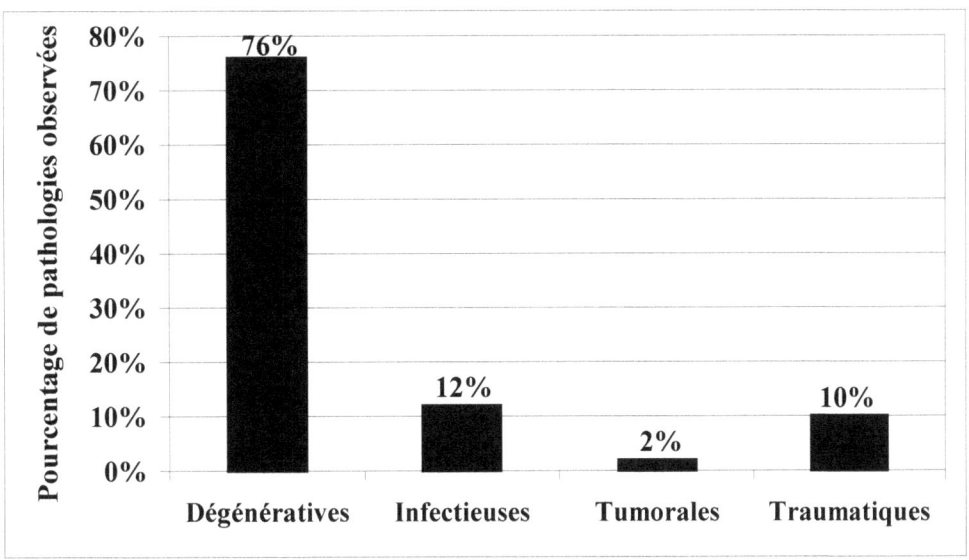

Figure 4. Groupes pathologiques observés sur 85 individus de la zone Nord.

trouvent comprises dans une fourchette allant de 147 à 180 cm, la stature moyenne étant d'environ 163 cm. Pour les sujets féminins, la fourchette se trouve plus réduite, de 152 à 168 cm, avec une stature moyenne de 160,3 cm.

La prévalence des pathologies observées dans la collection de Saint-Estève-le-Pont a été obtenue en calculant le rapport entre le nombre des individus adultes qui présentent au moins une atteinte pathologique (dégénérative, traumatique, infectieuse ou tumorale) et le nombre total des individus adultes constituant l'échantillon paléodémographique (figure 4).

L'examen macroscopique de la collection a mis en évidence la nette prédominance des **pathologies dégénératives**. Au sein de ce groupe, l'arthrose vertébrale touche les trois quarts de l'effectif ce qui n'est pas surprenant car l'arthrose vertébrale est une des pathologies les plus fréquentes dans les séries ostéoarchéologiques. Les fréquences les plus élevées concernent l'étage lombaire et notamment L3, L4 et L5. Le lumbago aigu et la sciatique vertébrale commune sont les principales manifestations de la détérioration discale lombo-sacrée (Ryckewaert, 1987; Pàlfi, 1997). Les autres arthroses touchent particulièrement les articulations du coude (3 cas), de l'épaule (2 cas) et sacro-iliaque (2 cas). Une forte prévalence d'ancarthroses est liée à des surmenages articulaires d'ordre professionnel (Berato et al., 1990), confortant l'attribution de ces individus à des catégories socio-professionnelles d'ordre manuel (Bello et al., 2000).

Les taux des pathologies traumatiques et tumorales se rapprochent de ceux des travaux conduits par B. Mafart (1983) et Gy. Pàlfi (1997). Les pathologies traumatiques que nous avons pu observer concernent particulièrement les avant-bras : 3 cas diagnostiqués. Cette distribution est assez commune dans le cas de populations ostéoarchéologiques d'époque médiévale (Grauer et Roberts, 1996). En ce qui concerne les pathologies tumorales, nous avons pu observer 1 cas d'ostéome bénin (tumeur ostéoformatrice) localisé sur les os frontaux du crâne. Cette localisation est un siège préférentiel pour cette forme tumorale (Dastugue et Gervais, 1992 ; Thillaud, 1996). La fréquence d'atteintes tumorales revient à des taux assez proches de ceux présentés dans la littérature (Gy. Pàlfi, 1997).

Enfin, en ce qui concerne les pathologies infectieuses, les atteintes périostées touchent essentiellement les os du membre inférieur, conformément à une distribution classique en clinique comme en paléopathologie. La distribution des atteintes périostées observées est la suivante : 1,08 % atteinte de la clavicule ; 1,08 % atteinte de la *scapula* ; 1,04 % atteinte de l'humérus ; 1,08 % atteinte du tibia ; 1,11 % atteinte de la fibula.

Toutefois, la collection de Saint-Estève-le-Pont présente généralement des fréquences d'atteintes périostées très faibles. Ces faibles valeurs pourraient trouver une explication dans le très mauvais état de conservation des surfaces corticales observées.

4. CONCLUSION ET PERSPECTIVES

Le site de Saint-Estève-le-Pont offre un répertoire dense de structures qu'il est encore difficile de dater précisément en raison de destructions et de réoccupations de l'espace. La première occupation remonte aux environs du IIIème siècle par l'installation d'une villa gallo-romaine. Succède le premier état de la chapelle qui apparaît vers le Vème siècle avec déjà une occupation sépulcrale importante. Cette occupation perdure jusqu'aux XIème – XIIème siècles avec une restructuration du bâtiment probablement vers l'An Mil. Enfin, l'espace sépulcral semble être abandonné pour l'installation d'une zone d'ensilage, peut-être associée à des fours communautaires. Au niveau des zones d'inhumations, le site présente un complexe dense et hétéroclite autour de la chapelle et, au nord, un cimetière plus homogène de tombes exclusivement rupestres.

Les résultats anthropologiques préliminaires de la collection ostéologique de la zone Nord datant du haut Moyen Age montrent une population que l'on peut qualifier de type "village" (importance de la mortalité des plus jeunes, *sex ratio* équilibré), population qui semble avoir un bon état sanitaire (sans compter le biais que représente le mauvais état de conservation du matériel) et qui présente des signes de surmenage d'ordre professionnel. La poursuite de l'étude archéologique permettra certainement d'apporter des éléments de réponses quant aux phases d'occupation et d'abandon de la chapelle. En ce qui concerne l'étude anthropologique, l'intérêt final résidera en la comparaison des résultats des individus inhumés autour de la chapelle avec ceux des individus inhumés dans la zone Nord. Le site de Saint-Estève-le-Pont représente de par ses vestiges archéologiques et son importante collection ostéoarchéologique un témoignage essentiel dans l'étude du haut Moyen Age en Provence, encore mal connu.

Adresses des auteurs

Aminte THOMANN, Silvia BELLO, Loïc LALYS, Pascal ADALIAN, Yann ARDAGNA, William DEVRIENDT, Morgane GIBERT, Olivier DUTOUR, Michel SIGNOLI
Unité d'Anthropologie - CNRS UMR 6578
Faculté de Médecine
Université de la Méditerranée
27, Bd Jean Moulin
13385 Marseille Cedex 5, FRANCE

Silvia BELLO
Dipartimento di Biologia Animale e dell'Uomo
Università degli Studi di Torino
17, Via Accademia Albertina
10100, Turin, ITALIE

Alain GENOT
Service Archéologique Municipal
Hôtel de ville
13130 Berre l'Etang FRANCE

Bibliographie

BAUD, C.A., GOSSI, M., 1980, Degree of mineralization of bone tissue as determined by quantitative microradiography : effect of age, sex and pathological conditions. In *Proceedings, Fourth international conference on bone measurement*, edited by Mazess, R.B. Toronto, 1978, p. 345-352. U.S. Department of Health and Human Services.

BELLO, S., THOMANN, A., ADALIAN, P., ARDAGNA, Y., GIBERT, M., MACZEL, M., VERGONZANNE, L., SIGNOLI, M., DUTOUR, O., 1999, *Etude anthropologique des sépultures du cimetière de Saint-Estève-le-Pont (Berre l'Etang, Bouches-du-Rhône)*, UMR 6578 – CNRS – Université de la Méditerranée – Service d'Anthropologie Biologique – Faculté de Médecine de Marseille, manuscrit, 91 p.

BELLO, S., LALYS, L., THOMANN, A., ADALIAN, P., ARDAGNA, Y., DUCOURNEAU, A., GIBERT, M., MACZEL, M., BOULE, E-L., DAGNAS, G., GENOT, A., DUTOUR, O., SIGNOLI, M., 2000, *Etude anthropologique des sépultures du cimetière de Saint-Estève-le-Pont (Berre l'Etang, Bouches-du-Rhône). Opération de sauvetage du 23 juin au 17 juillet 1999*, UMR 6578 – CNRS – Université de la Méditerranée – Service d'Anthropologie Biologique – Faculté de Médecine de Marseille 277 p.

BELLO, S., 2001, *Taphonomie des restes osseux humains. Effet des processus de conservation du squelette sur les paramètres anthropologiques*. Ph.D Dissertation, Università degli Studi di Firenze and Université de la Méditerranée, Florence.

BERATO, J., DUTOUR, O., ZARAKIAN, H., Acquaviva, P.C., 1990, Epidémiologie des affections rhumatismales dans une population antique. Etude de la nécropole du Haut Empire de Saint-Lambert (Fréjus, Var). *Revue du Rhumatisme*, 57/5, p. 397-400.

BROTHWELL, D.R., 1981, *Digging up bones. The excavation, treatment and study of human skeletal remains*. New York : Cornell University Press.

BRUZEK, J., 1992, Diagnose sexuelle à partir du squelette : possibilités et limites. *Archéo-nil*, p. 43-51.

BRUZEK, J., 2002, A methode for visual determination of sex, using the human tip bone. *American Journal of Physical Anthropology*, 117, p. 157-168.

BUIKSTRA, J.E., UBELAKER, D.H., 1989, *Standards for data collection from the Human skeletal remains*. Fayetteville Arkansas, Arkansas Survey Research, series 44, 206 p.

COLLARDELLE, M. (rap.), DÉMIANS D'ARCHIMBAUD, G., RAYNAUD, C., 1996, Typo- chronologie des sépultures du Bas-Empire à la fin du Moyen-Age dans le Sud-Est de la Gaule (travaux collectifs). In GALINIE, H., ZADORA-RIO, E (dir.), *Archéologie du cimetière chrétien*, actes du 2ème colloque A.R.C.H.E.A., Orléans, 29 septembre – 1er octobre 1994, Sociétés et cadres de vie au Moyen Age : approches archéologiques, G.D.R. 94 du CNRS, 11e supplément à la Revue Archéologique du Centre de la France, Tours, 1996, p.271-303.

DASTUGUE, J., GERVAIS, V., 1992, *Paléopathologie du squelette humain*. Boubée, Paris.

DUTOUR, O, 1989, *Hommes fossiles du Sahara : peuplements holocènes du Mali septentrional*. Paris : édition du CNRS.

FAZEKAS, I. G., KOSA, F., 1978, Forensis fetal osteology, Budapest, Akadémiai Kiado.

FEREMBACH, D., SCHWIDETZKY, I., STOUKAL, M., 1979, Recommandations pour déterminer l'âge et le sexe sur le squelette. *Bulletins et Mémoires de la Société d'Anthropologie de Paris*, t. 6, s. XIII , p. 7-45.

GAGNIÈRE, S., 1965, Les sépultures à inhumation du IIIe au XIIIe siècle de notre ère dans la basse vallée du Rhône. Essai de chronologie typologique. *Cahiers Rhodaniens*, XII, p.53-110.

GENOT, A., 2000, *Le site de Saint-Estève-le-Pont (Berre l'Etang, Bouches-du-Rhône, Opération du 15 avril au 30 octobre 2000)*. Rapport intermédiaire d'activité, 20 p.

GENOT, A., BELLO, S., THOMANN, A., ADALIAN, A., ARDAGNA, Y., GIBERT, M., MACZEL, M., VERGONZANNE, L., SIGNOLI, M., DUTOUR, O., 1999, *Etude anthropologique des sépultures du cimetière de Saint-Estève-le-Pont (Berre l'Etang, Bouches-du-Rhône, Opération de sauvetage du 1er au 19 février 1999)*, UMR 6578 – CNRS – Université de la Méditerranée – Service d'Anthropologie Biologique – Faculté de Médecine de Marseille – Service Régional de l'Archéologie de Provence-Alpes-Côte d'Azur, DFS sous la direction de A. Genot, 128 p.

GENOT, A., BELLO, S., THOMANN, A., ADALIAN, A., ARDAGNA, Y., GIBERT, M., SIGNOLI, M., DUTOUR, O., 2000, *Etude anthropologique des sépultures du cimetière de Saint-Estève-le-Pont (Berre l'Etang, Bouches-du-Rhône, fouille d'urgence du 21 juin au 16 juillet 1999 et fouille d'évaluation archéologique du 6 au 10 septembre 1999)*,

UMR 6578 – CNRS – Université de la Méditerranée – Service d'Anthropologie Biologique – Faculté de Médecine de Marseille – Service Régional de l'Archéologie de Provence-Alpes-Côte d'Azur, DFS sous la direction de A. Genot, 174 p.

GRAUER, A.L., ROBERTS, C.A., 1996, Palaeoepidemiology, healing and possible treatment of trauma in the Medieval Population of Helen-on-the-Walls, York, England. *American Journal of Physical Anthropology*, 100 : 531-544.

GUY, H., MASSET, C, 1997, Particularités taphonomiques des os d'enfants. In BUCHET L. (Dir.), *Actes des 7ᵉ Journées Anthropologiques « L'enfant, son corps, son histoire »*. Edition APDCA, p. 35-43

LALYS, L., 2000, *Etude anthropologique des squelettes exhumés de la nécropole de Saint-Estève-le-Pont (Berre l'Etang, Bouches-du-Rhône)*. Mémoire de DEA. Université de la Méditerranée.

LAMANDIN, H, 1978, Critère dentaire pour appréciation d'âge : étude de la translucidité et des canalicules, intérêt en odontostomatologie légale. *Revue d'Odonto-Stomatologie*, t. VII, n°2 : 11-119.

LEDERMANN, S., 1969, Nouvelles tables-types de mortalité. In *Travaux et Documents*, n° 53, INED.

MAFART, B., 1983, *Pathologie osseuse au Moyen Age en Provence*. Marseille : CNRS.

MASSET, C., 1990, Où en est la paléodémographie ?, *Bulletins et Mémoires de la Société d'Anthropologie de Paris*, t. 2, n° 3-4, p. 109-122.

MILES, A.E.W., 1963, The dentition in the assestment of individual age in skeleton material. *Dental Anthropology, Pergamon Press* : p. 191-209.

OLIVIER, G., AARON, C., FULLY, G., TISSIER, G., 1978, News estimations of stature and cranial capacity in modern man. *Journal of Human Evolution*, 7, p. 513-518.

ORTNER, D.J., PUTSCHAR, W.G.J., 1981, *Identification of pathological conditions in human skeletal remains*. Washington : Smithsonian Institution Press.

PÀLFI, Gy., 1997, Maladies dans l'Antiquité et au Moyen Age. Paléopathologie comparée des anciens gallo-romains et hongrois. *Bulletins et Mémoires de la Société d'Anthropologie de Paris*, t. 9, n° 1-2, p. 1-206.

PY, M. (dir.), 1993, Lattara 6 – DICOCER, dictionnaire des céramiques antiques en Méditerranée nord-occidentale. Edition de l'Association pour le Recherche Archéologique en Languedoc, Lattes.

ROBERTS, C., MANCHESTER, K., 1995, *The archaeology of desease*. 2th edition. New York, Ithaca : Cornwell University Press.

RYCKEWAERT, A., 1987, *Rhumatologie. Pathologie osseuse et articulaire*. Paris : Flammarion.

SHOGREN, M.G., TURNER, K.R., PERRONO, J.C., 1989, *Elko Switch Cemetery : an archaeological perspective*. The University of Alabama, Alabama State Museum of Natural History, Divison of Archaeology, Reprot of Incestigations, 58.

STEWART, T.D., 1957, The rate of development of vertebral hypertrophic arthritis and its utility in age estimation, *American Journal of Physical Anthropology*, 15 : 433.

STOUKAL, M., HANAKOVA, H., 1978, Die Länge des Längsknochen altslawischer bewölkerungen unter besonderer Berücksichtigung von Wachstumsfragen, *Homo*, 29, p. 53-69.

THILLAUD, P.L., 1996, *Paléopathologie humaine*. Kronos B.Y.

THOMANN, A., ADALIAN, P., ARDAGNA, Y., BELLO, S., GIBERT, M., SIGNOLI, M., DUTOUR,O., 1999, *Etude anthropologique des sépultures du cimetière de Saint-Estève-le-Pont (Berre l'Etang, Bouches-du-Rhône). Opération de sauvetage du 13 au 18 mars 1999*. UMR 6578 – CNRS – Université de la Méditerranée – Service d'Anthropologie Biologique – Faculté de Médecine de Marseille 22 p.

UBELAKER, D.H, 1978, *Human skeletal remains : excavation, analysis, interpretation*. Chicago : Aldine.

UBELAKER, D.H., 1989, *Human skeletal remains, 2ⁿᵈ edition*. Washington D.C. : Taraxacum press.

WALKER, P.L., JOHNSON, J.R., LAMBERT, P.M., 1988, Age and sex biases in the preservation of human skeletal remains. *American Journal of Physical Anthropology*, 76, p. 183-188.

L'ÉVOLUTION DES MODES D'INHUMATION EN PICARDIE (FRANCE) ENTRE LES IIIE ET VIIIE SIECLES

Luc HERMANN

Résumé. À travers l'analyse d'une vingtaine de sites de Picardie (nord de la France), cette étude retrace l'évolution des modes d'inhumation dans cette région entre les IIIème et VIIIème siècles. Nous constatons au milieu du Vème siècle et à la fin du VIIème siècle que les rites funéraires dans leur ensemble connurent des transformations profondes et significatives, reflétant par ce fait une modification des conceptions sociales et philosophiques du monde des vivants à ces deux époques.

Abstract. Through the analysis of about twenty sites of Picardy (north of France), this study recounts the evolution of the means of burial in this region between the 3rd and the 8th centuries. It is to be observed that during the middle of the 5th century and at the end of the 7th century, the burial rituals experienced significant and profound changes. These changes reflect a modification in the social and philosophical outlooks in the world of the living during these two periods.

I. INTRODUCTION ET SITES ETUDIES

Cette étude fut entreprise dans le cadre de mon mémoire de maîtrise à l'Université de Liège. Pour ce faire, j'ai étudié une vingtaine de sites en Picardie (nord de la France), c'est-à-dire dans les trois départements de l'Aisne, à l'est, de l'Oise, au sud-ouest, et de la Somme, au nord-ouest.

Environ 4100 sépultures furent étudiées en se basant sur les différents rapports de fouille publiés dans la Revue Archéologique de Picardie.

A. le département de l'Aisne

MARTEVILLE[1] est un faubourg de Vermand, au sud-est de cette localité, sur la rive gauche de l'Omignon. Vermand se situe à 10 kilomètres à l'ouest de Saint-Quentin. L'altitude est de 81 mètres. Il s'agit d'une butte exposée à l'ouest, à l'extérieur du faubourg, bordée au nord par l'ancienne chaussée romaine reliant Vermand à Saint-Quentin. Marteville était un quartier de Vermand à l'époque gallo-romaine. Vermand était un *vicus*, alors qu'à Marteville se trouvait un *fanum*, donc un sanctuaire suburbain avec des habitats. Les fouilles mirent au jour 59 inhumations, datées entre 360 et 380.

CAULAINCOURT[2] est un petit village situé à 3 kilomètres au sud-ouest de Vermand sur la rive droite de l'Omignon. Le site étudié est situé à l'ouest du village au sommet d'un versant crayeux dominant les marais de l'Omignon d'une trentaine de mètres. 145 sépultures furent mises au jour lors de fouilles de sauvetage, dont 10 en sarcophage. Seule une sépulture en sarcophage fut fouillée.

GOUDELANCOURT-LES-PIERREPONT[3] est situé à 20 kilomètres au nord-est de Laon. Le site, à une altitude de 100 mètres, est implanté sur une colline crayeuse orientée nord-est/sud-ouest à 1 kilomètre à l'est de Cuirieux. Au sud de la butte coule par intermittence un petit ruisseau : "le Cornu". 458 sépultures réparties en deux noyaux distincts furent fouillées. Le premier noyau contenait 324 sépultures, toutes orientées sud/nord. Le second noyau comprenait 134 sépultures, toutes orientées ouest/est. Ce cimetière débute au début du VIème siècle et s'achève à la fin du VIIème siècle. Les deux noyaux furent occupés simultanément. Des traces d'habitat mérovingien furent retrouvées à 150 mètres au sud du cimetière. Il s'agissait d'une unité agricole élevant le bœuf, le porc et le mouton mais ne pratiquant pas la culture céréalière.

VORGES[4] est situé à 7 kilomètres au sud-est de Laon. Le site est implanté au pied du Mont Pigeon culminant à 153 mètres d'altitude, sur son flanc ouest. Au pied du mont

---

[1] d'après LOIZEL, Michel, 1977, Le cimetière gallo-romain du Bas-Empire de Marteville (02). *Cahiers archéologiques de Picardie*, n°4, Amiens, p.151-203.
BLONDIAUX, Joël, 1986, Anthropologie physique du cimetière de Marteville à Vermand (Aisne). Fin du IVème siècle. *Revue archéologique de Picardie*, n°1-2, Amiens, p.29-33.

[2] d'après HARNAY, Véronique, 1995, *Rapport de fouilles de Caulaincourt (les Carrières)*, déposé aux archives départementales de la Somme à Amiens sous le n°1372W1, inédit.

[3] d'après NICE, Alain, 1988, La nécropole mérovingienne de Goudelancourt-lès-Pierrepont (Aisne). *Revue archéologique de Picardie*, n°3-4, Amiens, p.127-143.
CHARPENTIER, Michel, 1988, Résultats provisoires de l'étude anthropologique de la nécropole mérovingienne de Goudelancourt-lès-Pierrepont (Aisne). *Revue archéologique de Picardie*, n°3-4, Amiens, p.149-151.
MORAZZANI, Corinne, 1994, Etude anthropologique de la nécropole de Goudelancourt-lès-Pierrepont (Aisne). *Revue archéologique de Picardie*, n°1-2, Amiens, p.9-19.
NICE, Alain, 1994, La nécropole mérovingienne de Goudelancourt-lès-Pierrepont (Aisne). Présentation générale. *Revue archéologique de Picardie*, n°1-2, Amiens, p.3-7.
NICE, Alain, 1994, L'habitat mérovingien de Goudelancourt-lès-Pierrepont (Aisne). Aperçu provisoire d'une unité agricole et domestique des VIème et VIIème siècles. *Revue archéologique de Picardie*, n°1-2, Amiens, p.21-63.
BAYARD, Didier, 1994, La céramique de l'habitat mérovingien de Goudelancourt (Aisne). *Revue archéologique de Picardie*, n°1-2, Amiens, p.65-79.
RENARD, Gabriel, mars 1981 et 1983, *Rapport de fouilles de Goudelancourt*, déposé aux archives départementales de la Somme à Amiens, n°1372W3, inédit.

[4] d'après FLECHE, Marie-Pascale, 1988, La nécropole mérovingienne de Vorges (Aisne), in *Revue archéologique de Picardie*, n°3-4, Amiens, p.89-125.

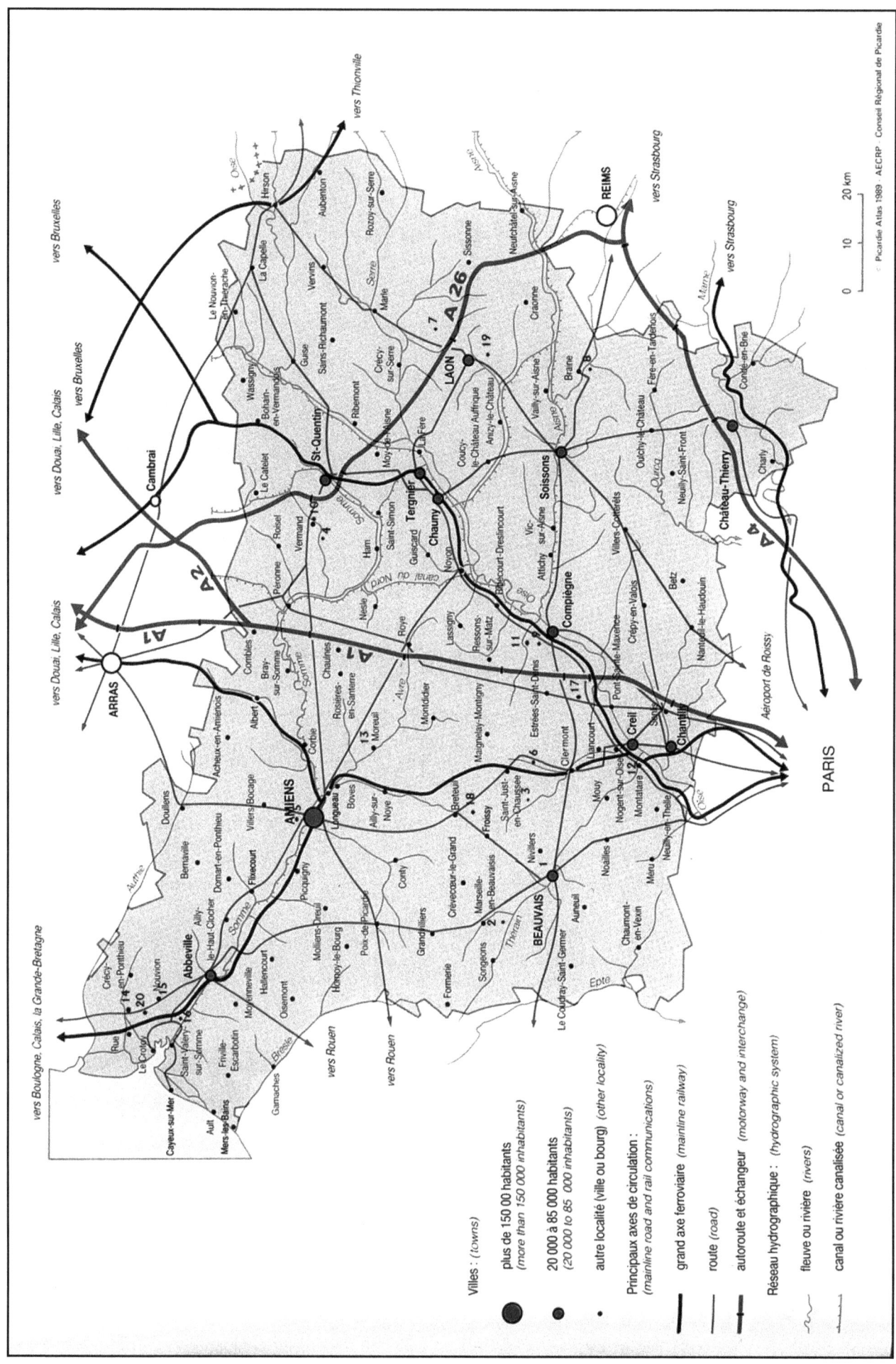

Figure 1. DESIRE, Emmanuel-Paul, *Picardie-atlas*, Amiens, 1989, p.19.

coulent plusieurs sources. 57 inhumations, orientées ouest/est, étaient alignées en plusieurs rangées parallèles, du bas vers le sommet du mont Pigeon. Elles datent du début du VIème siècle à la fin du VIIème siècle.

B. le département de l'Oise

Autour de Beauvais

BEAUVAIS. RUE DU PRESSOIR-COQUET[5] : Sur le site de l'ancienne voie romaine reliant Beauvais à Bavai, 12 sépultures, datées de la fin du IIIème siècle ou du début du IVème siècle furent exhumées.

BEAUVAIS. PLACE CLEMENCEAU[6] : 42 corps furent inhumés dans le substrat marécageux et humide, puisque le site est distant de 350 mètres du Thérain. Ce cimetière était situé *extra-muros*. Des datations C14 furent effectuées sur les inhumés des T.1608 et 1775. Pour le premier, la date calibrée se situe entre 692 et 957 et pour le second, entre 906 et 1148.

BEAUVAIS. L'ILOT DE L'HOTEL-DIEU[7] se trouve entre les rues Patin et Gambetta et le bld Lamette. Le site est installé à la base des flancs du mont Capron, hors de la ville, près des voies de communication de l'époque romaine. L'altitude du site est de 69 mètres. A l'ouest de l'îlot, 134 sépultures, datées entre le IIIème siècle et le Vème siècle, furent mises au jour.

BONNIERES[8] est une petite ville située sur la rive gauche du Thérain, à 12 kilomètres au nord-ouest de Beauvais. Le site étudié est implanté à la sortie ouest de la ville sur une butte marneuse qui domine à 103 mètres d'altitude la vallée marécageuse située à 88 mètres d'altitude. 110 inhumations, datées du VIème siècle et orientées ouest/est, furent exhumées.

BULLES[9] est située à 13 kilomètres au nord-ouest de Clermont et à 16 kilomètres au nord-est de Beauvais. Le site est implanté à 1,8 kilomètres au nord de Bulles, au lieu-dit "Saine-Fontaine", entre 100 et 105 mètres d'altitude, sur une colline orientée vers l'ouest, sur la rive gauche de la Brêche coulant à 85 mètres d'altitude. A 300 mètres à l'ouest se trouve une source. 1000 inhumations, dont 25 incinérations, furent mises au jour dans 832 fosses. Ce cimetière débute à la fin du Vème siècle et s'achève à la fin du VIIème siècle.

Autour de Creil

MONTATAIRE[10], dans l'agglomération de Creil, est située sur un plateau culminant à 80 mètres d'altitude dominant le confluent de l'Oise et du Thérain. Le site est implanté au lieu-dit "la Coquetière", en bordure du cimetière actuel et à 200 mètres au nord-est de l'église. Le site se trouve à 78 mètres d'altitude, à la pointe sud-est du plateau et domine d'une cinquantaine de mètres le Thérain au sud et l'Oise à l'est. La voie romaine reliant Senlis à Beauvais passait à proximité du site. 292 sépultures furent mises au jour, dont 270 en sarcophage et 15 en fosse. Le site fut occupé de la fin du Vème siècle jusqu'au début du VIIème siècle.

CUIGNIERES[11] est à 9 kilomètres au nord de Clermont, à 10 kilomètres à l'est de Bulles et à 21 kilomètres au nord de Montataire. Le site est implanté à 350 mètres à l'est du village actuel sur une butte orientée vers l'ouest, à 100 mètres d'altitude. L'ancienne voie romaine Saint-Martin-Longueau-Amiens était distante du site de 400 mètres. Entre le site et la voie furent mises au jour des traces d'habitat romain. 152 fosses, contenant à peu près 200 corps furent découvertes. Les sépultures se trouvaient au milieu de la pente du coteau. Elle sont datées du VIIème siècle.

Autour de Compiègne

SACY-LE-PETIT[12], dans le canton de Liancourt et dans l'arrondissement de Clermont est situé à 8 kilomètres au nord de Pont-Saint-Maxence et à 14 kilomètres au sud-ouest de Compiègne. Le site est implanté sur une légère butte dominant de deux ou trois mètres les terres environnantes. L'altitude est de 52 mètres. 49 inhumations furent mises au jour, comprenant 41 individus. Elle sont datées de la seconde moitié du VIème siècle et de la première moitié du VIIème siècle.

---

[5] d'après CARTIER, J. & F., 1967, Le cimetière gallo-romain à inhumation de la rue du Pressoir-Coquet à Beauvais, in *Revue du Nord*, n° 195, Villeneuve d'Ascq, p.637-657.

[6] d'après DESACHY, B., 1991, Les structures archéologiques de la place Clemenceau (Hôtel de ville de Beauvais, Oise). *Revue archéologique de Picardie*, n°3-4, Amiens, p.47-88.

[7] d'après DESACHY, Bruno & PETITJEAN, Martine, 1991, L'îlot de l'Hôtel-Dieu à Beauvais (Oise), in *Revue archéologique de Picardie*, n°3-4, Amiens, p.109-114.
PETITJEAN, Martine, 1991,Conclusion générale sur le chantier archéologique de l'Hôtel-Dieu. *Revue archéologique de Picardie*, n°3-4, Amiens, p.200-201.
BLONDIAUX, Joël, BOUALI, Marième, BUCHET, Luc & PETITJEAN, Martine, 1991, L'ouest de l'îlot de l'Hôtel-Dieu. *Revue archéologique de Picardie*, n°3-4, Amiens, p.161-199.

[8] d'après BERTHELIER-AJOT, Nadine, 1982, Le cimetière mérovingien de Bonnières (Oise). *Revue archéologique de Picardie*, n°4, Amiens, p.159-177.

[9] d'après LEGOUX, René, 1988, La nécropole mérovingienne de Bulles (Oise) : caractères généraux et particularismes. *Revue archéologique de Picardie*, n°3-4, Amiens, p.81-88.
LEGOUX, Yves & René, 1974, Le cimetière mérovingien de Saine Fontaine à Bulles (Oise). Etude des 155 premières sépultures. *Cahiers archéologiques de Picardie*, Amiens, p.123-180.

LEGOUX, Y. & R., 1978, Verrerie, vaisselle de bronze et céramique de la nécropole mérovingienne de Sainte-Fontaine à Bulles (Oise). *Cahiers archéologiques de Picardie*, Amiens, p.231-240.
LEGOUX, R., 1971-75, *Rapport de fouilles de Bulles*, déposé aux archives dép. de la Somme à Amiens, n°1367W3.

[10] d'après DECORMEILLE-PATIN, Claudie, BLONDIAUX, Joël & VALLET, Françoise, 1999, Le cimetière mérovingien de Montataire (Oise). *Revue archéologique de Picardie*, n°1-2, Amiens, p.83-182.

[11] d'après JACQUINEZ, Roger, 1969, Cuignières. *Documents et recherches, Bulletin de la société archéologique, historique et géographique de Creil*, n°63, Creil, p.1-16.
JACQUINEZ, R., 1977, Un habitat gallo-romain à Cuignères. *Revue archéologique du nord-est de l'Oise*, n°2, Compiègne, p.40-57.
LEGOUX, R., 1980, La nécropole mérovingienne de Cuignières (Oise). Chronologie par permutations matricielles et répartitions topographiques. *Cahiers archéologiques de Picardie*, n°7, Amiens, p.211-228.

[12] d'après DURAND, Marc & VANHAEKE, Lisa, 1987, La nécropole du Haut Moyen Age et le moulin médiéval de Sacy-le-Petit (Oise). *Revue archéologique de Picardie*, n°3-4, Amiens, p.83-114.

LONGUEIL-ANNEL[13] est située à 7 kilomètres au nord de Compiègne, sur la rive droite de l'Oise. Le site est implanté sur une butte orientée nord-ouest/sud-est. Cette butte en bordure d'un plateau domine l'ancien cours de l'Oise et le village d'une dizaine de mètres. L'Oise est distante de 200 mètres de ce site. 447 inhumés, dont 73 enfants furent exhumés des fosses creusées dans le sous-sol marno-calcaire. Ce site fut occupé à partir de la fin du Vème siècle jusqu'au VIIIème siècle ou au IXème siècle.

MELICOCQ[14] est situé sur la rive droite du Matz, à 3 kilomètres au nord de Longueil-Annel et à 8 kilomètres au nord de Compiègne. Le site étudié est situé sur une butte à 58 mètres d'altitude qui domine la vallée marécageuse située à 39 mètres d'altitude. 13 individus furent exhumés. Ce cimetière est daté des environs de 650.

C. le département de la Somme

Dans le Ponthieu

NOYELLES-SUR-MER[15], dans le canton de Nouvion, est distante de celle-ci de 5 km et située 2 km à l'est de la baie de Somme, sur la rive gauche du Dien, au confluent du Dien et de la Somme. Le site est implanté sur une butte à 26 mètres d'altitude. 31 sépultures, datées entre 350 et 380, furent mises au jour.

NOUVION-EN-PONTHIEU[16], dans l'arrondissement d'Abbeville, se situe à 7 km à l'est de la Baie de Somme. Le site est implanté sur une butte, entre 20 et 25 mètres d'altitude. Cette butte est située sur la rive droite du Dien. Les fouilles mirent au jour 469 sépultures, datées entre le IVème et la fin du VIIème siècle, et sept incinérations du Vème siècle.

VRON[17], dans le canton de Rue, est situé à 25 km au nord d'Abbeville et à 7 km au nord-est de Rue. Le site est implanté sur une pente calcaire orientée vers l'ouest. Au nord se trouve une petite vallée sèche et à 300 mètres au sud coule le ruisseau de Pendé. L'altitude est de 25 mètres. 325 sépultures, divisées en deux groupes, furent découvertes : - A l'ouest se trouvait un groupe de 110 sépultures, dont 9 incinérations. Ces sépultures datent de la fin du IVème siècle et de la première moitié du Vème siècle. Elles étaient toutes orientées sud/nord. - A l'est se trouvait un second groupe de 215 sépultures, toutes orientées ouest/est, excepté 3 sépultures, orientées sud/nord et qui font la liaison entre les deux groupes. Ces sépultures se situent entre le milieu du Vème siècle et la fin du VIIème siècle.

NAMPONT-SAINT-MARTIN[18], dans le canton de Rue, est implanté à 28 km au nord d'Abbeville. Le site se situe sur un promontoire surplombant l'Authie distante de 600 mètres. 4 sépultures, datées de la seconde moitié du VIème siècle, furent exhumées.

Autour d'Amiens

MOREUIL[19], sur la rive droite de l'Avre, est à 18 km au sud-est d'Amiens. Le site est implanté à 1 km à l'est de l'Avre, sur une butte dominant la vallée à une altitude entre 55 et 70 mètres. Le cimetière se trouvait au centre de la pente. 113 fosses, datées entre la fin du Vème siècle et la fin du VIIème siècle, furent exhumées.

COISY[20] est situé à 7 km au nord d'Amiens. Le site est implanté sur une butte à 106 mètres d'altitude. Le village actuel se trouve à 300 mètres au nord-est de cette butte. 40 fosses, datées du VIIème siècle, furent mises au jour.

VENDEUIL-CAPLY[21] est un ancien lieu cultuel et un ancien *vicus* romain aux sources de la Noye, à 2 km au sud de Breteuil, à 30 km au sud d'Amiens et à 25 km au nord-est de Beauvais. Le cimetière était implanté le long de la chaussée romaine reliant Amiens à Beauvais, à 2 km au nord du *vicus* romain et à 1 km à l'ouest des sources de la Noye. 188 sépultures, du milieu du VIème siècle au Xème siècle, ont pu être étudiées.

II. L'EVOLUTION DES MODES D'INHUMATION

A. L'implantation des cimetières

Jusqu'au milieu du Vème siècle, les défunts sont inhumés le long des routes et les cimetières s'étalent le long de celles-ci. Tous les cimetières sont implantés en dehors de l'habitat, à l'extérieur des murs de la ville. A partir du milieu du Vème

---

[13] d'après FREVILLE, Cécile & JOURNA, Robert, 1994, La nécropole mérovingienne de Longueil-Annel (Oise). *Revue archéologique de Picardie*, n°1-2, Amiens, p.87-178.
MAYART, Thierry, 1988, *Rapport de fouilles de Longueil-Annel*, archives dép. de la Somme à Amiens, n°1367W6.

[14] d'après JOURNA, R., JOURNA, A. & JAUSSAUD, M., 1973, La nécropole franque de Mélicocq (Oise). *Revue archéologique de l'Oise*, n°4, Compiègne, p.47-58.

[15] d'après PITON, D. & MARCHAND, H., 1978, Une nécropole du IVème siècle à Noyelles-sur-Mer. *Cahiers archéologiques de Picardie*, Amiens, p.199-229.

[16] d'après PITON, D. & SCHULER, R., 1981, La nécropole de Nouvion-en-Ponthieu (Somme), IVème-VIIème siècles. *Cahiers archéologiques de Picardie*, n°8, Amiens, p.217-284.
PITON, Daniel, 1985, *La nécropole de Nouvion-en-Ponthieu. Dossiers archéologiques, historiques et culturels du Nord et du Pas-de-Calais*, n°20, Berck-sur-Mer.

[17] d'après SEILLIER, Claude, 1986, Développement topographique et caractères généraux de la nécropole de Vron (Somme). *Archéologie médiévale*, XVI, Paris, p.7-32.
SEILLIER, C., 1989, Les tombes de transition du cimetière germanique de Vron (Somme). *Jahrbuch des römisch-germanischen Zentralmuseums Mainz*, Mayence, p.597-635.

SEILLIER, Claude, 1995, La présence germanique en Gaule du Nord au Bas-Empire. *Revue du Nord*, n°313, Villeneuve d'Ascq, p.71-80.

[18] d'après PITON, D., SCHULER, R. & BALANDRA, A., 1980, Découvertes gallo-romaines et mérovingiennes à Nampont-Saint-Martin (Somme). *Cahiers archéologiques de Picardie*, n°7, Amiens, p.281-291.

[19] d'après BAYARD, D., PITON, D. & SCHULER, R., 1981, Le cimetière mérovingien de Moreuil (80). *Cahiers archéologiques de Picardie*, n°8, Amiens, p.157-216.

[20] d'après MASSY, Jean-Luc, 1980, Nécropole mérovingienne à Coisy (80). *Cahiers archéologiques de Picardie*, n°7, p.292-301.

[21] d'après PITON, D., 1992-93, La nécropole du haut Moyen Age du clos de Vendeuil. *Vendeuil-Caply, Nord-Ouest archéologie*, n°5, Berck-sur-Mer, p.115-212.

siècle, les cimetières subsistent le long des routes, mais cet emplacement est avant tout lié à la proximité de l'habitat. Les défunts sont inhumés autour d'un noyau primitif d'inhumations. A la fin du VIIème siècle et durant le VIIIème siècle, voire au IXème siècle, comme à l'Hôtel-Dieu de Beauvais, les cimetières sont abandonnés et se regroupent autour des églises. A Vendeuil et à Montataire, le cimetière actuel se trouve au même endroit que le cimetière mérovingien. En fait, soit une église fut construite à proximité directe des sites, ce qui a favorisé le maintien des inhumations à cet endroit, soit le cimetière fut déplacé à proximité d'une église, afin que les défunts soient inhumés auprès des reliques d'un saint ("ad sanctos"). L'implantation d'une église, près d'un cimetière, a attiré l'habitat. Dans un premier temps, il y a eu une christianisation du lieu funéraire (Montataire, Vendeuil-Caply) et dans un second temps, c'est le cimetière qui se déplace vers le lieu de culte[22].

B. L'incinération en Picardie

L'incinération, très peu présente en Picardie, se retrouve principalement dans le Ponthieu, à Nouvion (7 cas) et à Vron (9 cas) mais aussi à Bulles (25 cas). Au total, 41 cas d'incinération, phénomène très marginal par rapport aux 4100 inhumations. Les incinérations sont placées dans une céramique ou dans un tissu comme à Nouvion ou encore dans un sac en toile ou dans un coffre en bois comme à Vron. L'incinération est bien délimitée chronologiquement. Elle apparaît au début du Vème siècle et disparaît au début du VIème siècle. L'incinération est donc un fait marquant du Vème siècle. L'apparition de l'incinération au Vème siècle peut être mise en rapport avec l'arrivée des Germains et leur installation en Picardie. A Vron et à Bulles, le même type de fibules à pied trapézoïdal, ansées ou discoïdes en bronze, caractéristiques de Basse-Saxe ou du sud de la Scandinavie, datées du début du Vème siècle, furent trouvées. La grande vague d'invasion a lieu vers 406-407. A cette époque, l'incinération refait son apparition et l'orientation des inhumations devient ouest/est. De plus, peu avant 400, le mobilier des sépultures est très riche et des contacts existent avec la Grande-Bretagne. Des marchands anglo-saxons se sont installés dans le Ponthieu pour effectuer des échanges commerciaux. A Vron et à Nouvion, les mêmes types de céramiques non tournées unies, à tessons ou à décor incisé, d'origine anglo-saxonne, datées de la seconde moitié du Vème siècle, furent mises au jour. Il pourrait donc y avoir une relation entre les contacts avec les Anglo-Saxons et l'apparition de l'incinération. D'après Salin[23], on retrouve régulièrement l'incinération en Grande-Bretagne chez les Angles. L'incinération serait donc bien d'origine germanique, mais anglo-saxonne et non franque[24].

C. L'orientation des sépultures

Du IIIème jusqu'au milieu du Vème siècle, l'orientation est généralement sud/nord (tête au sud, pieds au nord) comme à Nouvion, à Noyelles, à Vron et à Bulles. Il existe quelques exceptions, comme à Marteville, où la majorité des sépultures du IVème siècle sont orientées est/ouest. A Beauvais, sur le site du Pressoir-Cocquet, aucune orientation précise ne fut adoptée et à l'hôtel-Dieu, 127 sépultures sur 134 furent orientées ouest/est.

A partir du milieu du Vème siècle, l'orientation devient ouest/est. On constate notamment ce passage à Nouvion, à Vron et à Bulles. Cette orientation ouest/est perdure jusqu'à la fin du VIIème siècle et est une constante sur tous les sites picards, excepté à Goudelancourt, où les défunts furent séparés en deux noyaux distincts. Les 324 sépultures du premier noyau, du début du VIème siècle à la fin du VIIème siècle, sont orientées sud/nord, alors que les 134 sépultures du second noyau, du milieu du VIème à la fin du VIIème siècle, présentent un axe ouest/est.

A la fin du VIIème siècle et durant le VIIIème siècle, l'orientation reste ouest/est. Cependant, d'autres orientations se retrouvent fréquemment, comme à Bulles, où parmi les sépultures les plus tardives, 18 sont orientées nord/sud et 3 est/ouest. A Longueil-Annel, 9 sépultures du début du VIIIème siècle sont orientées sud/nord et à Montataire, 7 sépultures sont orientées nord/sud.

Pour de nombreuses sépultures, l'orientation manifeste un léger décalage vers le sud ou vers le nord. Ce décalage peut s'expliquer par les ruptures de pente créant une rupture dans l'orientation, par la différence de position du soleil entre l'été et l'hiver et aussi par le moment de la journée durant lequel la sépulture fut creusée. E. Salin a calculé ces variations et constate que pour la majorité des sépulture l'orientation est légèrement décalée vers le sud, témoignant du fait que les fosses auraient été creusées au lever du soleil et en hiver[25]. Depuis lors, d'autres observations effectuées confirment cette analyse[26].

D. L'évolution des contenants des corps

Aux IIIème et IVème siècles, les défunts sont inhumés en pleine terre, en cercueil de bois et parfois en sarcophages de pierre. Par exemple à Marteville, sur 59 inhumations, 17 défunts gisaient en pleine terre, 40 en cercueils de bois et 2 en sarcophages. A Noyelles, sur 20 observations possibles, 16 reposaient en cercueils et 4 en pleine terre. Il semble donc y avoir, malgré la diversité des contenants, une prépondérance de l'inhumation en cercueils de bois, ce qui fut aussi observé dans d'autres sites picards, comme à l'Hôtel-Dieu de Beauvais. Beaucoup de cercueils étaient assemblés à l'aide de chevilles de bois pour diminuer leur coût car le fer des clous était relativement rare (Marteville). Ils devaient être faits en série, car régulièrement, ils sont trop petits ou trop grands pour les enfants (Hôtel-Dieu de Beauvais, Longueil-Annel au VIème siècle). A Noyelles, des cercueils à double compartimentation, servant à séparer le défunt de son offrande alimentaire, furent mis au jour.

---

[22] d'après DURAND, Marc, 1988, Archéologie du cimetière médiéval au sud-est de l'Oise. *Revue archéologique de Picardie*, Amiens, p.118-120.

[23] d'après SALIN, Edouard, 1952, *La civilisation mérovingienne d'après les sépultures, les textes et le laboratoire*, t.2, Paris, p.4.

[24] d'après SALIN, E., 1952, *op.cit.*, Paris, p.11.

[25] d'après SALIN, E., 1952, *op.cit.*, Paris, p.194.

[26] d'après YOUNG, Bailey, 1977, Paganisme, christianisation et rites funéraires mérovingiens. *Archéologie médiévale*, VII, Paris, p. 20.

A partir du Vème siècle, les défunts sont inhumés soit en pleine terre, soit en cercueil de bois (Longueil-Annel). Cela reflète peut-être la condition sociale de l'inhumé, les défunts n'ayant pas les moyens de se faire construire un cercueil étant inhumés en pleine terre. A partir de la seconde moitié du Vème siècle apparaissent les coffrages de bois et à partir du milieu du VIème siècle, l'inhumation en sarcophage de pierre et en structures construites. A Longueil-Annel, 17 défunts furent inhumés en sarcophage monoxyle dans le deuxième et troisième quart du VIème siècle. Le sarcophage monoxyle est un demi-tronc d'arbre évidé, de forme elliptique. D'après Salin, le choix du sarcophage monoxyle est lié au fait qu'il ressemble à une pirogue[27]. Les pirogues étant creusées dans de demi-troncs d'arbres, le défunt serait placé dans ce type de sarcophage pour effectuer son voyage vers la mort.

A partir du VIIème siècle, on observe des dispositifs pour caler la tête du défunt, que ce soit en pleine terre (Longueil-Annel, Vendeuil, Beauvais (Clemenceau), Bulles, Sacy-le-Petit, Goudelancourt, Vorges) ou à l'intérieur du sarcophage (Longueil-Annel, Montataire, Vorges). Ces aménagements céphaliques servent à maintenir en place la tête du défunt afin qu'il regarde vers le ciel. A la fin du VIIème siècle et durant le VIIIème siècle, les sarcophages et les cercueils ne sont plus utilisés. Les défunts sont inhumés exclusivement en pleine terre, dont dans des fosses anthropomorphes (Longueil-Annel, Vendeuil, Beauvais (Clemenceau)). L'inhumation en pleine terre et l'anthropomorphisation de la fosse semblent être liées à la christianisation de la société.

L'ÉVOLUTION DU SARCOPHAGE DE PIERRE : Les sarcophages se retrouvent dans de nombreux sites. Ils apparaissent dès le Bas-Empire, au IIIème siècle (Beauvais et Marteville), puis sont abandonnés dans le courant du IVème. Ils réapparaissent dans la seconde moitié du VIème siècle. Ils sont rectangulaires et constitués de deux ou trois parties. Parfois, des sarcophages gallo-romains sont réutilisés (Bulles). Au début du VIIème siècle, ils deviennent trapézoïdaux et des sarcophages monolithiques commencent à être utilisés. A partir du milieu du VIIème siècle, ils ne sont plus que trapézoïdaux et monolithiques. Ils disparaissent finalement au VIIIème siècle. A partir du début du VIIème siècle, les sarcophages semblent être produits en série. On constate souvent que le fond du sarcophage fut coupé afin de pouvoir étendre les jambes du défunt (Montataire, Longueil-Annel) et que leurs dimensions sont standardisées (Montataire). Les sarcophages sont en calcaire, locaux (Montataire, Mélicocq) ou importés par voie fluviale dans un rayon d'une trentaine de kilomètres (Vendeuil, Bonnières, Bulles, Cuignières, Sacy-le-Petit, Longueil-Annel, Goudelancourt, Caulaincourt et Vorges). Ils sont presque absents des sites de la Somme (1 à Coisy et 3 à Moreuil). A Mélicocq, Bulles et Montataire, le défunt fut parfois inhumé dans un cercueil placé dans le sarcophage. Dans quelques cas (Bulles), le sarcophage fut déposé dans un coffrage de bois. Quelques sarcophages possèdent un décor à motif chrétien (croix), comme à Montataire et à Vorges. Dans quelques cas (Montataire, Vorges, Bulles), le couvercle du sarcophage fut découvert. Ils sont plats ou en bâtière. Le couvercle en bâtière est plus tardif que le couvercle plat.

E. Le mobilier contenu dans les sépultures

Du IIIème au Vème siècle, le mobilier, présent dans de nombreuses sépultures est très riche. Parmi ce mobilier, une ou plusieurs céramiques communes et verreries sont déposées à la tête du défunt (Marteville, Noyelles, Nouvion, Vron). De plus, on trouve parfois aux pieds du défunt des plats en céramique sigillée ou en métal sur lesquels fut déposée une offrande alimentaire, constituée de poulet, d'œufs, de poisson ou de mouton, comme à Marteville (6 cas), Nouvion (3 cas), Noyelles (9cas) et Vron. Par contre, on constate à l'Hôtel-Dieu de Beauvais l'absence du mobilier et de l'offrande alimentaire dans les sépultures. Dans quelques sépultures furent déposées des pièces de monnaie, souvent contenues dans une aumônière placée à la ceinture (16 cas à Noyelles; 7 cas à Marteville; 1 cas à Bulles; 11 cas à Nouvion; 5 cas à Vron). Ces monnaies furent rarement déposées avec l'offrande alimentaire (2 cas à Noyelles), dans la main du défunt (1 cas à Noyelles, à Marteville et à l'Hôtel-Dieu de Beauvais); ou dans sa bouche (1 cas à Marteville et à Bulles; 4 cas à Nouvion; 7 cas à Vron). Le dépôt de pièces de monnaie dans la bouche porte le nom d'obole à Charon car, d'après la tradition, cette pièce devait servir à payer Charon, afin que l'âme du défunt puisse franchir le Styx[28]. On peut s'interroger sur la pertinence de l'expression "obole à Charon", car la majorité des sépultures romaines ne renfermaient pas de monnaie et parmi celles en contenant, la plupart se trouvaient dans une aumônière.

Dans la première moitié du Vème siècle, le mobilier diminue en quantité; une ou deux verreries ou céramiques sont placées à présent aux pieds du défunt. La présence de pièces de monnaie devient également plus rare (Vron). Les défunts sont habillés. A partir du milieu du Vème siècle, le mobilier est exclusivement déposé aux pieds du défunt et l'offrande alimentaire disparaît. Des armes sont placées dans les sépultures masculines. La céramique est présente dans presque toutes les sépultures. La céramique est généralement locale (Moreuil et Bulles), commune, avec des formes fermées et est souvent décorée à la molette. Une grande variété de décors existe, comme à Nouvion et à Bulles. A Montataire, pour l'ensemble des périodes, la céramique est pratiquement inexistante.

A partir du milieu du VIème siècle et durant le VIIème siècle, la quantité de mobilier diminue fortement et la verrerie devient quasi inexistante dans les sépultures. Parmi les objets déposés, certains ont à présent un caractère chrétien, comme des pyxides portant des chrismes gravés trouvés à Moreuil et à Vendeuil, deux croix en bronze à Vorges et une coupe à décor de chrisme et d'orants à Bulles. Le dépôt de pièces de monnaie est abandonné complètement, excepté à Cuignières où 4 sépultures de la fin du VIème siècle renfermaient une pièce de monnaie. Le dépôt de pièces de monnaie est donc une coutume romaine qui disparaît à l'époque mérovingienne à la fin du Vème siècle. L'obole ne se maintient donc pas, contrairement à ce que dit Young[29], durant cette période, si ce n'est à Cuignières.

---

[27] d'après SALIN, E., 1952, *op.cit.*, Paris, p.126.

[28] d'après YOUNG, Bailey, 1977, *op.cit.*, Paris, p.49-50.

[29] d'après YOUNG, Bailey, 1977, *op.cit.*, Paris, p.49.

A la fin du VIIème siècle et durant le VIIIème siècle, le mobilier disparaît complètement des sépultures et les défunts n'étaient probablement plus habillés (Beauvais (Clemenceau), Longueil-Annel, Vendeuil, etc.).

III. CONCLUSIONS

On observe deux grandes ruptures dans l'évolution des modes d'inhumation en Picardie entre le IIIème et le VIIIème siècle : La première rupture a lieu au milieu du Vème siècle. On observe un changement d'orientation des sépultures (ouest/est et non plus sud/nord), une diminution générale du mobilier funéraire et un changement dans celui-ci (disparition des monnaies et de l'offrande alimentaire, mais apparition des armes. Le mobilier est déposé aux pieds et non plus au chevet du défunt). La seconde rupture a lieu à la fin du VIIème siècle. On observe une diversification des orientations des sépultures; une disparition du mobilier; l'inhumation est exclusivement en pleine terre, dont dans des fosses anthropomorphes ou dans des fosses à dispositif céphalique pour maintenir la tête en position verticale et enfin, un abandon des cimetières "en campagne", c'est-à-dire hors des murs de la ville, pour une installation des cimetières autour des églises.

Une première évolution entre le IIIème siècle et le VIIIème siècle concerne l'implantation des cimetières

Jusqu'au milieu du Vème siècle, les défunts sont inhumés le long des routes et les cimetières s'étalent le long de celles-ci. Les morts avancent au fur et à mesure du temps, comme s'ils suivaient eux-mêmes le trajet de la route. L'idée du voyage domine dans cette conception.

A partir du milieu du Vème siècle, les cimetières subsistent le long des routes, mais cet emplacement est avant tout lié à la proximité de l'habitat. Les morts, jusqu'au VIIème siècle, sont dissociés du monde des vivants. Du IIIème siècle au milieu du Vème siècle, aucun lien entre les vivants et les morts n'est établi, car les morts doivent accomplir leur voyage pour sortir du monde des vivants. A partir du milieu du Vème siècle et jusqu'à la fin du VIIème siècle, des correspondances s'établissent entre les vivants et les morts. Les sépultures ne sont plus étalées le long des routes mais se développent de manière concentrique autour d'un noyau primitif. La route et la proximité de sources déterminent l'implantation des vivants qui, eux-mêmes, installent les morts hors de leur monde tout en gardant un contact avec eux. Le cimetière se développe de manière concentrique autour des sépultures les plus anciennes, comme un village se développe de manière nucléaire autour du patriarche. Le monde des morts devient le reflet du monde des vivants et est structuré de la même manière, comme si la mort n'est qu'un autre état pour les vivants. La structure sociale se reflète dans la mort, comme si la mort est identique à la vie.

A la fin du VIIème siècle, les cimetières sont abandonnés et se regroupent autour des églises. L'Eglise, la vie religieuse et les saints constituent à présent le centre de la vie sociale. La société patriarcale est devenue ecclésiale. La religion devient le moteur de la vie sociale et le saint, le modèle de la société.

Les morts pénètrent à l'intérieur des villes, à l'intérieur du monde des vivants. Les vivants, s'ils veulent accéder à la vie éternelle promise par l'Eglise, doivent transiter par le monde des morts, puisque celui-ci enserre les églises. La mort est donc le passage entre la vie terrestre et la vie éternelle.

La seconde évolution concerne la présence du mobilier funéraire et à travers lui, le statut social des défunts

Du IIIème siècle jusqu'au début du Vème siècle, les défunts sont inhumés avec énormément de mobilier, principalement des céramiques et des verreries, mais aussi des pièces de monnaie. Outre les significations rituelles de ce mobilier, celui-ci reflète surtout le statut social du défunt. Il accomplit un voyage vers une autre vie dans laquelle les objets inhumés lui permettent de vivre de la même manière que lors de son vivant. L'offrande alimentaire, par contre, est surtout un viatique pour le défunt durant son voyage vers la mort. Les pièces de monnaie, plus qu'une obole à Charon, reflètent la condition sociale du défunt. Elles disparaissent à la fin du Vème siècle, car le statut social se marque par la présence d'autres objets.

Durant le Vème siècle, le mobilier s'appauvrit. Cela n'est que le reflet de l'appauvrissement de la population suite aux invasions germaniques. A la fin du Vème siècle, le mobilier réapparaît, mais en moindre quantité. Le statut social du défunt se marque surtout par la présence d'armes pour les hommes. La société mérovingienne étant une société guerrière, le guerrier a un statut social élevé que ce soit chez les vivants ou chez les morts. La présence de son arme montre qu'il garde son statut social dans la mort. Il est d'abord un guerrier avant d'être un individu. La société mérovingienne est construite autour de cette caste et le cimetière reflète cette structuration sociale. Les femmes sont inhumées avec leurs objets de parure, conservant elles aussi leur rang social dans la mort. Cette société très hiérarchisée est structurée de la même manière dans le monde des morts.

A la fin du VIIème siècle, le dépôt funéraire est abandonné. En fait, le mobilier sort de la sépulture pour être donné à l'Eglise. Le christianisme permet la vie éternelle par les prières et ces prières peuvent être obtenues par la donation de biens. Le statut social du défunt ne va plus se marquer dans la sépulture, mais dans le monde des vivants, par les prières effectuées pour lui par l'Eglise. L'Eglise domine à présent la hiérarchie sociale et la caste des guerriers mérovingiens se soumet à cette nouvelle hiérarchie. Un nouvel ordre social est établi, dans lequel dominent la prière, la caste religieuse et plus particulièrement le saint autour duquel veulent être inhumés les défunts afin de bénéficier de sa protection.

La troisième évolution concerne la volonté de protéger le corps du défunt

Du IIIème à la fin du VIIème siècle, le corps est inhumé dans la terre. Il est constamment isolé de celle-ci par un linceul, par des blocs de pierres, par un cercueil ou par un sarcophage. La fosse creusée dans la terre appartient au défunt. Celui-ci humanise le sol dans lequel il repose. Cet espace devient sacré et s'oppose à la terre profane environnante. Le corps est protégé par un contenant, comme s'il fallait qu'il subsiste. Cette protection du corps, cette volonté de le maintenir intact répond à la volonté des vivants de protéger leur propre corps. Le mort et le vivant sont identiques; leurs corps doivent être protégés de la même manière. Les différences ou l'absence de contenants semble résulter de contraintes matérielles ou financières. Les défunts inhumés en pleine terre avant le VIIème siècle semblent l'être suite au peu de moyens financiers dont ils disposent.

La protection du corps s'est accentuée à l'époque mérovingienne. Au milieu du Vème siècle, le défunt est à peu près systématiquement inhumé dans un contenant. Il doit être séparé de la terre, avoir sa propre habitation. Dans celle-ci, d'autres défunts de la même famille peuvent le rejoindre. Ils sont protégés par le même contenant, comme une famille par le même toit. L'implantation des cimetières sur des collines assure aussi la protection des sépultures, les protégeant des débordements des rivières pouvant se produire dans la plaine.

A la fin du VIIème siècle, les défunts sont à nouveau inhumés en pleine terre, enveloppés simplement dans un linceul. Le linceul évoque Lazare et si la protection du corps n'est plus aussi importante, c'est parce que le défunt devient esprit et non plus matière. Les fosses deviennent anthropomorphes et des emplacements céphaliques sont aménagés. Le défunt a une attitude de prière dans la mort et la terre est aménagée comme si le corps avait toujours été conçu pour elle. La mort est une étape. Elle fait le lien entre la matière qu'est le corps du vivant et l'Esprit auquel accède le défunt par la vie éternelle.

Adresse de l'auteur

Luc HERMANN
Les Closures, 6
B-4970 Stavelot; BELGIQUE
Email : lhermann2@hotmail.com

Bibliographie

ALEXANDRE-BIDON, Danièle & TREFFORT, Cécile, 1993, A réveiller les morts. La mort au quotidien dans l'Occident médiéval, Lyon.

ARIES, Philippe, 1975, Essais sur l'histoire de la mort en Occident du Moyen Age à nos jours, Paris.

ARIES, Philippe, 1977, L'homme devant la mort, Paris.

BONNABEL, Lola & CARRE, Florence (dir.), 1996, Rencontre autour du linceul, Reims.

BUCHET, Luc (dir.), 1986, Le matériel anthropologique provenant des édifices religieux, Paris.

COLLARDELLE, Michel, 1996, Terminologie descriptive des sépultures antiques et médiévales. In Archéologie du cimetière chrétien, GALINIE, Henri & ZADORA-RIO, Elisabeth, Tours, p.305-310.

DEPEYROT, Georges, 1994, Richesse et société chez les mérovingiens et carolingiens, Paris.

DESIRE, Emmanuel-Paul, 1989, Picardie-atlas, Amiens.

DIERKENS, Alain, 1981, Cimetières mérovingiens et histoire du haut Moyen Age : chronologie, société, religion. Acta historica Bruxellensia, IV, Histoire et méthode, Bruxelles, p.15-70.

DUDAY, Henri, 1990, Observations ostéologiques et décomposition du cadavre : sépulture colmatée ou en espace vide. Revue archéologique du Centre de la France, t.XXIX, n°2, Vichy, p.193-196.

DUDAY, H. & MASSET, C. (dir.), 1986, Anthropologie physique et archéologie, méthodes d'étude des sépultures, Paris.

DURAND, Marc, 1988, Archéologie du cimetière médiéval au sud-est de l'Oise. Revue archéologique de Picardie, Amiens.

DUVAL, Y. & PICARD, J.-CH. (dir.), 1986, L'inhumation privilégiée du IVème au VIIIème siècle en Occident, Paris.

DUVAL, Yvette, 1988, Auprès des saints, corps et âme. L'inhumation "ad sanctos" dans la chrétienté d'Orient et d'Occident du IIIème au VIIème siècle, Paris.

GALINIE, Henri & ZADORA-RIO, Elisabeth, 1996, Archéologie du cimetière chrétien, Tours.

HENRION, Fabrice & HUNOT, Jean-Yves, 1996, Archéologie et technologie du cercueil et du coffrage de bois. In Archéologie du cimetière chrétien, GALINIE, Henri & ZADORA-RIO, Elisabeth, Tours, p.197-204.

LEMAITRE, Jean-Loup (dir.), 1986, L'Eglise et la mémoire des morts dans la France médiévale, Paris.

PERIN, Patrick, 1980, La datation des tombes mérovingiennes. Historique-Méthodes-Application, Genève.

PERIN, P., 1987, Des nécropoles romaines tardives aux nécropoles du Haut-Moyen Age. Remarques sur la topographie funéraire en Gaule mérovingienne et à sa périphérie. Cahiers archéologiques, n°35, Paris, p.9-30.

SALIN, Edouard, 1950-59, La civilisation mérovingienne d'après les sépultures, les textes et le laboratoire, 4 tomes, Paris.

TREFFORT, Cécile, 1996, L'Eglise carolingienne et la mort, Lyon.

TREFFORT, C., 1993, Les meubles de la mort : lit funéraire, cercueil et nattes de paille. In A réveiller les morts. La mort au quotidien dans l'Occident médiéval, ALEXANDRE-BIDON, D. & TREFFORT, C., Lyon, p.207-221.

YOUNG, B., 1977, Paganisme, christianisation et rites funéraires mérovingiens. Archéologie médiévale, VII, Paris, p.5-81.

WOODWORKING IN THE EARLY MIDDLE AGES IN CENTRAL AND NORTHERN EUROPE: PRODUCTION AND PROCESSING TECHNIQUES OF HANDMADE ITEMS

Paolo DE VINGO

Abstract: Wood, one of the best workable raw materials and, at the same time, one of the most easily perishable, was largely used for the manufacturing of several products in the early Middle Ages. However, as this material rapidly decomposes due to its biological activity, it is only preserved in dry contexts, in constantly damp environments or in highly acid soil, and therefore the possibility of proving its existence is a basic archaeological element. Referring to the early Middle Ages in western Europe, wood items are generally found in burial-grounds as a complement to the outfit, as well as in settlements, wells, cisterns, submerged lake or river deposits and finally in peat bogs, namely in all those contexts where particular climate conditions have made it possible to preserve such items. In the early Middle Ages, despite a partial lack of written documents, the archaeological research and the improvement in excavation techniques allowing experts to identify important traces in the archaeological deposit testify to a large use of wood items in daily life, whose production embraces largely diversified typologies. The morphological features of wooden finds allow us to make assumptions about the manufacturing techniques that would interact with handmade items either by themselves or by a combined action. Woodworking in the early Middle Ages seems to be limited to three basic classes of workers: joiners, carpenters and woodcarvers, whose diversified working characteristics and techniques gave birth, in the late Middle Ages, to three different guilds, thus underlining the presence of different skills in production activities. Tools for daily work reflect this difference, and that's why lathes, jointer planes, saws and axes were typical joiner's tools, whereas hammers, chisels and hatchets were mainly used by carpenters, and finally gouges, iron bits and burins represented the basic tools of woodcarvers, which generally proved to do their work accurately and with great skill. A number of these tools, belonging to the outfit of male burials, were found in northern Germany and central France, and this makes us assume that such craftsmen played a leading function within the community. It is important to point out that woodworking existed both in rural areas and within urban settlements, but it represented two different aspects of an extremely complex and fascinating problem that cannot be considered as a standardised one. This is why archaeological research should be interpreted in a new way, thus taking into account even the hidden shades of a handicraft tradition whose contents will have an impact and an important meaning in the following centuries.

THE STRUCTURE AND MECHANICAL CHARACTERISTICS OF WOOD

Wood has always had a fundamental importance in all ancient societies because of its wide availability in nature. It was used for most of the objects of daily use, from utensils to buildings, from furniture, including household furnishings and containers with various functions, to means of transport, not to mention artistic objects (Mannoni-Giannichedda 1996, 105).

In spite of the quantity of wooden artefacts produced and used, it is difficult to find them intact today. If wood is not carbonised, it is subject to rapid deterioration. But in constantly dry or humid contexts, the biological activity is blocked, and it is possible to guarantee its conservation (Castelletti 1988, 421-424). In north-central Europe, the bottoms of wells and cisterns, lake and river deposits below water level, and peat moss represent the environments where it is possible to recover wooden artefacts (Lusuardi Siena 1994, 319). These finds, if studied in detail, can have great informative potential.

Wood, being a basic resource made up of trunks of plants, possesses a rather complex internal structure (Cagnana 2000, 215-218). A cross-section of a young tree shows a series of concentric cylindrical layers from exterior towards the interior: the *bark,* the *wood* and the *pith.* Each layer is composed of tissues that serve to support the plant and to conduct nutritive liquids from the roots to the leaves and vice versa. With the growth of the plant, between the layer interior to the bark, called the *phloem,* and the *wood* or *xylem,* a thin cylindrical layer of living cells is formed called the *cambium,* which will continue to produce annual layers of new wood internally and new bark externally as long as the plant lives. In this way the change is obliged to move externally. After a few years, a cross section of the trunk reveals a series of annual concentric layers; from the periphery towards the centre, through these layers, strips of conducting tissues called *medullary rays* are insinuated.

The following annual layers, or *rings,* are visible because of their colour differences, with alternating light and dark shaded circles. In the spring, in consequence to the resumption of growth activity, a great quantity of sap ascends from the roots. The ringed portion that the cambium is forming, is extremely rich in *xylem rays* that facilitate the upward movement of liquids. A light and tender wood is born, especially in conifers, called spring wood or *sapwood.* In the period between the end of summer and the beginning of autumn, when the plant is reducing its activity, the wood that is formed has fewer ducts, is darker, harder and more compact: it is summer wood or *heartwood.* With age, the interior layers of the wood die; their cells fill with strongly coloured substances which become the heart of the wood; dark, resistant and also prized (Gretter 1972, 14-17).

The exact placement of the cells, their relative dimensions, their distribution and the details of certain cell structures reveal the characteristics of a particular species or genus. As a result, the structure of the wood can also be recognised by examining sections of the tree, which can be either *transverse, longitudinal radial* or *longitudinal transverse cross-sections.*

The transverse cross-section is a horizontal cut through the tree that shows the annual rings and the *xylem rays* of the plant. These rings of lymphatic vessels, fibres and/or tracheids, are concentrated in the primary phloem or pith, and appear as bands of small pores. Instead, *medullary rays* irradiate from the centre of the tree and are seen as wide or thin lines. In many species the rings can be invisible to the naked eye, and in others the *medullary rays* can be more prominent, especially if they were subject to certain kinds of decay.

The *longitudinal radial cross-section* is a vertical section taken through the length of the tree along one of its rays. In this section the pores forming the rings appear as a series of long, thin lines crossed at right angles by shorter lines (the rays) that in some oak species can be grouped in "flame-shaped" sheets.

The *tangential longitudinal cross-section* is a vertical section across the length of the tree and at a right angle compared to the axis of the rays. The section is formed by bands of fine and disconnected lines, stripes or brief ellipses (Allen 1994, 2-3).

As far as the technical characteristics of wood are concerned, the hardness, or resistance to incision, exceeds that of the softest rocks only in few woods. However, many types of wood can be hardened by a brief exposure to heat. Notable differences exist between the various types of mechanical resistance; the resistance to pressure along the fibres is about a quarter of that of the most compact stones, but it's about the same as the resistance to traction when in the same direction, therefore ten times superior to that of the hardest stones. Only a few types of wood, or certain parts of wood, resist impact long enough to be able to make mallets for works that do not require much energy, because wood weighs from a third to a fifth less than stone. On the whole, one can say that wood is not fit for making cutting tools, and is best for light-weight penetrating and striking tools: it is optimal for tools that must be flexible (Mannoni-Giannichedda 1996, 105-106).

THE WORKING CYCLE: PRELIMINARY PREPARATIONS

On the tree felling site, jobs relative to the cutting, the barking, branch removal and the preparation to cut into logs could be done (McGrail 1987, 26).

The best period to eliminate the bark was the spring: it was removed along with the alburnum (Cagnana 2000, 219-220), which was often the part of the trunk least resistant to the attacks of insects and fungi (Rival 1991, 104). Plinius illustrates the phases relative to the barking and the conservation of the trunks prepared in this way: "....*Caedi tempestivum quae decorticentur et teretes ad templa ceteraque usus rotundi cum germinant, alias cortice inestricabili et carie subnascente ei materiaque nigrescente....tigna et quibus aufert securis corticem a bruma ad favonium aut, si prevenire cogamur, arcturi occasu et ante eum fidiculae, novissima ratione solstitio...."* (*Naturalis Historia, liber XVI.188-189)*. Moreover, in the Medieval age, the bark trade must have had an important economic role considering that oak bark was employed in tanning hides (Goodburn 1992, 109).

Another type of work presumably done in the forest consisted of cutting the trunks into logs if necessary. Axes were used for this purpose. In England, inventories attest to the use of saws only from the 15th century while their use will not be affirmed until the 17th century. In fact, these tools allowed for less loss of raw material and major profits (Goodburn 1992, 110).

The most commonly used tools in carpentry were axes and hatchets, chisels, saws, awls and bow drills. The tools had iron blades and wooden handles. The hatchets could be distinguished from the axes because the cut was not perpendicular, but parallel to the handle and also functioned as a plane. They were used for the preliminary preparations while the axe, of the "hooked" type with its curved blade, was used for shaping and successive refinishing (Parenti 1994, 28-30). The saws were of the "pulling" type, and being rather long were often operated by two male individuals. Cutting trunks to obtain boards came after barking and fixing the trunk to the ground with a sort of vice, vertical to the length of the tree, from top to bottom; sometimes they were simply cleaved with wedges. Chisels of various dimensions had rectangular blades terminated by a flat point, while the punches and awls had curved blades and pointed tips. The gouges were characterised by one spoon shaped end and the other extremity was shaped like a trapezoidal spatula (Aufleger 1996, 602-603). One of the most important applications of this type of tool regarded woodcarving. It was carved in a way to form a design that reproduced the semicircular shape of the gouge itself, giving the impression of a series of grooves. The technique of engraved decorations which necessitated the removal of wood from the background was quite simple and widely diffused (Symonds 1993, 249-251).

In early Medieval written sources there is a distinction between woodworkers (*faber lignarius* or *lignorum artifices*) and carpenters (*carpentarii*). One can hypothesise of the existence of workshops where the two types of craftsmen performed diverse roles and functions. The possibility that they held affluent positions in the single communities can be deduced by the numerous tools found in early Medieval graves (Mooisleitner 1988, 209-210) the most interesting being the remains of Hérouvillette in the north of France. In the grave of one male there was a deposit of many goods including both utensils for metal working, such as hammers, anvils, burins, pliers and shears as well as tools for wood working, augers for perforating and gouges (Aufleger 1996, 602-603).

The transport of wood was done by beasts of burden or by floats (Muillez 1982). Where navigable waterways existed, rafts were widely utilised because they were very quick and economical (Meiggs 1982, 333). Regarding the Italic peninsula, some antique sources give testimony to their use along waterways (Rival 1991, 108). In one such example, Vitruvius (*De Architectura, II.9, II.46, II.53*) described the means of transport of larch-wood and pine by river navigation along the tributaries of the Po river: the trunks would be loaded on large barges or they were tied to each other, forming a big raft that facilitated transport. Towing with beasts of burden was documented by Diodorus Siculus *(Biblioteca liber XIV.42.4)*.

After the felling and the successive transport, the trunk begins to dry, that is to say it loses both the water that is found freely in the cellular cavities as well as the water absorbed by the trunk during transport. From the moment that the water has evaporated, the quantity of the sap is subsequently reduced, determining a change in the property of the wood, such as increasing its rigidity, its resistance to compression and warping, and decreasing its resistance to traumatic events (Cagnana 2000, 220-222). The drying of the wood also determines its tightening which if verified in the longitudinal sense is quite dense. If this occurs in the radial or tangential sections, it can be the cause of marked warping. Moreover, wood dries more quickly on the surface: the sap tends to rise up by way of osmosis, causing superficial cracks (McGrail 1987, 27). To avoid warping and cracking due to rapid drying, practical and efficient solutions were utilised: the bark was not removed (*Theophrastus, Historia Plantarum, III.8.7*) or the wood was covered with dung (*Theophrastus, Historia Plantarum, V.5.6*). If one wanted to control the drying and in some way speed it up without causing damage, deep, circular incisions were made at the base of the tree. Vitruvius (*De Architectura, II.9.6-9 e II.11*) and Plinius wrote how this technique was widely utilised during the Roman era: "...*Nec novellae autem ad materiem nec veteres utilissimae. Circumcisas quoque in medullam aliqui non inutiliter relinquunt, ut omnis umor stantibus defluat....*" (*Naturalis Historia, XVI.192-193*).

After cutting, wood can be subject to various phenomena of decay other than that caused by tightening, such as the attack of fungi, corrosion or mechanical damage. As far as mycological attacks are concerned, one can differentiate between humid and dry putrefaction. The first develops caused by external humidity that enters through cracks and spaces in the wood, causing it to ferment the sap and transform the wood into black *humus*. In contrast, the second type develops from the natural humidity of the wood that is transformed into dry crumbly yellow or brownish matter (Rival 1991, 107-108).

THE CONVERSION OF WOOD

The process of transforming a tree into beams with established shapes and dimensions is called conversion. To learn how a plant has been converted and which tools were used, it is necessary to reconstruct a section of the trunk, distinguish the type of conversion, namely which part of the log was used (orientation of the log) and identify the method of conversion, that is, how the log had been cut (Goodburn 1992, 111-112). Conversion influences the aspect of the wood, determines the configuration of the grain, and establishes the properties of the piece, also revealing its weaknesses (Allen 1994, 3).

The most common types of conversion are: the squaring up of the sides and ends, dividing the wood in two parts lengthways, cutting it into four parts, dividing into segments that radiate from the centre (the growth apices meet the sides of the plank at approximately a right angle), cutting into parallel slices (the rings are nearly parallel to the sides of the plank), "natural" grain cutting (the growth rings meet the sides of the plank between a 30° and 60° angle). To obtain different kinds of cuts, the carpenters had substantially three possible techniques of log conversion at their disposal, and each one required the use of different tools. The work could be accomplished by cleaving, reducing or squaring up and sawing. The technique of conversion by radial cleaving was based on empirical knowledge of the anatomy of wood, causing the carpenter to choose wood with straight fibres (Rival 1991, 104-105). This way was preferred also because by following the natural lines of division (grain) without breaking the cells, one maintained all the mechanical properties of the wood (Rival 1991, 125).

Oak cleaves best in the radial sense compared with all the other types of wood. For example, ash is more resistant to radial cleaving even if neither the halving nor the quartering is practicable. In contrast, pine divides better longitudinally, that is along the growth rings, as with many other soft woods where the differences between sapwood and heartwood are well-defined along the tracheids, long vertical cells (McGrail 1987, 30-31). Green woods are more adapted to cleaving compared to partially dried woods (Rival 1991, 125) because their natural splitting planes, parallel to the xylem rays, follow the length of the trunk (McGrail 1987, 31). Some of the tools utilised for cleaving consisted in a very hard wooden wedge, for example, cornel beaten with a wooden mallet (Rival 1991, 125; Goodburn 1992, 99). Metal handled wedges were found in the Danish territories (Olsen-Crumlin Pedersen 1967, 10) and in Medieval France (McGrail 1987, 152) while "T" axes have also been documented (Goodburn 1992, 113). The boards obtained by splitting are less subject to warping and breakage once dried. Moreover, this method reduces the presence of knots which cause weaknesses in the wooden structure (McGrail 1987, 31).

In reducing or squaring up, the trunks were straightened by eliminating the rounded parts (Rival 1991, 128).

The use of saws for converting the trunks into planks was very widespread in the Mediterranean during the Classic era, while it seems that in northern Europe its use appears only in Medieval centuries and only with the 14th century becomes the most utilised conversion method. This method is still used today as it allows the best use of the trunk with the least waste of raw materials (McGrail 1987, 31-32; Goodburn 1992, 113-114). The boards can be sawed beginning with the whole trunk, either with the bark or with the log squared up. In the first case, irregular planks are obtained, because it is impossible to trace references in trunks covered with bark. In the second case, on the other hand, straightened, squared-up boards can be obtained. Both methods produced only two or three radial planks (Rival 1991, 134). Sawing could also be used to obtain double curved or very large elements, but it presented problems because it consumed a notable quantity of raw material, while the pieces obtained in this way were less resistant and could easily split (Gianfrotta-Pomey 1980, 271). Finally, Theophrastus (*Historia Plantarum, V.6.2*) furnishes some guidelines for this kind of cut. It is easier to do with humid wood, even if there is the problem of more difficulty moving the saw. In addition, it must be performed parallel to the wood fibres, otherwise the pith could be destroyed. The parallel cut allows the conservation of all the mechanical characteristics, while an oblique cut opens the piece up to attacks of various nature and if put under stress to weaken (Rival 1991, 135-136).

THE ARTIFACTS PRODUCED

The objects produced were used in daily life, to satisfy the needs of the domestic environment (Mille *et alii* 1993, 255-258), play (Colardelle-Verdel 1993, 263-266), agriculture, the military, and free time. In north-central Europe, the availability of consistent forest resources allowed the use of oak, birch, ash, maple, walnut, white pine, alder, willow, elm, woodland pine, hawthorn and box-wood, obviously distinct in their diversity of use based on the type of wood and the objects produced.

The knowledge of the individual properties and potentials of woods is also revealed in the craftsmen's capacity to associate different species in making the same object based on the function of each single part. Ways of connecting the structural components of an object are largely diversified even if they are often only a hypothesis, because no direct confirmation has been provided by the state of the single elements. The assembly of planks was made with tenon and mortise joints, and with grooves and wooden pegs inserted into the proper cavities. Edge joints could have been made at right angles or they could be corner joints with numerous variants, dovetail or butterfly joints. Glues made from animals were probably used, whereas joints were reinforced using wooden pegs, nails and wooden pins, ties made of leather or rope and sometimes twisted gut or copper and iron wires (Wolf 1997, 381-388).

The main function of wooden objects was in the domestic environment, where it is plausible to find artefacts utilised in daily life, such as benches, stools, trunks, tables, cupboards and shelves. These represented the fundamental components of simple, functional furniture in direct rapport with what the external environment provided. The seats of the stools and tables were built of thick pieces of wood placed on three or four legs which were either rounded or squared off, with the corners rounded and smoothed. The upper part of the leg was inserted with pressure and sometimes blocked with a wedge while the lower part was always placed with a marked splay compared to the horizontal plane of support and positioned at an angle for more stability and resistance. The chests were constructed using the principles of insertion and joining. The chest was formed in a parallelepiped shape composed of six boards, placed on each side including the lid and the bottom. The former could have been hinged directly to the anterior board, which is the solution that guaranteed the best functionality compared to simply posing the top onto the superior borders of the four assembled boards. If one wanted to establish better stability, nails were inserted into the rear and front boards. The posterior part could be characterised by the presence of a simple decoration done on the sanded surface with a chipping or engraving carving technique: this depended on the ability of the craftsmen and the availability of man-hours necessary to do the work (Symonds 1993, 243-257). The cupboard was a crate used for the preservation of food and materials, with a covering obtained by the overlapping of unfinished boards, obtained by splitting with a hatchet, put together and joined by wooden pegs (Wolf 1997, 380-381).

Although furniture is often found, most of the objects were made up of plates, spoons, lids and pestles (Von Hessen 1990, 258-259). They were produced from a single piece of wood, while buckets (Mille *et alii* 1993, 241-242) and small barrels were obtained by assembling several single staves.

The plates could have been of differing dimensions, but the use of serving plates differing from single plates is to be excluded. Such an aspect is testified to from the images taken from miniatures, where the tables were not laid with single serving plates, but each table companion took the desired quantity of food out of the main serving dish. This plate may have been decorated with engravings obtained by light indentations with palmette or geometric designs. The plates were made from green or semigreen logs that after being hewn, took on the form of a stocky plate. The plate was then fixed unto a pole lathe, turned, and lines were designed on the borders using a gouge (Mille *et alii* 1993, 238-241).

While plates were not utilised for individual use, the bowls were, where stews and other semisolid foods were served. After a careful analysis with a binocular microscope of the patina of the internal surface of the containers, the following hypothesis was confirmed. In addition, the numerous scrape marks present on the bottom suggest the use of spoons for eating meals. The dimensions of the latter were more or less standardised and they were built of a handle and an oval-shaped end. They were carved from long, straight branches that were between 6 and 12 cm in diameter. When cut to the necessary length, the hewn spoons were finished on a block with a very sharp curved knife. The spoons also had the same patina found on the bowls confirming the hypothesis that they were used contemporaneously with the dishes (Mille *et alii* 1993, 244-245).

Another wooden object that made up part of the household goods was the lid: circular and flat shaped. It was posed on vases and pots to close the opening. Some lids present a small notch for the passage of a spoon handle. "Scrapers" also existed: a type of spatula with a long handle blocked into a hole with a small pin. Their use was probably tied to spreading flour on a pastry board and focaccia dough onto stone baking sheets probably already placed directly on the fire (Mille *et alii* 1993, 245-246).

If meal utensils required few man-hours, the realisation of barrels and buckets was trusted to able craftsmen, who were needed to assemble staves, bottoms, and hoops. In the Ligurian territory, the quantity of coopers was so prevalent in both rural and city environments that they were the first to organise a "guild" in the city of Genoa. The preparation of the staves was long and laborious. The oak was cut down in winter and then the staves were obtained from a single log. After three years of drying, they were finished with a jack-plane and then carefully assembled. The hoopings were made of either cane, arranged close together and tied with wicker, or iron. The choice of material was determined by the final use of the barrel: the first type was utilised for transporting cured meats, and the second for the conservation of liquids, wine overall (Baratta 1997, 110). Wine put considerable pressure on the staves and had to be contained inside the barrels with iron hoopings. The species of wood used was not of secondary importance: both oak and chestnut could be used (Mannoni 1976, 230-231) like the bucket recovered in Genoa, Liguria (Italy) in a post-Medieval stratigraphy in Portofranco (Calderara 1976, 375-378) confirmed by a palaeobotanical analysis.

Wooden buckets could have had completely different uses from that of liquid or semisolid food containers. The tombs of individuals recognised as having Germanic ethnic origins offer numerous examples starting from the 4th century up until the 7th century. The buckets were often associated with rich burial goods. Interpreted as drinking containers for horses, typically found in the tombs of cavalry officers, the wooden buckets were also found in female tombs and evidently they must be considered as indicators of the wealth and social class of the defunct. Widespread from Rhineland to Normandy, these buckets often stand apart by their decorative metallic borders with stylised human figures etched in triangles, and by the handle attachments, built with bronze handmade, open-worked plaques and often terminating in a zoomorphic figure. These types of containers come from a burial in Krefeld (Germany), from the cemetery of Pry (Belgium) and from that in Bâle-Bernerring (Switzerland) with a chronology going from the first quarter of the 6th century to the end of 7th century (Lusuardi Siena 1994, 323-325).

Major care and revision of the excavation documentation has allowed the recovery of other important elements in the early Medieval funerary outfits that are pertinent to the Germanic populations such as funerary structures, sepulchral rooms, funeral beds and coffins: the latter consisted of simple hollowed logs, but other examples formed of wooden boards nailed together and decorated with ornamental elements also existed (Lusuardi Siena 1994, 325). Examples of this can be found in materials recovered from a Frankish or perhaps Alemanic graves (Doppelfeld 1964, 160-164) as an expression of craftsmanship of notably high quality as well as an index of ancient funerary traditions: in Cologne (Doppelfeld 1960, 90-94), Lauchheim, Oberflacht and Langenlonsheim (Aufleger 1996, 599-601).

The documentation of stratigraphic excavations relative to the early Medieval settlements furnishes the most complete picture of the variety of wooden objects utilised not only in the household but also in farming and crafts. Handles for scythes, axes and hammers have been found, together with mallets, made of a stump conical head and a short cylindrical handle. Beside these objects of common use, some "measuring sticks" were found. They were distinguished from normal walking sticks by the presence of regular notches. They were triangular in section and one side had notches positioned at an interval of about 40 millimetres. The use of this tool is uncertain: perhaps it was a grain measure used in selling (Mille *et alii* 1993, 246-247).

In the excavation in the Medieval village of Charavines in north-central France, very important data relative to the wooden tools used for spinning wool have been acquired dating from the end of the 10th to the beginning of the 11th centuries: spindles, spools and bobbins. The first had different dimensions; the larger ones for spinning and the smaller ones for the loom. They had a little nut on the top and a slightly flared body. It took a good craftsman to make them because the spindles were moulded from maple logs that were still green. After being left to dry, they were turned so that a series of black circles were left on the long neck of the spindle, that represented the blocking points of the product on the wheel. According to some interpretations, these could have measured the quantity of yarn that was wound around the spindle. The sizeable quantity of exhibits suggests the presence of a successful craftsman, which not only produced utensils for the inhabitants of the village but also for the surrounding communities. This hypothesis is based on the fact that weaving is primarily a feminine activity, and considering the consistent quantity of spindles recovered, it is plausible that production was destined to satisfy the requirements of other communities (Mille *et alii* 1993, 247-251).

If it is possible to document the existence of combs, chairs, dressing tables and looms in the female burials, arrowheads, javelin points, lance points, sword sheaths, knives and bow grips all appear in the male graves. Inside the vast and complex Germanic cultural world, military equipment represented private property and could not be inherited. Therefore it had to accompany the defunct into the afterlife. From the types and combinations of the diverse weapons, it is possible to understand the possible social condition of the owner as well as the combat techniques he used.

The presence of javelin points and arrowheads in the tombs is an absolutely typical element. These weapons were used primarily by foot soldiers and were never submitted to a typological-technical evolution that modified their use by the passage through an intermediate form. Whether Franks, Bavarians or Alemans, three general typologies of arrowheads were found inside the graves throughout the course of the 7th century: the first, a swallowtail, the second, a willow leaf, and the third, a triple barb. The possibility of mixture of different kinds of weapons in use by the Germanic populations is documented however by the historic sources. Ammianus Marcellinus in book XVI, chapter 12 of the History, reveals how in the battle of Strasbourg set in the second half of the 4th century, darts and javelins were employed by the Alemanic warriors against the Roman infantry: "....*Spicula tamen verrutaque misfuroris non cessabant, ferrataeque arundines fundebatur, quamquam etiam comminus mucro feriebat contra mucronem, et loricae gladiis fundebantur, et vulnerati nondum effuso cruore ad audendum exsertius consurgebant......*" (Selem 1998, 236-237).

One of the most interesting artefacts that represent the collective memory of the military technology in its primordial phase is definitely the bow, and the different types of arrows that can be correlated to its employment. In the case of the Germanic populations, a working craft of local woods like yew and ash allowed the production of bows made of one piece of wood (self bows), reflex bows and also composite bows made of wood, horn and fibrous materials, often with reinforcements in bone. The bowstrings were made of animal tendons, the wooden part was reinforced by the insertion of bone in the two inferior margins while the grip, placed on the curve in the simple type of bow, was slightly asymmetrical in the composite bow; however, it was counterweighted by several layers of strips of leather to assure that the structure flexed with a balanced and gradual pressure to power ratio. The total length of the bow can be hypothesised with an average value calculated between 160 and 180 centimetres while the pull load must have reached 35 to 40 kilograms, allowing a maximum range between 250 and 300 metres, with a lethal efficiency reached at about 60-70 metres (Wolf 1997, 387).

The arrow shaft was made of light woods such as willow or poplar so as to absorb the vibration caused when the arch was pulled, and presented diverse types of iron tips with differing dimensions and weights depending on the various uses and the typology of ownership. Inside the burial of a male individual in the Alemanic necropolis in Niederstotzingen, rare examples of arrowheads were documented at the cemetery site. The particular conservation conditions have allowed the documentation of the fragmented remains of arrow shafts that a botanical analysis has shown to have been made of beech and birch (Paulsen 1967, 122-123). The arrowheads were nested into the shaft by a tang and blocked in place with a tie or also by circular bands, as demonstrated in the find at Niederstotzingen of a thinly laminated collar made of iron (Paulsen 1967, tomb 3c, 182-185). On the heel of the shaft, that was approximately 60-70 centimetres in length, a notch was present that allowed to nock the arrow, while bird plumes were positioned on both sides in order to guarantee the desired direction and force of the arrow. The arrows were gathered together tip down in a leather quiver probably around 80 centimetres long with a semicircular opening. It is presumed that loops and a shoulder strap were fixed along the straight sides of the container (Wolf 1997, 388).

The shield was one of the real symbols of the warrior, the exemplification of his social status and role. He received it the first time he was accepted among warriors; therefore, abandoning it was considered as a deeply offensive and disgraceful act. If the warrior died while fighting, he was carried away lying on his shield. During assemblies warriors would approve resolutions by hitting the boss (umbo), namely the metallic part of their shields. This object, of either round or elliptical shape, was the main defensive equipment throughout the early Middle Ages. The shield consisted of wooden strips, sometimes covered with one or more layers of leather and decorated with iron or bronze fittings; the diameter ranged from 30 to 76 centimetres, whereas according to the rivets found the thickness varied from 12 to 30 millimetres. A hole in the centre allowed the warrior to clasp an iron grip across the inner face of the hole, and this hole was protected by a metal boss about 15 centimetres wide, usually hammered out of a single piece of iron, though occasionally a flat sheet of metal was merely bent to form a cone. The boss was secured to the wood by four or five rivets with heads measuring as much as 50 millimetres wide (Sandler 2000, 43).

The reconstruction of the fragments from the Sutton-Hoo shields produced a diameter measuring 91.5 centimetres long. This shield, made of lime-wood and covered with leather, was decorated with ornamental metal pieces, including a stylised dragon and a finely worked iron umbo which can be compared to a similar pattern excavated in a Swedish grave-slip (Sandler 2000, 43).

Author's address

Paolo DE VINGO
University of Turin
Archaeology Research Doctorate
SAAST Department
via G.Giolitti 21/e, 10123 Torino ITALY
Email: Aldebaran@aleph.it

Bibliography

ALLEN S., 1994, The illustration of wooden artefacts: an introduction and guide to the depiction of wooden objects, Oxford.

AUFLEGER, M., 1996, Holzarbeiten und Holzbearbeitung. In Alltagskultur im Frankenreich. Die Franken. Wegbereiter Europas, Mainz: Verlag Philipp Von Zabern, p.599-604.

BARATTA G., 1997, Le botti: dati e questioni. In Techniques et économie antiques et médiévales. Le temps de l'innovation. Colloque d'Aix-en-Provence (Mai 1996), edited by D. Garcia, D. Meeks. Paris: Editions Errance, p.109-111.

CAGNANA A., 2000, Archeologia dei materiali da costruzione, Mantova: Società Archeologica Padana.

CALDERARA A., 1976, Restauro di un secchio in legno del XVI secolo proveniente dagli scavi di Genova. Archeologia Medievale III, Firenze: Edizioni All'Insegna Del Giglio, p.375-378.

CASTELLETTI L., 1988, Dendrocronologia. In Restauro dei monumenti. I ciclo di lezioni sulla ricerca applicata in archeologia. Certosa di Pontignano (28 settembre-10 ottobre 1987), edited by R. Francovich, R. Parenti. Firenze: Edizioni All'Insegna Del Giglio, p.421-454.

COLARDELLE M., VERDEL E., 1993, Les jeux. In Les habitats du lac du Paladru (Isère) dans leur environnement. La formation d'un terroir au XIe siècle, edited by M. Colardelle, E. Verdel. Paris: Editions de la Maison des Sciences de l'Homme, p.263-266.

COLES J.M., 1982, Ancient woodworking techniques: the implications for archaeology. In Woodworking before A.D. 1500. Papers presented to a Symposium at Greenwich in September 1980. British Archaeological Reports International Series 129, Oxford: BAR Publishing, p.1-6.

DOPPELFELD O., 1960, Das fränkische Frauengrab unter dem Chor des Kölner Domes. Germania, 38, p.89-113.

DOPPELFELD O., 1964, Das fränkische Knabebgrab unter dem Chor des Kölner Domes. Germania 42, p.156-188.

VON HESSEN O., 1990, Oggetti di legno dell'altomedioevo. In L'ambiente vegetale nell'altomedioevo, Settimane di Studio del Centro Italiano di Studi sull'AltoMedioevo, (30 marzo-5 aprile 1989), XXXVIII, Spoleto, p.257-260.

GIANFROTTA P.A., POMEY P., 1981, Archeologia subacquea, Milano.

GOODBURN D., 1992, Woods and woodlands: carpenters and carpentry. In Timber Building Techniques in London c.900-1400. An archaeological study of waterfront installations and related material, London: University Press, p.106-130.

GRETTER I., 1972, L'ultimo verde, Trento.

MC GRAIL S., 1987, Ancient boats in North-Western Europe. The archaeology of water transport to AD 1500, London: University Press.

MANNONI T., MANNONI L., 1976, Per una storia regionale della cultura materiale: i recipienti in Liguria. Quaderni Storici 31, Genova, p.229-251.

MANNONI T., GIANNICHEDDA E., 1996, Archeologia della Produzione, Torino: Einaudi.

MILLE P., COLARDELLE M., VERDEL E., 1993, Les objects de bois. In Les habitats du lac du Paladru (Isère) dans leur environnement. La formation d'un territoire au Xie siécle, edited by M. Colardelle, E. Verdel. Paris: Editions de la Maison des Sciences de l'Homme, p.238-258.

MOOISLEITNER, V.F., 1988, Handwerk und Handel. In Die Bajuwaren, Salzburg, p.208-219.

MEIGGS R., 1982, Trees and timber in the Ancient Mediterranean World, Oxford: University Press.

PARENTI R., 1994, I materiali da costruzione, le tecniche di lavorazione e gli attrezzi. In Edilizia residenziale tra V e VIII secolo, edited by G.P. Crogiolo. Mantova: Padus, p.25-37.

PAULSEN P., 1967, Alamannische Adelsgräber von Niederstotzingen (Kreis Heidenheim). Veröffentlichungen des Staatlichen Amtes für Denkmalpfllege Stuttgart, Reihe A, Vor –Und Frühgeschichte, Heft 12/1, Stuttgart: Verlag Müller & Graff.

RIVAL M., 1991, La charpenterie navale romaine, Paris.

SANDLER F.L., 2000, Sutton Hoo. In Enciclopedia dell'Arte medievale, edited by Angiola Maria Romanici. XI, Milano: Arti Grafiche Ricordi, p.42-44.

SELEM A., 1998, Ammiano Marcellino. Le Storie, I-II volume, TEA: Milano.

SIENA LUSUARDI S., 1995, I manufatti in legno. In Ad Mensam. Manufatti d'uso da contesti archeologici fra tarda antichità e Medioevo, edited by S. Lusuardi Siena. Udine: Del Bianco Editore, p.319-332.

SYMONDS R.W., 1993, Il mobilio nell'epoca postromana. In Storia della tecnologia 2. Le civiltà mediterranee e il Medioevo, edited by C. Singer, E.J. Holmyard, A.R. Hall, T.I. Williams. Torino: Bollati & Borlinghieri, p.243-261.

WOLF, R., 1997, Schreiner, drechsler, bottcher, instrumentenbauer. Holzhandwerk im fruhen Mittelalter. In Die Alamannen, Stuttgart: Theiss, p.379-388.

MIGRATED GROUPS AND LOCAL POPULATIONS: INTEGRATION AND CONTRAST IN THE WESTERN ALPS BETWEEN THE ROMAN PERIOD AND THE EARLY MIDDLE AGES

Paolo DE VINGO

Abstract: The Alps have always played a major role in the history of the European land, though with different functions through the centuries. These mountains, in fact, were a natural boundary between central and western Europe on the one hand and southern Europe on the other, but they never represented an insuperable barrier separating the different German populations settled near this articulated mountain range. In the early Middle Ages, the Alpine lands were not a homogeneous political union. In western Switzerland the Burgundian kingdom, which had stemmed from the military needs of the Romans, was surrounded by the Franks, which subjected and absorbed it in 543 A.D.. From the northern lands, some compact groups of Alemannians and Bavarians pressed against the Alpine barrier, whereas in northern Italy the situation was quite chaotic. In 569 A.D., the Lombards occupied the northern lands in Italy, leading to the establishment of new territories inhabited by different German groups with their own diversified political and social patterns: the Franks, the Alemannians and the Bavarians beyond the Alps, whereas the Lombards consolidated their presence in central and northern Italy. The remains inherited from the original settlement of the Burgundians are just a few, and their number starts to increase only since the Frankish occupation. Among the typical items are a number of belts for both male and female clothing; some of them had large-sized plates decorated with Christian designs. The presence of weapons among the grave goods of male burials is completely exceptional, and the rare recovered examples belonged to men of Frankish or Alemannic groups. A contrasting settlement feature is observed in the Italian Lombard graves, where both male and female grave goods are clearly defined. Women used to wear a Germanic costume with a couple of stirrup-shaped fibulae and a pair of smaller fibulae, bags and amulets hanging from their belts, whereas on their neck they used to wear glass and stone beads necklaces. Men were buried with the traditional fighting equipment: a double-edged, long sword, a lance with willow leaf head and a round shield with the iron boss, basically of conic shape; the belt that held the sword was usually decorated with simple bronze or iron plates.

INTRODUCTION

The Alps have always held a significant role in all of the periods of European history, holding different but equally important functions. In fact, this articulated mountainous system functioned for long tracts as a natural border between the Northern and Southern areas of the European Continent. They never represented an insurmountable barrier in the absolute sense of the word, because the mountain chain allowed numerous communication possibilities between the north and south. These interactions were made directionally through phases of importation and exportation and in the filtering function performed by the Alps (Von Hessen 1997, 193).

In late antiquity the western and eastern alpine areas formed part of four different provinces: the *Viennensis,* the *Lugdunensis the first,* the *Maxima Sequanorum* and the *Raetia the first* (Martin 1986, 147) inhabited by a large nucleus of a local roman population who went on to join distinct groups of Germanic populations during the 5th and 6th centuries: Burgundians, Franks, Alemannians and Bavarians who each held a diverse but significant role in the destiny of an evolving Europe. The relationships among these ethnographic entities and the phenomena of their integration and juxtaposition constitute a channel of research and advanced study of very interesting components (Colardelle 1983, 12-14).

In 569 the occupation of the northern areas of the Italic peninsula by the Lombards determined the formation of territories occupied by distinct Germanic ethnic groups with very diverse political and social structures: Franks, Alemannians and Bavarians beyond the limits of the Alps, while the Lombards consolidated their presence in the north-central Italic territories (Privati 1983, 10-15).

Under the pressure of Germanic populations, a part of the autochthonous populations in the alpine areas retreated into certain secure and isolated areas, usually in valleys at rather high elevations, continuing their existence. Small necropolises pertaining to these groups are often found which contain late antiquity burial goods and other objects which better reflect local characteristics (Von Hessen 1997, 193).

In western Switzerland, more or less large necropolises of the Burgundian population have been conserved that in the last decade have been the object of intense stratigraphic excavations. The objects recovered in the graves are relatively scarce in the first part of the 6th century, but the situation is also exactly identical to the autochthonous population. Only after the conquest of the Burgundian reign by the Franks, new forms appear among the objects recovered which were similar to those of the Franks. Typical examples include men's and women's belts with bronze and iron appliqués: the latter were silver plated and had geometric motifs etched on the silver surface, otherwise Christian figures were present which reflected Mediterranean models. Among the Germanic populations, the Lombards left the most evidence in the alpine valleys and foothills of the Alps, because of their custom of burying their dead with grave goods. Even if it is a fairly generalised fact that this custom was used only from the second half of the 7th century and was followed by a progressive abandonment during the course of the subsequent century (Crosetto 1998, 217).

Burial goods were therefore the expression of the conception of the unearthly world and important indicators of the social position of each defunct. The objects of the outfit consisted of costume elements, which were put in the tomb as functional accessories of the clothing worn by the dead (buckles, pins, belt parts) and real and actual burial offerings, which goes to say objects deposited on purpose such as cavalry equipment and weapons for the men, and ornamental objects for the women, to which ceramics and utensils can be added, placed as a funeral offering for either men or women. The composition of the outfit followed fixed rules and a study concerning burial goods and the combinations of funeral offerings allows the extrapolation of the rules that were followed with regularity in funerary practices. The long, double-edged *spatha* appears in adult men's tombs and is completely absent in the burials of infants and adolescents. This type of weapon represents a fixed component of the adult male burial goods and appears with much regularity in all the necropolises examined in the two different contexts. In almost all of the male tombs the remains of shields, usually the umbo and the handle, are also found. Along with the helmet and armour, the shield is the most common weapon of defence. It could be considered the necessary companion to the *spatha,* a weapon that could be used in close combat or in individual fights. Its missing in certain tombs where the *spatha* is present could be justified by the fact that the shield was made of entirely organic materials and therefore had deteriorated. The lance was placed in the grave goods with less frequency while the supplementary armament with armour, helmet, reflex bow with reinforcements in bone and arrows should be considered a "hyper-armament" and must therefore be interpreted with a prevalently sociological eye. A subordinate role in the necropolises pertaining to the southern alpine strip of territory is attributed to the *sax,* being that this weapon is found in only a very limited number of graves. The quantitative data on its diffusion is in strong contrast with that of the contemporaneous transalpine graves, where the *sax* was the most frequently documented weapon found in the male burials. Ceramics were not deposited in adult male individual tombs, but were reserved for women, and children and adolescents of both sexes. In the transalpine regions the funeral use of placing bronze ware is found without distinction in both masculine and feminine tombs, while in the southern territorial areas it is found only in those of adult men. Finally, for specific funerary customs, some forms of conditioning existed linked to age and sex: the placing of clothing components, the utensils, foods and coins or other personal effects were not subject to fixed rules but constitute variable elements (Rupp 1997, 26-27). The goods most documented in the feminine tombs were clothing accessories. In a particular way, belt buckles show with a certain regularity a number of typologies that in some cases one can define as standardised while in other examples they are peculiar to an ethnic group in a an individual and characteristic sense. Other important components are fibulae, in particular arch-shaped and disc-shaped ones and other pins utilised as both hairpins and to close robes on the front side. Shoe accessories are also quite frequent, such as the decorations on the ties and the shoes themselves.

An analysis of the female burial goods based on clothing accessories produces, at first glance, an image of their class costume. A time-ordered typological examination on a significant number of necropolises pertinent to both territories has allowed us to recognise those burial complexes where important transformations occurred in the fundamental components of feminine dress from those that did not register any change. This has allowed us to identify the populations that abandoned traditional funerary customs and embraced the local uses of placement. Notwithstanding these limitations, the feminine burial outfit seems to follow precise canons. As a matter of fact, two distinct types have been recognised: the first group includes those tombs with richer ornaments and with a quantity of various grave offerings, while the second burial grouping has a reduced outfit. However, this reduction does not seem to have a sociological origin. In fact, the simplification of the outfit constitutes a successive development, because only the burials with pins can be considered chronologically reliable. In the southern region, in particular, the tombs with reduced burial goods do not demonstrate any temporal relationship to the generation of immigrants already emerging from the beginning of the 7th century, while the burials with fibulae, ornaments of high artistic quality and many various objects are pertinent to both the immigration phase and the following one. In necropolises with very similar dating and positioned close to each other, funerary customs were practised that differed in a few fundamental aspects: women presumably of the same rank were buried with a common funeral composition, yet prepared in different ways (Rupp 1997, 27-28).

ISSUES RELATIVE TO THE WESTERN ALPINE ARCH

Of the four ethnic groupings indicated *(cf. supra)* the Burgundians, after submitting to a disastrous defeat in 436 at the hands of the Roman General Aetius, were the object of a forced relocation, for strategic, military and political reasons, from central and southern Germany to the *Sapaudia* area where they had to share the territory with the autochthonous population: «...*Sapaudia Burgundiorum reliquiis datur cum indigenis dividenda....*» (Bierbrauer 1993, 10). The military practicality of this choice can be identified in the necessity to guarantee control of the alpine passes towards the territories of the Italic peninsula and the lower Rhone valley. The possibility that the integrative phenomena were successful can be proven by the discovery of a gold ring with a seal found near Sierre: it was attributed to a high ranking Burgundian official that probably carried out important duties on the part of the Roman political authority in the Rhone valley (Amrein 1997, 239). The formation of the Burgundian reign happened according to the canons and principles of territorial division utilised for the *foederati,* similar to that which also characterised the eastern German areas (Bierbrauer 1993, 10) as was confirmed by the Chronicles of Mario d'Avenches regarding the occupation of Lyon in 456: «...*Burgundiores cum Gallis senatoribus diviserunt...*» (Bierbrauer 1993, 10). The region of the *Sapaudia* must have been located in the territory surrounding Geneva to the slopes of the Jura of Nurenburg in southern Switzerland. This first geographical redistribution met with successive transformations that initially brought a sizeable territorial expansion towards the North to the high plain of Langres, towards the Northeast up to the middle valley of Aare, towards the South to the Durance river and then in 532 a territorial downsizing that became deeply connected with the historic-political issues linked to the establishment of the Frankish reign (Bierbrauer 1993, 10-11). An approximate quantification of the total number of Germanic individuals quartered in the *Sapaudia* could be hypothesised at around twenty thousand units: a number that substantiates the hypothesis of coexistence with the predominant population of the Romanised Autochthons (Bierbrauer 1993, 11-12).

The rapport of interaction between the distinct ethnic groups within this geographic area can be examined by further study of the results obtained in a long archaeological intervention at the necropolis of Sézegnin in the commune of Avusy, 12 kilometres south-west of Geneva, where between 1973 and 1979 a total of 710 tombs were excavated (Martin 1986, 149). The phases B and C of the necropolis did not correspond with burials of individuals of Germanic origin during the early Middle ages. The funeral rites that characterise the Frank and Alemannic cultures in the 6th and 7th centuries were not found in Sézegnin. In only one male grave, the long combat blade known as a *sax* was found deposited, but even if the dead person was a Germanic warrior, it is more plausible to identify him as an individual of Frankish origins than Burgundian (Privati 1983, tomb 502). If between the 5th and late 7th centuries, a culturally homogenous group coming from southern areas by spontaneous migration, but at the same time totally distinct from the predominant population, had settled near Sézegnin, they should have left evidence of the Germanic culture use of placing the individuals buried in their traditional daily costume. On the basis of these conclusions, the occurrence of forced immigration of small tribal nuclei has been hypothesised, but in a period preceding the early Medieval times, probably set around the first or second third of the 5th century. The above hypothesis would coincide historically with the quartering of the Burgundians in the *Sapaudia*. In fact some male tombs can be traced back to a primordial phase A of the employment of burial sites in Sézegnin. These tombs held deposits of bows, arrows and axes that made up combat objects typical of the burial typology linked to the Luboszyce culture of the 2nd to 4th centuries of the eastern Germanic populations (Bierbrauer 1993, 12). In the following period chronically relative to the phase B burials, only three female individuals rendered very interesting information. In one of these graves a plated belt buckle was found (Martin 1986, 174-175) while a common characteristic was the artificial deformation of the cranium: the cultural horizon that this custom expresses appears to be a trademark characteristic of Hunnish nomads. Regarding this fact, it is useful to note that the Burgundians were allied with the Huns and subject to their control previous to 443 (Bierbrauer 1993, 12).

This observation would seem to demonstrate that the Burgundian population reached the alpine region with a level of acculturation much more substantial than any other Germanic group settled inside the Roman territory: as a matter of fact, they had lost almost every characteristic cultural trait. This fact is not only explainable through the simple phenomena of acquisition of dominant ethnic traits in the absolute sense and in a literal way, but it is also possible that a Burgundian cultural substratum had already been influenced during the settlement phase between the Rhine and the Main river, beginning from the late 4th century from western Germanic cultural models. Fibulae made in "cloisonné" style can be traced back to this typology coming from Saint-Sulpice (tomb 97 and tomb 133) and Saint-Prex, as well as a pair of small clasps decorated with geometric forms in "Kerbschnitt" style also found at Saint-Sulpice. The production of these female clothing elements can be attributed to artisan workshops that operated regionally, but considering the stylistic contents and relation to the eastern Germanic-Ostrogothic type, it is also plausible that they come from Ostrogoth workshops identified on the Italic peninsula. In fact, from 494 to 507 a close relationship was established between Theodoric and Gundobald (Bierbrauer 1993, 12).

One part of the Burgundian tombs from the late 5th and early 6th centuries were found on the borders of the *Sapaudia*, in the territory that up until 532 was under Burgundian rule, even though there is no current evidence to our knowledge of a dense Burgundian settlement in the plains areas of this zone (Bierbrauer 1993, 12).

The presence of the first elements of grave goods in Burgundian areas dates back to the first half of the 6th century and bears witness to the development in this period of the custom of burials with grave goods. Plated fibulae and belt buckles figure in among the elements of the highest artistic quality along with other complementary objects (pins, double-hooked clasps, shoe buckles, pearl necklaces, ferrules, pendants and rings).

An extended Burgundian area can be distinguished by the characteristic influence of a relative homogeneity, despite the presence of certain types of bronze clasps shaped like flies and snake-like ones with animal decorations of oriental origin, in consequence to the Burgundian expansion that occurred between 457 and 500 in *Sapaudia;* clasps attributed to the Rhine influence dated from the first half of the 6th century must be added to these finds. In the second half of the 6th century, one notes the development of regional models, in particular in the Lemanic, Genevan and Faucigny regions, that spread through the northern alpine populations of Roman-Gallic tradition, thanks to the rapid assimilation of Burgundian immigrant populations followed by the Franks in the 6th and 7th centuries (Raffaelli 1997, 213).

These models substantiate the existence of artisan workshops of a regional character still scarcely sufficient that continued the Germanic tradition of workmanship and decorative styles. At the beginning of the 6th century we find some indications of the social condition of the Burgundian craftsmen in the Gombette laws. They were slaves, but their importance was shown by the fact that in the case of homicide, the law established equal legal compensation to that of free men. Their technical ability in raised cells or "cloisonné" enamelling, niello-work, damascening or plating was limited by the scarcity of metals and of an art which, however minor, was masterly in its use of materials and polychromy. The ornamental characters of Germanic origin were adapted to the new Aryan and Catholic sensitivities after having submitted to the poetic and Danubian influences which recalled the Greek, Mid-east and Siberian ones, during migration, and followed by the Mediterranean adaptations caused by contact with the Christian world (Raffaelli 1997, 213).

Between the 6th century and first quarter of the 7th, the D type bronze-plated belt buckles from the Genevan and the Faucigny regions use decorative ornamentation with Christian themes, such as "Christ's entrance into Jerusalem", "Daniel in the lion den", "Daniel and Abacus divide a plate of bread", or otherwise Christianised like "Hippogryph about to drink from the cup of life", with Latin inscriptions and with the names of Germanic personages around the borders. In the late 6th century, in Roman-Burgundian women's clothing, the type D buckles were substituted by iron models, almost always damascened, of the B type. These also had the typical tags or bangles of decorative rectangular trimming with a braided motif or of the second animalistic style. The type B buckles were documented in a wider area than the type D ones, in conformity with their chronology, which is to say their increased use in grave goods, which reached its peak in the initial period (Bierbrauer 1993, 14). Analogously, in the Lemanic region, the type L (Lutry) presents three people praying comparable to "Three Jews in the furnace", or the S type (Saint-Sulpice) showing a person praying or "The Lord of the animals" Christianised of Siberian or Oriental origins. The R type was influenced by the DB types (group of the Jura) and S (Saint-Sulpice). The most recent belts are the type A ones, which are composed of two parts, and appear in the second half of the 7th century. In this case there is a long, heavy belt buckle with counter-trimming which was damascened then plated, taken from Eastern Frankish models (Bierbrauer 1993, 14).

The Frankish presence is documented in a sporadic way in the territorial strip including the high Savoy and the central-western Alps until the first third of the 6th century by small discoidal buckles, as well as S-buckles with bicephalus monsters and shield-shaped buckles, used typically in North-eastern Gaul (Raffaelli 1997, 213). The only difference there can be identified at the moment when the Burgundian territory was absorbed into the Frankish reign: in a particular way in the Trans-Jurassian region, among plated buckles of the D type with bronze trimming and the various typologies of damascened accessories in rectangular and trapezoidal iron (7th to the start of the 8th centuries). This last aspect could correspond to a period of transition when, after the definitive Frankish conquest in 534, the Burgundian territory, characterised by its strong Roman-Gallic cultural matrix, would have been opened to the Frankish influence. The use of damascening and of iron appears from the second half of the 7th century (Raffaelli 1997, 214).

The plated buckles of the A type distinguish the northern "Burgundian area" from the Burgundy region in the Alps. They are often associated with or immediately subsequent to the "Berna-Soletta" type plated buckles (7th to the early 8th centuries) with late armament coming from Northeast Gaul and characteristic of Austrian excellence. The B type, although widespread in the Trans-Jurassian regions are the subject of controversy regarding their dating (from the first half of the 7th century to the start of the 8th century), and remain therefore little utilised; they generally characterise the female burials. The same thing is true for the double-hooked clasps widely widespread in the region and whose use may not be correlated to the clothing, but rather for closing the shroud. Finally, in the second half of the 7th century and the beginning of the 8th, some studded plated buckles of Aquitanian type or from Neustria bear witness to a temporary influence of that culture (Raffaelli 1997, 214).

The burial goods of the early Medieval times in Savoy are scarce and of late epoch. For the most part, there are cases of discovery or antique reports. Numerous burials lack grave goods, in particular those in cases of stone slabs. This suggests the loss of the importance of funeral offerings, subordinated to the problem of perishable materials. The dating of the type C counter-plating of Grésy-sur-Aix may be attributed to the late 7th century or the early 8th century, while the plated buckle of Montricher-Albanne has not been chronologically determined (Raffaelli 1997, 214).

The goods from the necropolis at Collet de la Madeleine, near Lanslevillard, include some finds of plated buckles for ordinary type shoes, comparable to the objects discovered near Balme (La Roche-sur-Foron) which date back to the end of the 6th and 7th centuries, an ordinary counter-plating of a belt from the 6th century and some lost objects (Raffaelli 1997, 215).

The plated buckle from Saint-Marcel-en-Tarentaise is a T type (Tolochenaz) and shows a motif "with praying figures" of late epoch (the first quarter of the 7th century) that corresponds to the diffusion of a model more frequently traced back to the territory of the Rhone and in the Burgundy than the same Lemanic region (Raffaelli 1997, 215).

The archaeological site of Cognin is very well documented. In fact, in the necropolis of Cognin IV in a female grave situated in the ancient Gaul-Roman hypocaust, a type B buckle with crossing animal figures has been brought to light (silver and bronze plated on iron) dated between the third quarter of the 7th and the beginning of the 8th centuries. The young female individual of alpine type showed an artificial cranium deformation as was the custom used in the Eastern Germanic populations.

In the necropolis of Cognin IV only graves dug in simple earthen pits have been identified with few examples of various caskets and very simple grave goods composed of double-hooked clasps which, in the case of Cognin, would be dated between the end of the 7th and the first half of the 8th centuries (Raffaelli 1997, 215).

Burials with ceramic objects are very rare in the Savoy and seem to be of late epoch. Coinciding with the disappearance of funerary "store-rooms" and the maintenance of burials in use, a hiatus in ceramic production in Savoy during the early Medieval times was registered. This is a direct consequence of Christianisation. Yet, in the necropolis of La Pèrette at Montmélian, some pitchers have been brought to light which were intentionally broken following the tradition that was used in ancient burial rituals. Subsequently, small glasses or pitchers appeared near external tomb store-rooms like at Faverges or at Yvoire, starting from the end of the 6th century. The simple viaticum container most likely held Christian symbolic symbols. In the Lemanic region, funerary pottery was not recovered prior to the second third of the 6th century and corresponds to the diffusion of a new Frankish style (Raffaelli 1997, 216).

The presence of weapons was an overall exception in the Savoyard grave goods (scramasax, spatha and arrowheads). When weapons have been documented, they were generally late epoch and typically Frankish or Alemannic. The *scramasax,* rarely present in the high Savoyard necropolis, is absent in the Savoyard Alpine valley as an exception to the untold ancient discoveries of Saint-Marcel-en-Tarentaise, Collet de la Madelaine and Roc-des-Puits Brisés. They were always late examples of the aforementioned *scramasax* (Raffaelli 1997, 217).

From the start of the 6th century, the central-western Swiss Alps became a region which bordered the Frankish reign. Diverse fortresses, like for example the Large castle at Bellinzona, were responsible for defence against raids from the Germanic populations from the North and in particular the Franks. In 590, the territory of the Tessin canton fell under the dominion of the Lombards (Amrein 1997, 239).

Political, cultural and linguistic development in the various regions of modern Switzerland depended on the influx exercised by the Germanic populations on the autochthonous groups. Archaeological excavations done in the course of the last few years in the Leman lake region, in the Swiss uplands in the sub-alpine Sottoceneri region, has allowed the gathering of further information about the period from the 5th to the 8th centuries. As to the central-western Alps region, our knowledge is still scarce and lacking (Amrein 1997, 239).

Regarding the study of History in the early Medieval period in Switzerland, there are both written and archaeological sources available. The latter consist of finds discovered inside graves: the discoveries in a living context, on the other hand, are quite rare. Regarding the often unilateral character of archaeological sources, one must consider the fact that between the 4th and early 6th centuries the Autochthonous population generally buried their dead practically without grave goods, or only accompanied by some simple objects, for example an iron belt buckle (Amrein 1997, 239).

There is no doubt that the Roman roads that crossed the alpine passes were utilised during the Medieval centuries, even if the entire Roman road network was not maintained in working order. The most important connection between the North and South was situated west of the Alps and extended from the North Sea to the Mediterranean, passing through the Sâone-Rhone valley and Marseilles. The alpine passes regained notable importance starting from the 6th century, probably in the wake of politics actuated in Italy by the Frankish reign in continual expansion. A studded helmet from the 6th century, recovered near the estuary of the Rhone at the Leman lake, was perhaps lost by a high-ranking Frankish officer during an expedition into Italy (Amrein 1997, 240).

In the sub-alpine valleys most of the population was buried according to the Autochthonous custom without any kind of grave goods as shown in the necropolises at Lavorgo in the Leventina valley and Castro in Val di Blenio. Some necropolises recovered in Sottoceneri, at Muralto, Mezzonico or Bioggio, clearly demonstrate the continuity of the occupation up until the early Medieval period, that probably extended to Sopraceneri region (Amrein 1997, 240).

Near Bellinzona, some tombs associated with a rich burial outfit reveal a probable limited Lombard presence. At Castione, to the North of Bellinzona, various male graves containing arms have been discovered. Castione is an important crossroads of alpine passes (San Bernardino, Lucomagno, Greina, Nufenen), which explains the Lombard presence destined to control the alpine passes. Near the San Martino Church in Sonico, dating back to the early Middle Ages, a cross shaped buckle was found in the grave of a female. This type of buckle was worn especially by women in the Central and Eastern Alpine regions. It is difficult to establish if the defunct was perhaps a Lombard woman from outside the group or an exponent of the autochthonous population (Amrein 1997, 240).

The wealthy dominating classes also controlled the access roads to the Northern Alps, as revealed by a find recovered at Altdorf in the Uri Canton, for example. The founder of the San Martino church was buried within the time period between 660 and 680. The precious burial outfit showed that the defunct was of Alemannic origin and belonged to the social class of the freemen. His remains represent the most advanced archaeological evidence of the penetration of the Alpine massif by the high-ranking Alemannic representatives. There isn't any information provided regarding the population who lived in proximity to the church. It is a plausible hypothesis that the alpine passes that parted from Central Switzerland and were utilised during the Roman era, which is to say the Brünig, the Surenen and probably already the St Ghottard, continued to be utilised also in the early Medieval centuries (Amrein 1977, 240).

CONCLUSION

As the archaeological panorama shows, it is possible to establish that the Eastern Germanic culture was subject to two processes of acculturation in some fundamental aspects: in the first place the probable adjustment of clothing customs and typology to those of the Eastern Germanic populations (Alemannians and Franks) prior to 443; in the second place, the rapid process of Romanisation throughout the course of the 6th century. The first of these acculturation processes determined the impossibility of no longer being able to distinguish the Burgundians, as opposed to what happened to all of the other Germanic migrations, like those belonging to the Eastern Germanic populations departing from their settlements in the Sapaudia. No sure hypothesis about the Burgundian aristocracy can be made either by cause of the fragmentary aspect of the archaeological evidence.. All of these objects that can be connected to Germanic lineage within the tombs of individuals of elevated rank make their appearance, especially in the Northern zones of the Burgundy, in tombs that can be identified as of Frankish origin subsequent to 532. The lack of rich tombs, however, might also be justified by the process of Romanisation that, as much as in the creation of other Germanic States, mostly interested the ruling classes, particularly in the urban settlements. Not taking into consideration the exception of the late 6th and early 7th centuries (burials of individuals pertaining to the ruling class in religious buildings), the information relative to the social structure and burial customs of members of the ruling class was only obtained from written documents (Bierbrauer 1993, 14).

From the two factors presented – the process of Romanisation and the lack of rich tombs – also depends on the lack of evidence about the possibility that would confirm the existence of an artisan factory that could be defined as specifically Burgundian. The few golden artefacts dating from the first period (443-532) strongly reflect the Merovingian-Germanic-Eastern influence, in the case of Burgundian graves, or perhaps can be traced back to Frankish burials (Bierbrauer 1993, 14).

The artistic production of the late 6th and 7th centuries, limited from the archaeological point of view to clothing accessories (in particular type B and D belts and disc-shaped buckles), strongly shows the Latin influence in certain shapes (type B and D belts with rectangular bangles) and especially in the models (phytomorphic ornamentation made naturalistic with human and animal figures, braided motifs, and Christian symbology); the same can be said of the disc-shaped buckles. The Germanic aspect is manifested beginning from the late 6th century only in the use of second style animalistic elements (Bierbrauer 1993, 15).

Author's address

Paolo DE VINGO
Università di Torino
Dottorato di Ricerca in Archeologia
Dipartimento SAAST
via G.Giolitti 21/e
10123 Torino ITALY

Bibliography

AMREIN H., 1997, *Le Alpi Svizzere centro-occidentali durante l'altoMedioevo*. In Ori delle Alpi, edited by L.Endrizzi, F.Marzatico. Quaderni della Sezione Archeologica 6. Trento: Temi, p. 239-241.

BIERBRAUER V., 1993, *Burgundi*. In Enciclopedia dell'Arte Medievale IV. Roma: Marchesi Grafiche Editoriali, p.10-15.

COLARDELLE M., 1983, *Sépulture et traditions funéraires du V au XIIIe siècle ap. J.-C dans les campagnes des Alpes françaises du Nord*. Grenoble.

VON HESSEN O., 1993, *Reperti dell'Alto Medioevo provenienti dalle Alpi*. In Ori dalle Alpi, edited by L.Endrizzi, F.Marzatico. Quaderni della Sezione Archeologica 6.Trento: Temi, p.193-196.

CROSETTO A., 1998, *Sepolture e usi funerari medievali*. In Archeologia in Piemonte. Il Medioevo, edited by L.Mercando, E.Micheletto. Torino: Umberto Allemandi & C., p.209-232.

MARTIN M., 1986, *Romani e Germani nelle Alpi Occidentali e nelle Prealpi tra il lago di Ginevra e il lago di Costanza. Il contributo delle necropoli*. In Romani e Germani nell'arco alpino (secoli VI-VII), edited by V.Bierbrauer, C.G.Mor. Annali dell'Istituto Storico italo-germanico. Quaderni 19, Bologna: Il Mulino, p.147-200.

PRIVATI B., 1983, *La nécropole de Sézegnin (Avuys-Genève), Ive-VIIIe siècle*, Genève-Paris.

RAFFAELLI P., 1997, *Accessori metallici e parure della Burgundia provenienti dal corredo funerario savoiardo del V-inizi del secolo VIII d.C*. In Ori delle Alpi, edited by L.Endrizzi, F.Marzatico. Quaderni della Sezione Archeologica 6. Trento: Temi, p.213-217.

RUPP C., 1997, *La necropoli longobarda di Nocera Umbra (località il Portone): l'analisi archeologica*. In Umbria longobarda. La necropoli di Nocera Umbra nel centenario della scoperta. Roma: De Luca, p.23-40.

LES FOUILLES DES CHÂTEAUX FORTS DE CASTELLNOU DE BAGES, CALLUS, ET BOIXADORS A LA FRONTIERE MERIDIONALE DE LA MARCHE HISPANIQUE

Àlvar CAIXAL MATA, Alberto LÓPEZ MULLOR, Ainhoa PANCORBO
& Javier FIERRO MACÍA

Résumé : Entre les années 1998 et 2000, des recherches archéologiques ont été développées aux ruines des châteaux forts de Castellnou de Bages, Callús et Boixadors, placés sur l'ancienne frontière méridionale du royaume carolingien avec le califat de Cordoue. Ces recherches-ci ont constitué une partie des études historiques et archéologiques qu'on y a réalisé avant de la restauration des sites, qui est déjà faite à Castellnou de Bages et qui aux autres deux lieux est en train d'être effectuée. Tous ces travaux, ont été développés par le Service du Patrimoine Architectonique Local de la Diputació de Barcelone.

Abstract: Between 1998 and 2000, have been developed archaeologicals researches at the ruins of the castle of Castellnou de Bages, Callús and Boixadors, placed at the ancient southern frontier of the Carolingian Kingdom with Cordobas's Caliphate. These researchs have constitute a part of the historical studies that we have it done before the restoration of the archaeological site, that have been already done at Castellnou de Bages and that is doing at the other two places. The Local Architecture Heritage Service of the Barcelona Country Council had been developed all those works.

CASTELLNOU DE BAGES[1]

Nous traiterons, d'abord, sur l'actuelle maison paroissiale de Castellnou de Bages. Ce village est placé dans la province de Barcelone, quasiment à son centre géographique. Il est caractérisé par le peuplement disperse en maisons rurales, nommées «masias» en catalan, situées dans un territoire escarpé et boisé. Le centre urbain de l'agglomération, enclavé dans une clairière avec une magnifique visibilité vers le massif du Montserrat, est composé de la mairie, une maison qui fait la fonction de restaurant, une auberge pour colonies écolières de vacances et l'église de Saint André avec sa maison paroissiale ci-jointe.

Le temple, de style roman lombard, a une certaine renommée puisqu'il s'agit d'un exemple typique de plan basiliquel qui se conserve très bien. La maison paroissiale, cependant, était plongée dans une grande prostration depuis qu'elle avait été saccagée et incendiée en juillet 1936, au début de la guerre civile espagnole (1936-1939). Celle-ci, dont nous possédons deux photographies antérieures à l'incendie, avait un plan rectangulaire et possédait trois étages et un toît à deux pentes. À la façade principale il y avait aussi un typique grand balcon soutenu par un porche placé au rez-de-chaussée.

Jusqu'au début de l'intervention de notre Service, l'on avait considéré que la maison manquait de valeur architectonique et, pratiquement, elle était condamnée à la démolition. Derrière l'église il y avait une espace vraiment négligé, couvert de garrigue et enlaidi par un cimetière minuscule, où, au long des dernières années, l'on avait ajouté des blocs de tombes en niche. Compte tenu de ces antécédents, la mairie de Castellnou de Bages a demandé une fois de plus l'intervention de la Diputació[2]. En ce cas-ci, afin d'ordonner et embellir l'espace qui touchait la partie postérieure du temple, et aussi pour transformer son cimetière, si ancien.

Les premières recherches archéologiques développés sur place, très sélectives, ont démontré que le cimetière, en plus des tombes contemporaines placées dans les niches, contenait dans son sous-sol une intéressante nécropole, autant du moyen âge que de l'époque moderne, se remontant, au minimum, jusqu'au Xème siècle. Les tranchées stratigraphiques préliminaires ont rendu évident le bon état des tombes médiévales. C'était le cas contraire des modernes, qui se pressaient en peu d'espace, à cause de la croissance économique et démographique de l'époque.

En conséquence, la fouille totale de la nécropole, indispensable pour agrandir et mettre au jour le cimetière au même lieu qu'il occupait, on l'augurait longue, laborieuse et, sans doute, d'un coût respectable, surtout si l'on prenait en considération le budget initial de l'intervention, que l'on no le prévoyait guère important. D'ailleurs, il ne semblait pas très justifiée l'élimination radicale de la nécropole, où reposaient les citoyens de Castellnou depuis le Xème siècle, telle que semblait exiger un premier projet d'agrandissement du cimetière actuel, qui finalement a été refusé.

Tout de suite, le critère de l'intervention architectonique, dont la direction général a été assumée par M. Antoni González, architecte chef, a changé radicalement, puisque

---

[1] Sur les études archéologiques à ce site, on peut voir: López Mullor, 1999 a et b.

[2] Notre institution avait déjà restauré l'église paroissiale aux années soixante du XXème siècle, sous la direction de M. Camil Pallàs, à l'époque architecte chef.

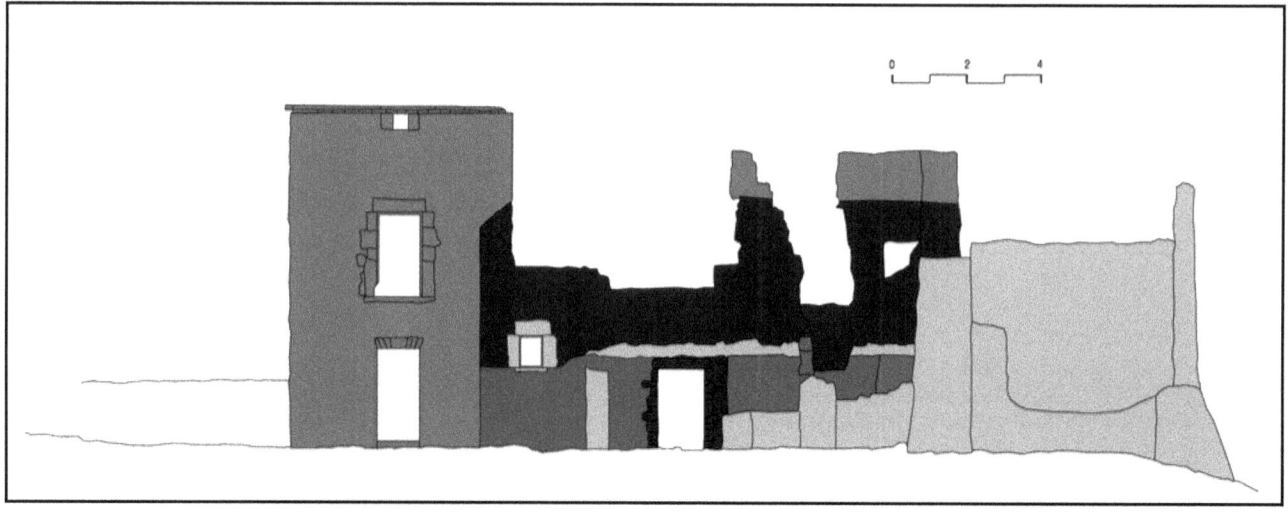

Figure 1. Façade de l'ancienne maison paroissiale de Castellnou de Bages (province de Barcelone) avec des indications chromatiques des différentes phases chronologiques.

l'on a considéré que les ruines de la maison paroissiale, préalablement consolidées, pouvaient loger le grandissement du cimetière. Cette alternative-ci permettait conserver *in situ* presque la totalité de la nécropole médiévale et, à la fois, mettre en valeur la tête du temple, qui avait été longtemps mi-caché, aussi bien que l'utilisation publique de ses alentours méridionaux, qui n'avaient eu aucun usage pendant plus de cinquante ans.

L'idée de la conservation et réutilisation de la maison paroissiale nous semble un bon exemple de l'action quotidienne de notre Service, orientée à la conservation d'un patrimoine pas toujours de grande catégorie, mais d'un intérêt indubitable pour les municipes où il se trouve et qui, sans une action continue sur lui, disparaît d'une façon presque honteuse.

En ce qui concerne à la recherche archéologique, notre intention était d'obtenir la plus grande quantité d'information avec la minimale dépense possible. De plus, en ce cas, nous avons essayé de laisser le gisement pratiquement intact. C'est pourquoi, après d'avoir ouvert les tranchées préliminaires à la nécropole, qui se sont révélées si outils pour l'orientation postérieure de l'action du Service, on a réalisé l'étude stratigraphique des couches déposées sur les ruines de l'ancienne maison paroissiale et aussi de leurs murs.

Tout d'abord, et comme étape indispensable pour avoir une connaissance exacte de la configuration de l'édifice, on a fouillé la couche de destruction formée au juillet 1936, dont le matériel a été abondant et hétérogène. À côté des fossiles directeurs, comme par exemple un pistolet de petit calibre, fabriqué aux années vingt, probablement oublié par l'un des incendiaires, on a mis au jour une grande quantité de céramique de l'époque moderne, qui a indiqué la datation de l'une des reformes de la maison au XVIIème siècle, lorsque l'on a ajouté des murs de pisé au premier étage. En plus de la fouille de la couche d'incendie, on y a fait de différents sondages sur certains endroits significatifs de l'édifice. De cette façon, nous avons obtenu la datation absolue de nombreuses structures.

L'enregistrement généralisé des unités stratigraphiques et l'analyse des relations entre les parements et les autres éléments constructifs ainsi que l'identification typologique des différentes fabriques, nous ont permis établir une séquence évolutive de l'histoire d'un bâtiment apparemment si modeste et anodin.

Selon ce qu'on a pu apprécier, la maison, même en ruines, reflet de façon fidèle les avatars de l'histoire du village, mieux que l'église, dont les restaurations l'ont réduit à un style relativement homogène. Ainsi, la recherche archéologique a indiqué que le moment de formation du bâtiment, placé au Xème siècle ou un peu avant, correspond à la construction d'un château fort, comme conséquence de l'implantation du système féodal, où les limites paroissiales et seigneuriales étaient souvent superposées. Alors, il s'agissait d'un édifice de moyennes dimensions et de plan rectangulaire, ce qui dans la documentation médiévale catalane apparaît sous le nom de «sala», textuellement, salle. Cet espace était caractérisé par la présence de l'appareil dénommé *opus spicatum*, témoigné longuement chez nous dans les édifices haut médiévaux, et dont l'apogée il faut le situer à la deuxième moitié du Xème siècle. Une telle datation est d'accord avec les renseignements fournis par la fouille de la nécropole où l'on a trouvé une sépulture anthropomorphe découpée au terrain naturel. Cette classe d'enterrement, connue autant en Catalogne qu'en Castille, bien que dans cette dernière région elle puisse être un peu plus tardive, possède dans notre territoire une fourchette chronologique bien délimitée, comprenant depuis la moitié du Xème jusqu'aux premières années du XIème siècle. En outre, la série de documentation écrite connue sur le temple commence l'année 981, ayant la première référence du château fort l'année 1020, à l'occasion d'un transfert féodale de sa propriété.

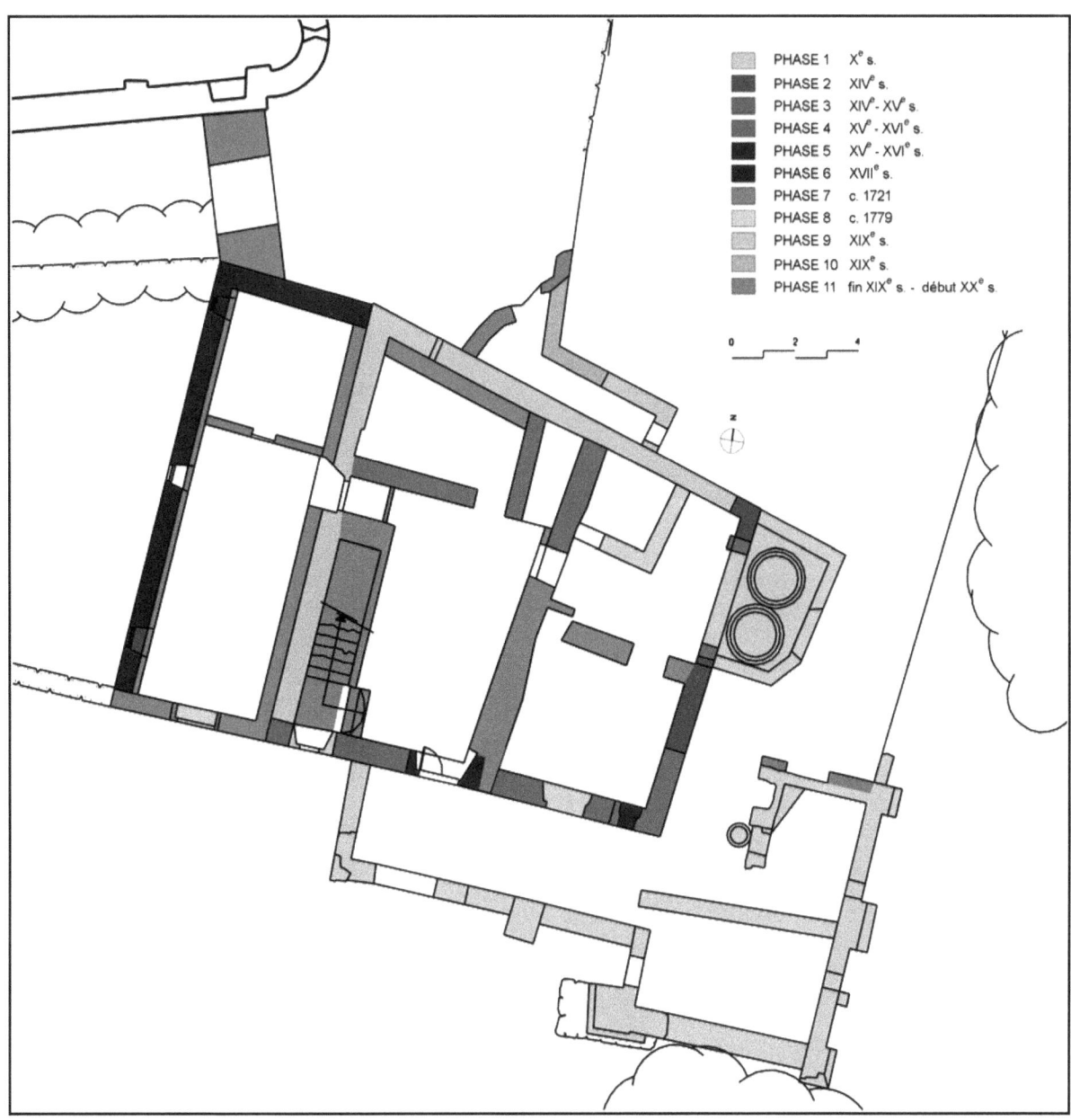

Figure 2. Plan de l'ancienne maison paroissiale de Castellnou de Bages (province de Barcelone) avec des indications chromatiques des différentes phases chronologiques.

Après, le bâtiment fait foi de l'essor qui en Catalogne est caractéristique du haut moyen âge et qui s'éteint aux dernières décennies du XIVème siècle. Cette deuxième phase était moins explicite puisqu'elle était caractérisée par un appareil de maçonnerie en pierre locale placée en assises rudimentaires très peu éloquentes. Néanmoins, il ne possédait pas des fragments de céramique interpolés entre les pierres, en guise de cales, ni des petits éléments lytiques de fonction identique, qui apparaissent dans les édifices ruraux depuis la fin du moyen âge. D'ailleurs, tel qu'il se passait avec l'*opus spicatum*, l'élément de cohésion était un mortier de chaux à peine visible. Tout cela nous fait affirmer que nous sommes devant une œuvre bas médiévale, postérieure, peut-être, au XIIIème siècle, vu l'absence d'assises.

À cette époque-là, le corps principal du bâtiment acquit son tracé actuel, car les façades méridionales et orientales furent bâties. L'appareil des façades respectives était fait en pierre presque non travaillé placée en assises, comprenant de fragments de tuiles ou de petites pierres en guise de cales. Tout cela nous le fait situer vers le XVème siècle. En cet état-ci, peut-être, se trouvait la maison paroissiale le 1425, lorsqu'elle fuit cité dans les documents écrits pour la première fois dans son rôle de résidence du curé.

Dans le XVIIème siècle, jusqu'au début de la guerre dénommée des «Segadors» (1640-1652), au temps du roi Philippe IV, quand le pays vit une croissance soutenue, à Castellnou les signes de récupération sont bien évidents. C'est alors que le premier étage du corps principal de la maison prit son aspect actuel, selon la date proportionnée par la céramique procédant des murs tombés. Ceux-ci, comme nous l'avons expliqué ci-dessus, étaient de pisé et, peut-être, ils ont remplacé des autres antérieurs faits en pierre.

À partir de la fin de la guerre suivante, celle de Succession (1701-1714), qui a intronisé en Espagne la dynastie des Bourbons, de nouvelles et grandes réformes sont produites, dans une conjoncture à la hausse généralisée. Ces œuvres-là sont finies l'année 1721, date qui apparaît sur une inscription au linteau du balcon de la façade principale de la maison. Elles sont l'exemple d'une bonne situation économique des paroissiens qui, d'après un document du 1742, continuaient à payer la dîme en grain, la déposant dans un grenier placé à la maison paroissial ; au rez-de-chaussée du corps occidental, peut-être.

Tout au long de ce siècle-là, le renouvellement de la maison est constant. L'on y ajoute les dépendances destinées à l'élaboration du vin, pas étranges dans les bâtiments de ce type. L'occupation vinicole du clergé est justifiée par une grande éclosion de ce genre d'activités, qui sont attestés en Catalogne jusqu'au début du XXème siècle, et qui ont entraîné le plantage de vignes sur une grande partie de la superficie cultivable du pays.

Pendant la deuxième moitié du XIXème siècle, à l'époque de la floraison industrielle catalane, qui a eu son expansion principale au bassin du Llobregat, pas très loin de Castellnou, il parait que notre petit noyau agricole cesse, une autre fois, d'avoir part à la redistribution de la richesse. Malgré tout, entre 1887 et 1917, des travaux d'entretien sont développés à la maison, d'après les documents écrits.

Peu avant de 1936, de nouveau selon les sources littéraires, l'édifice a été reformé superficiellement, bien que l'incendie du début de notre dernière guerre civile ait fini, pour l'instant, une histoire si longue. Voilà, donc, un parcours archéologique par un site qui pratiquement n'a pas été fouillé.

CALLÚS

Le village de Callús est à une dizaine de kilomètres de celui de Castellnou de Bages. Les ruines du château fort sont placées au sommet d'une petite colline au bord du fleuve Cardener, affluent du Llobregat. Il faut dire que les ruines se trouvent au côté de l'ancienne église paroissial et très près du chemin de fer qui vient des mines de sel de Súria et Cardona, qui ont été exploitées depuis l'époque romaine, dont l'importance stratégique est évidente.

La première mention de la fortification dans la documentation écrite date de l'année 940[3]. D'ailleurs, le temple est attesté depuis 977[4]. Voilà, comme nous l'avons déjà vu à Castellnou de Bages, l'association entre les deux constructions féodales par excellence : le château fort et l'église. Cependant, en ce cas-ci, le temple a été fortement bouleversé, et ses structures médiévales ont été cachées au-dessous d'un nouveau bâtiment au début du XIXème siècle[5]. Le château, à son tour, est resté bien conservé du point de vu archéologique parce qu'à la fin du moyen âge il a essuyé une destruction soudaine.

La mairie de Callús a eu l'intention de mettre en valeur et restaurer les vestiges de la fortification. C'est pourquoi notre Service a été demandé et, comme d'habitude, nous y avons commencé en développant la recherche historique documentaire et la fouille archéologique[6].

Au moment du début des travaux, qui ont eu lieu au long des années 1999 et 2000, les ruines du château fort n'étaient que le périmètre d'une tour de plan circulaire, de 7 m de diamètre et 1,50 m de hauteur. Aussi y avait de petits indices de l'enceinte fortifié extérieur. Tous les parements visibles étaient bâtis avec de petites pierres de taille unies avec du mortier de chaux et placées en assis peu réguliers. La fouille, donc, on l'a orienté à la découverte extensive de toutes les ruines et à leur datation absolue.

De cette façon, au long des travaux nous avons trouvé, d'abord, une couche très épaisse, formée comme conséquence d'un incendie. Autant la céramique qui y était mise au jour que la documentation écrite – qui a fourni un renseignement inattendu : la date de l'assaut du château, 1464[7] -, ont coïncidé à indiquer que le site a été abandonné à cause de sa destruction partielle, lors d'une guerre civile qui a affronté la noblesse catalane avec le roi d'Aragon, Jean II, et qui a eu lieu entre 1462 et 1472. Précisément, au long de ce conflit, qui a représenté le début de la longue fin du système féodal chez nous, de nombreux châteaux forts ont été détruits.

Au-dessous de la couche de destruction, nous avons trouvé d'abondants vestiges architectoniques significatifs. Les uns conservés *in situ*, comme la base des murs de certaines structures adossées à la tour, lesquelles avaient délimité de différentes dépendances, et les autres procédants de la chute des éléments aériens : tuiles, colonnes, pieds-droits, objets de fer, chaînes. En plus, il y avait les témoignages de la bataille : des pointes de flèche, des fragments d'épées et poignards, des projectiles sphériques d'artillerie faits

en pierre. Finalement, de la céramique, qui nous a donné des précisions chronologiques. Notamment, celle de Valence décorée en bleu ou de reflets métalliques et celle de Barcelone, toujours peinte en bleu. Mais nous nous sommes occupés de ce sujet plus longuement dans l'autre communication qui apparaît dans ce volume.

---

[3] Malheureusement, ce document n'est arrivé à nous qu'à travers d'un résumé du XVIIIème siècle, qui appartenait aux anciens archives du monastère de Sant Benet de Bages (ORDEIG, 1999: 388 et doc. 481).

[4] ORDEIG, 1999: 887-888 et doc. 1233, daté du 26 avril de 977.

[5] Malgré tout, l'église de Saint Sadurní a conservé sa fonction paroissiale jusqu'à 1941, lorsque le nouveau temple au noyau urbain de Callús a été inauguré (SALA, SERRA, FONS, 1996: 46-47).

[6] Le projet de restaurations des ruines du château fort a été élaboré par le personnel technique de notre Service sous la direction générale de M. Antoni González Moreno-Navarro, architecte chef.

[7] Grâce à un document conservé au Arxiu Històric Comarcal de Manresa, on sait que, le 28 janvier 1464, des gens de la ville de Manresa, avec l'appui de pièces d'artillerie, assiégeaient le château fort de Callús. Le résultat de cet attaque-la a été la destruction presque totale de la forteresse (AHCM/AM.I-22. *Manual del Consell*, 1463-1465).

Figure 3. Photographie aérienne du château fort de Callús (province de Barcelone) pendant les fouilles, juillet 2000.

Figure 4. Photographie aérienne du château fort de Boixadors (municipe de Sant Pere Sallavinera, province de Barcelone) pendant les fouilles, juillet 2000.

Tout de suite, la fouille a permis d'identifier les parties essentielles du château fort : le rempart, la porte –avec un système d'accès compliqué-, la tour, dont les vestiges sont devenus, de plus en plus, hautes de 4,5 m, et de nombreuses dépendances répandues par tout le périmètre fortifié, entourant la tour, à l'exception du versant méridional, où il y avait une petite cour. Cette série d'éléments confierait le château au moment de l'incendie mais leur formation a été diachronique.

Sur ce sujet, il faut signaler que la fouille et l'étude stratigraphique des vestiges trouvés ont démontré que la tour a été bâtie au long de deux phases. La fabrique la plus ancienne, qui a été doublée par l'appareil de petites pierres taillées décrites plus en haut, a été construite avec de grandes dalles allongées se disposant en angle, c'est à dire formant l'appareil appelé *opus spicatum*. Nous avons déjà dit, en traitant du château fort de Castellnou de Bages, que cet appareil, en Catalogne, est typique de la deuxième moitié du Xème siècle environ. C'est comment la datation du 940, proportionnée par la documentation, elle est d'accord avec celle qu'indique l'*opus spicatum*.

Autrement, il convient ajouter que la fouille a mis au jour la première enceinte fortifiée, contemporain du château du Xème siècle, dont les vestiges étaient placés sous le pavé de la cour. Ce dernier espace, tel que se confierait au moment de l'incendie, a été formé au XIIIème siècle, lorsque le rempart extérieur a été modifié.

Comme résumé des travaux qui y sont menés, lesquels n'ont pas encore complètement fini, nous avons pu établir une succession chronologique de différentes phases d'occupation du site. La séquence commence au Xème siècle, avec la construction de la tour et d'un petite enceinte fortifiée au sommet de la colline. Cette structure défensive surveillait la frontière avec al-Andalus qui, à ce moment-là, était bien définie par le fleuve Cardener.

Deux cent ans plus tard, vers le premier quart du XIIIème siècle, le périmètre du rempart que nous avons découvert est construit. C'est alors que la tour originaire est doublée avec de nouveaux parements, à l'intérieur aussi bien qu'à l'extérieur. À cette époque-là, les différentes dépendances intérieures du château fort sont bien définies : autant celles domestiques que celles que l'on utilisait pour le stockage des matières premières procédants de la culture des champs voisins, comme par exemple des réservoirs, dépôts et entrepôts. Également, il est possible de situer dans cette période les éléments de colonne –chapiteaux, bases et fûts- retrouvés à la fouille de la couche d'incendie.

Entre le premier quart du XIIIème et le début du XVème siècle, l'on a développé au monument une série de reformes et rallongements architectoniques, qui en ont transformé l'apparence, surtout en ce qui concerne à la distribution intérieure et au renforçage des remparts et des bastions. Enfin, la recherche archéologique et celle de la documentation écrite, comme nous l'avons vu ci-dessus, ont constaté que le château fort fut pris d'assaut lors de la guerre civile nommée populairement de Jean II contre la Generalitat (1462-1472). Depuis ce moment-là les ruines du château fort de Callús sont restées abandonnées et ensevelies.

BOIXADORS

Le château fort de Boixadors, placé à trente kilomètres à ponant de celui de Callús, se trouvait aussi sur la frontière entre la Marche Hispanique et le Califat de Cordoue. Comme dans les deux autres cas exposés ci-dessus, ce château fort est conforme aux caractéristiques basiques de ce genre de bâtiments de défense d'origine féodal : près de l'église paroissiale de Saint Pierre et placé au sommet d'une colline, depuis laquelle on a une magnifique visibilité du territoire, qui atteignait les voies de communication aussi bien que les châteaux voisins.

L'ensemble des bâtiments qui composent la forteresse est dominée par une tour de plan circulaire, utilisée comme donjon, aux alentours de laquelle il y a des structures, fruit de nombreuses reformes et élargissements du château. Parmi ces dépendances, il faut mettre en relief la salle principale, à levant de la tour, où est l'accès actuel au château fort. D'ailleurs, il y a la cour qui dispose d'un niveau souterrain, et aussi deux éléments défensifs qui, avec la tour ronde et les remparts périmétriques, confèrent au château son aspect de forteresse. Il s'agit d'une tour d'angle, au Nord-Est, et d'une tour carrée, à levant. Le niveau inférieur, que nous venons de citer, est divisé en deux espaces : une petite dépendance qui, pendant le XIXème siècle, a servi à colombier, et une citerne.

Lors que le site a été cédé à la mairie de Sant Pere Sallavinera, municipalité à laquelle il appartient, celle-ci a demandé l'aide de notre Service à fin de le restaurer[8]. Comme d'habitude, nous y avons mis au jour une recherche archéologique préalable aux travaux, développée au long des années 2000 et 2001, qui a affecté la plupart des dépendances du château, bien que nous n'ayons atteint la roche que dans une. Dans le reste de l'ensemble, pour l'instant, les fouilles ne sont arrivées qu'aux niveaux du XVIème ou de XVIIème siècle, selon les secteurs. Néanmoins, les renseignements obtenus pendant ces recherchés ont permis configurer l'évolution du monument et en établir les phases principales d'occupation.

La notice documentaire la plus ancienne du château de Boixadors, remonte à l'année 1085[9]. La datation du donjon, doit se situer près de ce moment-là, tenant en compte sa technique constructive et son style. La fouille n'a pas apporté d'autres renseignements puisque la tour s'appuie directement sur la roche naturelle. À l'époque, elle ne serait entourée que de quelques structures isolées, desquelles il en reste seulement la première assise d'un pan de mur. Par ailleurs, dans cette phase, la propre roche fut utilisée comme pavé.

Ce n'est que vers l'année 1300 que l'on dispose de nouveaux renseignements sur le site. On sait, grâce à la documentation écrite, que la famille Boixadors a joué un rôle très remarquable dans l'expansion occidental de la Couronne d'Aragon, de sorte que, tout au long du XIIIème siècle, elle fut récompensée avec la concession d'importantes possessions[10]. C'est alors que la tour est restée entourée par une enceinte fortifiée documentée, notamment, dans la fouille de la salle principale. Bien que

---

[8] A. González, architecte chef du notre Service, a dirigé les travaux de restauration réalisés à ce site.

[9] BENET, JUNYENT, MAZCUÑAN, 1992: 499-500.

[10] LLODRA, 2001: 22.

la tour d'angle n'ait été objet d'aucun sondage archéologique, ses caractéristiques formelles la rattachent à cette première enceinte fortifié. À ce temps-là, le château fort avait deux portes. La principale était ouverte au pan du mur déjà cité et l'on y arrivait à travers d'une rampe dallée. L'autre, placée près de la tour d'angle, avait des dimensions très réduites, ce qui suggère qu'il s'agisse d'une porte secondaire, à la guise de poterne.

Pendant la deuxième moitié du XIVème siècle, un nouveau corps a été ajouté au versant de levant de l'ensemble. Il était celui que nous dénommons la cour et qui, d'après ses caractéristiques formelles, était en origine une salle noble couverte avec une voûte en berceau. La nouvelle muraille a laissé à l'arrière plan un secteur du périmètre fortifié bâti vers l'année 1300 dont une grande partie du dallage restait très malmené. C'est à cause de ces travaux que la porte principale a été modifiée, en élevant son seuil aussi bien que le niveau du sol, qui a été pavé avec une couche de chaux.

Il faut attendre aux alentours de l'année 1500 pour la réalisation d'une autre réforme importante, affectant la totalité de l'ensemble, qui a donné lieu à un agrandissement considérable de la forteresse. Le rempart du 1300 est relégué de nouveau à l'arrière, précédé par de nouvelles défenses qui ont entraîné de changements dans la distribution de l'enceinte, car la plupart des dépendances médiévales restait annulée. C'est alors aussi que l'on a bâti le corps connu comme salle principale. À ponant, dans l'espace entre les deux périmètres défensifs, celui du 1300 et celui du 1500, l'on a bâti un chemin de ronde en bois. Tout cela a été mis en évidence d'après une couche où les accumulations de charbons étaient alignées avec les boudins du parement du mur de ponant.

Pendant la première moitié du XVIème siècle, une suite de réformes, qu'il faut mettre en relation avec la transformation et emmagasinage des premières matières agricoles, confèrent au château fort un nouvel aspect. C'est alors que, à toucher de la tour, l'on a bâti un pressoir et un four à pain et on y a réalisée deux canalisations. La première, d'écoulement, et la deuxième pour mener de l'eau procédant du donjon jusqu'à la citerne placée au-dessous de la cour.

C'est évident que dans cette époque-là, assez moderne, le château fort de Boixadors n'est plus une grande forteresse militaire, mais plutôt une résidence seigneuriale secondaire, dont les métayers s'occupaient de l'entretien des dépendances aussi que de l'exploitation des vignes. Malgré quelques réparations, certaines dépendances du château ont fini par être abattues vers l'année 1600. En revanche, au levant, l'espace de résidence a continué à être utilisé et l'on a bâti un nouvel édifice rattaché au corps principal.

Peu après, le périmètre muré du château fort a été renforcé par des murs talusés. C'est alors quand on bâtit aussi la tour carrée à levant de l'enceinte, dont l'étage inférieur était un dépôt de plan circulaire avec une voûte en ogive. En 1728, d'après la date proportionnée par trois monnaies trouvées dans la salle principale, cet espace fut objet de grandes réformes à fin de l'articuler en trois niveaux.

Tout au long du XIXème siècle, la plupart des dépendances du château sont tombées en désuétude. Les paysans qui y habitaient ont du partir à cause du mauvais état de l'ensemble, qui, depuis les années cinquante, est resté complètement abandonné jusqu'au 1971, quand notre Service, demandé par la mairie pour la première fois, y a développé la restauration de l'église et du donjon.

Adresse des auteurs

Àlvar CAIXAL MATA, Alberto LÓPEZ MULLOR, Ainhoa PANCORBO PICÓ, Javier FIERRO MACÍA
Diputació de Barcelona
Service du Patrimoine Architectonique Local
187, rue du Comte d'Urgell
08036 Barcelone, ESPAGNE
Email : Lopezmal@diba.es

Bibliographie

BENET, A., JUNYENT, F., MAZCUÑÁN, A., 1992, Sant Pere Sallavinera. Castell de Boixadors. *Catalunya Romànica, XIX. El Penedès. L'Anoia*. Barcelona: 499-501.

LÓPEZ MULLOR, A. 1999 a, Dos estudios recientes de arqueología del patrimonio edificado. *XXV Congreso Nacional de Arqueología. Actas*. Valencia, 1999: 161-177.

LÓPEZ MULLOR, A. 1999 b, Arqueología del patrimonio edificado. Una definición y dos ejemplos. *Actas del congreso internacional "Restaurar la Memoria". Métodos, técnicas y criterios en la conservación del Patrimonio mueble e inmueble*. Valladolid, 1999: 139-166.

LLODRÀ, J.M., 2001, *Estudi històric i documental del conjunt de Boixadors*. Servei del Patrimoni Arquitectònic Local de la Diputació de Barcelona. (Inèdit).

ORDEIG, R., 1999, Els comtats d'Osona i Manresa. *Catalunya Carolíngia, IV*. Barcelona.

SALA, LL., SERRA, M., FONS, R., 1996, *Callús. Història en imatges (1850-1975)*. Centre d'Estudis del Bages. Manresa.

LA CÉRAMIQUE MISE AU JOUR À LA COUCHE D'ABANDON DU CHÂTEAU FORT DE CALLÚS (BARCELONE, ESPAGNE)

Ainhoa PANCORBO, Alberto LÓPEZ MULLOR & Àlvar CAIXAL MATA

Résumé : A l'occasion de la restauration du château fort de Callús, qui est en train d'être réalisée par le Service du Patrimoine Architectonique de la Diputació de Barcelone, nous y avons réalisé des fouilles archéologiques. Ces travaux on mis au jour une série de couches d'abandon datées de l'année 1464, environ, qui ont livré de la céramique vernissée, surtout originaire de la région de Valence, et aussi des productions communes catalanes de pâte grise ou oxydée. Ces matériaux ont permis leur comparaison, notamment, avec ceux de trouvés à la ville de Barcelone et, en général, de Catalogne, et a donné des renseignements bien illustrants à propos des contextes céramiques de cette époque-là.

Abstract: At the time of the Callus castle restoration, being done by the Local Architecture Heritage Service of the Barcelona Country Council, we have undertaken archaeological excavations. These works have revealed abandonment strata dated to 1464. We find varnished ceramics, coming from the Valencia region and also common Catalan productions of grey and rusted paste. The materials have made possible the comparison with those found at Barcelona and, in general, in Catalonia. They have also yielded important data about the ceramics contexts of this period.

Nous avons déjà parlé dans une autre communication à ce congrès du parcours historique et archéologique de trois forteresses médiévales catalanes étant sur la frontière méridionale de la Marche Hispanique. C'est à dire, en face du territoire dominé par les musulmans.

Maintenant nous présentons un panorama bref de la céramique la plus significative que nous avons mis au jour dans l'une d'elles. Il s'agit du matériel trouvé à la couche d'abandon du château fort de Callús. Parmi les événements historiques qui ont conditionné l'abandon de cette forteresse, il faut se rappeler l'incendie qui l'a détruite. Ça s'est passé l'année 1464, dans une époque particulièrement peu éloquente sur nos sites. L'épidémie de peste noire qui a battu la Catalogne pendant la deuxième moitié du XIVème siècle, lié à une série de circonstances politiques et économiques peu favorables ont donné lieu a une importante crise qui, selon les données de l'archéologie, elle n'a fini qu'au début du XVIIème siècle. La mauvaise situation économique a déterminé que, tout au long de cette période, les réformes sur les bâtiments autant publiques que particulières ont été très pauvres. C'est pourquoi nous ne possédons que quelques ensembles céramiques de cette époque-là.

Dans ce cadre la découverte de Callús est intéressante puisqu'elle nous montre, bien stratifiées, de certaines céramiques que nous ne connaissions pratiquement qu'à travers de la bibliographie. C'est le cas, par exemple, de la céramique valencienne décorée. D'autre part, cette série a été utile pour étudier la céramique commune du bas moyen âge, comprenant des formes très traditionnelles, comme la marmite, dont l'origine est bien attesté, mais non la fin de sa production, qui restait absolument sombre du point de vu chronologique.

Conséquemment, nous ferons tout de suite une rapide révision de la typologie et la datation des pièces, vraiment fragmentaires, mais pour nous intéressantes, trouvées à la fouille de ce petit château fort.

LA CÉRAMIQUE MÉDIÉVALE DE CUISINE

La céramique grise était déjà présente aux gisements catalans depuis les VIIème-VIIIème siècles, étant le fossile directeur des ensembles céramiques jusqu'au XIIIème siècle. Malgré l'apparition et le développement, désormais de plus en plus rapide, des céramiques glaçurées, dont la prépondérance a son début au XIVème siècle, la céramique grise ne cesse pas de se produire.

Du point de vu technique, il s'agit des exemplaires faits au tour, majoritairement de cuisson réductrice, ce qui leur donne une couleur gris foncé, alors qu'il y a aussi des exemplaires bicolores : Marron aux superficies extérieures et grises à l'intérieur. Un troisième groupe de céramique de cuisine, minoritaire, présente une cuisson oxydante, bien qu'à Callús, on n'en ait trouvé que quelques tessons informes.

Le type le plus abondant c'est la **marmite** de profil en esse, bord rabattu et lèvres arrondis (pl. I.1-4). Bien que la fouille n'ait proportionné que quelques bords, il faut supposer que leur base serait concave telle que celle de la plupart des exemplaires pareils trouvés aux sites voisins. Il s'agit d'un type avec une chronologie très étendue qui comprend depuis le XII^{ème1} jusqu'au XV^{ème2} siècle et qui, conséquemment, présente beaucoup de variations. La plupart des marmites (pl. I.1-3) sont bicolores, avec des

---

[1] Datant de cet époque l'on a localisé des exemplaires dans l'ermite de la Mare de Déu de Bellvitge, l'Hospitalet de Llobregat (LÓPEZ MULLOR, 1988: 29-30, pl. V.1.) ou à Sant Quirze de Pedret, Cercs (LÓPEZ MULLOR, CAIXAL, FIERRO, 1997).
[2] BELTRÁN DE HEREDIA, 1994: 117, 141, n° 62.

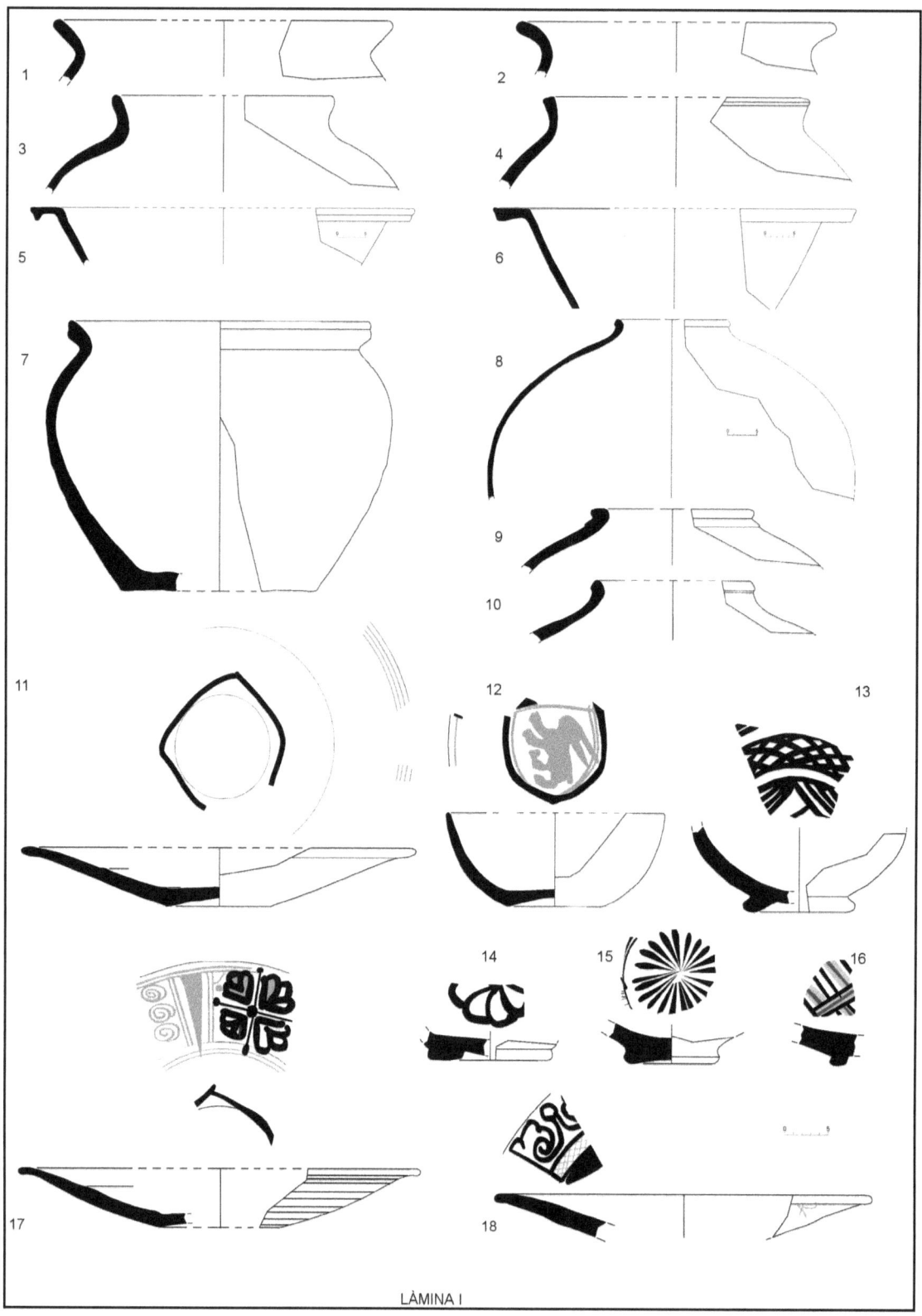

Planche I. Céramique grise médiévale (XIIIème-XVème ss.) : 1 à 4, marmites. 5 et 7, terrines. 8 à 10, jarres. Céramique oxydée médiévale (XIIIème-XVème ss.) : 6, terrine. Céramique catalane décorée en vert et manganèse (XIIIème-XIVème ss.) : 16, assiette creuse, présentant un château au fond intérieur. Céramique valencienne décorée en bleu (XIVème-XVème ss.): 13, écuette avec des palmettes. Céramique valencienne décorée avec des reflets métalliques (XIVème-XVème ss.): 15, écuette présentant une palmette ouverte au fond intérieur. Céramique valencienne décorée en bleu (XIVème-XVème ss.): 13, écuette avec des palmettes. Céramique valencienne décorée des reflets métalliques (XIVème-XVème ss.): 15, écuette présentant une palmette ouverte au fond intérieur. Céramique valencienne décorée des reflets métalliques et de la peinture bleue (XIVème-XVème ss.): 11, plat avec un écu en bleu au fond intérieur et trois circonférences concentriques au bord. Le reste du décor est impossible de déterminer. 12, écuette, avec un blason bleu au fond de la pièce, présentant un lapin doré a l'intérieur. 17, plat présentant un blason bleu au fond intérieur et un orle composée par des roses gothiques bleues et spirales dorées. 18, plat décoré avec le motif des couronnes. Céramique bleue de Barcelone (XVème-XVIème ss.): 14, écuette avec une rose fermée.

des inclusions, notamment quartz et mica, visibles aux deux superficies des pièces. L'exemplaire 4 de la planche I présente la lèvre de profil triangulaire et légèrement biseauté.

Toujours dans le même groupe des marmites, il y a un type bien différencié des autres, représenté par un exemplaire, presque complet, de profil aussi en esse, mais avec la lèvre bifide et la base plate (pl. I.7). On n'a pas trouvé des parallèles pour cette pièce dans la céramique grise. Toutefois, son profil est fréquent dans les types glaçurés primitifs datant du XIVème ou XVème siècle.

Un deuxième groupe c'est formé par des **jarres** de corps globulaire, bord étroit et lèvre plate, avec de la pâte assez fine et de couleur gris clair (pl. I.8-10). Il s'agit d'un type déjà attesté sur d'autres gisements catalans où il a été daté du XIVème siècle. Cependant, il ne faut pas oublier la manque des ensembles clairs du XVème siècle.

Il faut souligner aussi la trouvaille de deux exemplaires de **bassins** de pâte grossière avec un diamètre de la bouche de 30 cm environ. Ils présentent un bord sorti vers l'extérieur et aplati horizontalement, avec une grosse lèvre bifide. C'est un type peu habituel dans ces productions mais qui a pu être daté vers la deuxième moitié du XVème siècle[3] (pl. I.5-6).

LA CÉRAMIQUE DÉCORÉE EN VERT ET MANGANÈSE

La première céramique avec de la glaçure stannifère produite en Catalogne fut celle au décor vert de cuivre et brun de manganèse. Traditionnellement, l'on l'a remontée au IXème siècle en Syrie, d'où elle aurait passé au Nord d'Afrique et, pendant le Xème siècle, elle serait arrivée à la péninsule Ibérique. Malgré tout, ce n'est qu'au XIIIème siècle que l'on la trouve chez nous après la conquête d'une partie des territoires islamiques[4]. Son étape la plus expansive a eut lieu vers le milieu du XIVème siècle tandis qu'à la fin de sa production, au long du XVème siècle elle a été progressivement substituée par de nouvelles productions, surtout par la céramique valencienne décorée en bleu et en reflets métalliques. Ses principaux centres producteurs furent Barcelone[5], aussi que Manresa et Gérone.

Ces pièces présentent une pâte grossière avec des parois épaisses. Le décor s'applique sur l'émail blanc stannifère, pas très bon, qui couvre seulement la superficie intérieure des types ouverts.

La fouille n'a proportionné qu'un seul fragment de cette céramique (pl. I.16) correspondant à la base d'une assiette creuse, avec le pied annulaire. Malgré les dimensions du tesson on y peut distinguer le décor d'un château dont le dessin est fait en manganèse et le remplissage en vert.

LA CÉRAMIQUE VALENCIENNE À REFLETS MÉTALLIQUES

L'origine de la production céramique à reflets métalliques a été placée sur un lieu indéterminé du monde islamique, d'où elle fut transmise à la péninsule Ibérique lors des invasions musulmanes. Pendant le XIVème siècle, le reflet métallique aussi que la technique de l'oxyde du cobalt furent introduites à Valence par des potiers de Malague. Le centre producteur principal se trouvait à Manises, qui commençât son activité entre les années 1305 et 1310[6] et dont les pièces bientôt furent connues et appréciées partout, s'exportant vers l'Italie, la France et la moitié septentrionale de l'Espagne. Peu après, d'autres centres très proches de Manises, comme Paterne ou Mistala, dans la même région de Valence, ont aussi commencé à produire cette œuvre dorée, en utilisant le même répertoire décoratif et formel.

Les manufactures les plus anciennes, datant de la première moitié du XIVème siècle, étaient très semblables à celles produites au sud de l'Espagne, prédominant parmi elles les décors d'influence islamique. Par contre, pendant le XVème siècle, naquit un nouveau répertoire, plus chrétien, caractérisé par les couronnes, les figures d'anges, les blasons... Les exemplaires trouvés à Callús peuvent être attribués à cette deuxième étape et datés vers le milieu du XVème siècle.

Cette céramique est caractérisée initialement par la grande qualité technique de l'œuvre. Elle possède des pâtes bien dépurées mais avec de petites inclusions de mica, et de couleur beige, rosée ou orangée. Les pièces sont toutes couvertes d'un émail stannifère blanc ou jaune.

Les fragments mis au jour à Callús sont quantitativement significatifs, étant plus nombreux ceux qui ont la combinaison du reflet et bleu que ceux de seulement dorés. Il faut dire aussi que les pièces nous sont arrivées très fragmentées et, de plus, le reflet a souvent disparu par l'action de l'eau.

Les types de petites dimensions, notamment des plats et des écuettes sans anses sont les plus abondants. Il y a aussi deux exemplaires avec de petites anses triangulaires. Les plats, ils ont un profil plat et bas, avec un bord large et une lèvre légèrement tournée. Ils présentent le fond extérieur concave, n'ayant pas de pied.

Les motifs décoratifs attestés sont les suivants :

Blason : Motif central. Il faut souligner la trouvaille d'un jeu composé de trois plats et trois écuettes avec le trait d'un blason dessiné en bleu. Il s'agit d'un décor habituellement combiné avec d'autres en bleu (roses, « alafias »...), ainsi qu'en doré (spiraux, feuilles...). Malheureusement, la plupart des exemplaires, pas

---

[3] BOLÒS, MALLART, 1984: 66-67, fig. 2.44; BARRACHINA, 1983: 173-174, fig. 20.

[4] CIRICI, 1977: 74.

[5] C'est le seule centre producteur qui a été documenté sur les sources écrites. CASANOVAS, 1983: 24.

[6] LÓPEZ ELUM, 1984: 173.

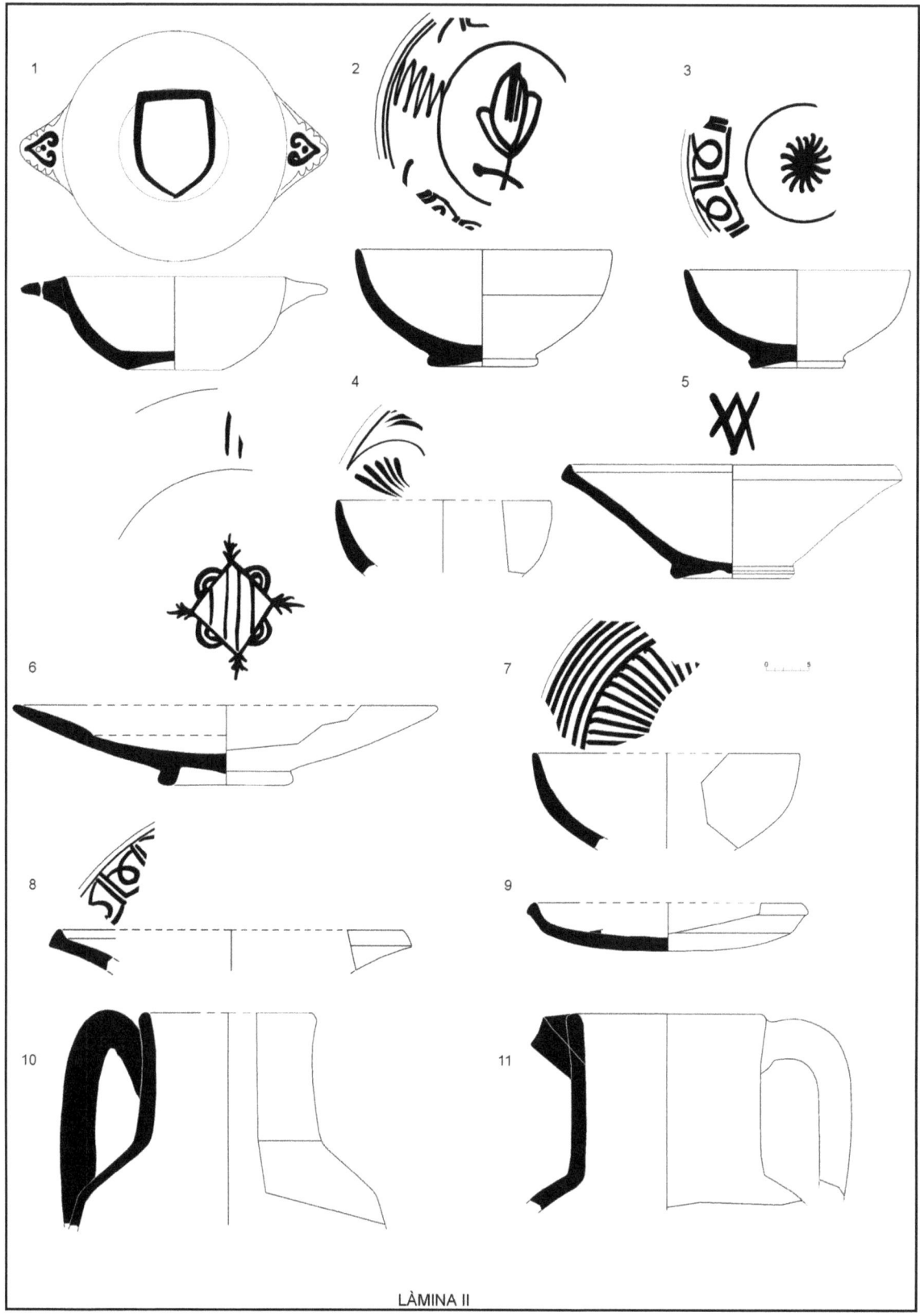

Planche II. Céramique valencienne décorée des reflets métalliques (XIVème-XVème ss.): 4, écuette avec le motif de la palmette ouverte. Céramique valencienne décorée avec des reflets métalliques et de la peinture bleue (XIVème-XVème ss.): 1, écuette présentant un blason bleu au fond intérieur et deux anses triangulaires décorées en bleu avec le profil d'une feuille. Céramique bleue de Barcelone (XVème-XVIème ss.): 2, écuette décorée d'une fleure en bouton au fond intérieur et du motif des alafias et lignes ondulées au bord. 3, écuette décorée d'une étoile à quinze rayons épais au fond interne et du motif des alafias sur le bord. Céramique bleue de Barcelone (XVème-XVIème ss.): 5, plat décoré de chevrons opposés sur le fond intérieur. 6, plat décoré avec le blason royal, quadrangulaire. 7, écuette présentant les rayons d'une étoile entourés par des circonférences concentriques. 8, plat avec le motif des alafias au bord intérieur. Céramique catalane de glaçure plombifère (XIIIème-XVIIIème ss.): 9, couvercle du type dénommé «d'arc de pont», glaçure miellée à l'intérieur et à l'extérieur, avec des taches vertes. 10, jarre, glaçure verte sombre à l'extérieur et verte olive à l'intérieur. 11, jarre, glaçure verte olive à l'intérieur et à l'extérieur.

seulement ceux de Callús, ils ont perdu le décor en reflets. Leur chronologie a été établie au XVème siècle. (Pl. I.11-12 et II.1).

Lapin : Motif central. Il s'agit du seul élément qui a pu être distingué dans le blason de l'une des écuettes. Cet animal, peint en doré et entouré d'un deuxième blason doré de trait encore plus fin, remplit l'intérieur du trait en bleu. Nous n'avons pas pu documenter aucun motif pareil. (pl. I.12)

Rose gothique : Motif de l'orle. Deux tessons, appartenant aux bords des plats avec du blason au fond interne, présentent-ils un décor avec des roses en bleu de cobalt. La composition est formée à partir d'une croix, aux angles de laquelle il y a des feuilles trilobées. Ce motif apparaît souvent alterné avec des décors géométriques dorés. À Callús, ce sont des spiraux. Les feuilles sont aussi presque toujours remplies en reflet métallique. Bien que nos pièces soient trop petites pour en déterminer la composition des décors, à partir des exemplaires pareils, du XVème siècle, nous pouvons conclure qu'elles apparaissent en nombre de deux ou de quatre et disposées symétriquement. Les spiraux nous aident à préciser un peu plus cette chronologie, ayant été datées par Mme. Martínez Caviró du troisième quart du XVème siècle[7]. (pl. I.17)

Série des couronnes : Ce décor consiste à la répétition de couronnes en oxyde de cobalt disposées de façon différente, en plats, pots et écuettes –à Callús ce ne sont que plats- et aussi alternées avec des décors dorés. Ce motif est propre du XVème siècle e l'on le trouve sur des tableaux contemporains[8] (pl. I. 18).

En ce qui concerne à la céramique décorée uniquement aux reflets métalliques, assez rare à Callús, on y a pu distinguer deux motifs décoratifs différents : les palmettes et les éperons.

- **Palmettes** : Il s'agit de motifs très stylisés, formés par une palme entouré d'un trait courbé ou d'une circonférence disposée en médaillons, un central et trois latéraux. Au site, l'on a mis au jour tessons avec ce décor appartenants à écuettes de profil hémisphérique, semblables à ceux que nous venons de voir. Le seul type de base que l'on y a trouvé présente le fond extérieur concave et le pied échelonné. La fourchette chronologique attribuée à ce décor s'étend de la fin du XIVème à la fin du XVème siècle[9]. (pl. I.15 et II.4)

Eperons : Motif composé d'is grègues disposés l'un dans l'autre, formant part d'une bande décorative. D'habitude, ils se trouvent accompagnés d'autres motifs, bien qu'à Callús les pièces soient trop petites pour attester cette dernière information.

LA CÉRAMIQUE VALENCIENNE DÉCORÉE EN BLEU

Au long de la première moitié du XIVème siècle commença à apparaître à Valence la céramique décorée en oxyde de cobalt sur un fond blanc stannifère. Elle est très étendue aux gisements du bas moyen âge si bien qu'elle s'y impose et déplace la céramique décorée en vert et manganèse. Il s'agit d'une production traditionnellement attribuée au centre de Paterne, standardisée et bon marché, qui envahit la Catalogne de la fin du XIVème et la première moitié du XVème siècle.

Ses pâtes sont fines, avec quelques vacuoles et des inclusions de quartz et de mica, et leurs couleurs sont crèmes ou beiges rosées. L'émail, prenant un aspect opaque et dense, est beaucoup plus riche que celui des productions en vert et manganèse, et couvre toute la pièce, même le fond extérieur des types fermés.

Les pièces attribuées à cette production, minoritaires, sont apparues tellement fragmentés que c'est difficile à en déterminer les types et les décors. De cette façon nous n'avons pu que reconnaître deux motifs décoratifs différenciés :

Les motifs radiaux, qui sont représentés par des rayons d'une étoile ou d'une roue et qui apparaissent entourés de six circonférences concentriques. (pl. II.7)

Les palmettes, très différentes de celles des productions dorées, sont richement combinées avec d'autres motifs décoratifs. Notre exemplaire présente deux bandes et un médaillon central. La bande supérieure bien qu'elle ne soit pas visible, est souvent occupée avec des traits stylisés qu'on a appelé orle de « vagues et de poissons ». La bande inférieure est réticulée alors que d'habitude elle présente de palmettes. Enfin le médaillon central est rempli par une palmette inscrite dans une circonférence. Ce type de décor est daté depuis le début du XIVème au milieu du XVème siècle[10]. (pl. I.13).

LA CÉRAMIQUE BLEUE DE BARCELONE

L'expansion du commerce céramique fut décisive pour l'introduction de la technique de l'oxyde de cobalt en Catalogne, qui bien tôt acquérit une telle importance qu'il fut imité. D'après la documentation écrite, des artisans de Manises furent appelés à Barcelone[11], qui probablement fut le principal centre producteur. Toutefois, il faut rappeler que la localisation des poteries utilisant cette technique est encore un sujet plein d'interrogeants.

---

[7] MARTÍNEZ CAVIRÓ, 1983: 116 et 142.

[8] Id: 139.

[9] BARRACHINA, 1983: 155-157, fig. 17, 27-28, photos 57-58, deuxième quart du XVème s.; MARTÍNEZ CAVIRÓ, 1983: 135, fig. 108, XVème s.; LLUBIÀ, 1967: 160, fig. 251, fin du XVème s.; NAVARRO, 1986: 578-579, pl. 2, depuis la fin du XIVème au dernier quart du XVème s.

[10] AMIGÓ, 1986: 77, fig. 9.52, vers le milieu du XVème s.; LERMA, 1984: 190, 194, fig. 11.2, deuxième moitié du XIVème et début du XVème s.; SOLER, 1992: 65, fig. 26, début du XIVème s.

[11] LLUBIÀ, 1967: 139, 152-153.

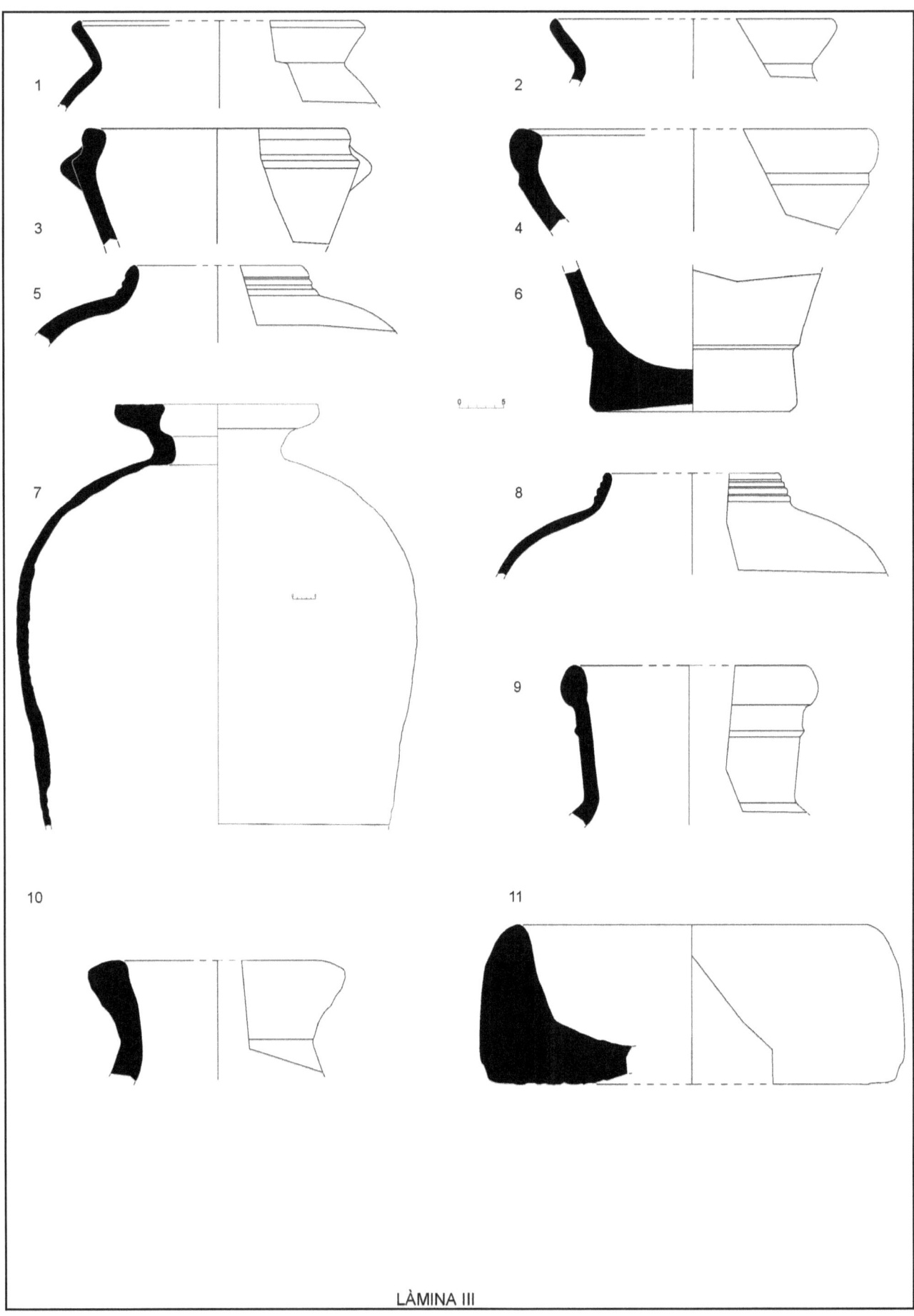

Planche III. Céramique catalane de glaçure plombifère (XIIIème-XVIIIème ss.) : 1 et 2, marmites ; 3, mortier. Glaçure verte olive à l'intérieur et à l'extérieur. Pâte rougeâtre avec de particules de quartz et de mica de grain fin. 4, mortier. 6, mortier, glaçure verte sombre à l'intérieur. 8, seau de puits, glaçure verte à l'extérieur. Céramique commune oxydée (XIVème-XVème ss.): 5, seau de puits. 7, 9 et 10, amphores. 11, mangeoire.

Les premiers exemplaires connus de cette production datent de la première moitié du XVème siècle, où elle convivait avec la céramique décorée en vert et manganèse, dont ils ont pris la typologie, jusqu'à les déplacer. Vers le milieu du XVème siècle cette céramique a vécu son étape d'apogée. C'est aussi le moment où les sources écrites sont plus prolifiques, et grâce auxquelles l'on connaît l'existence d'au moins cinq ateliers de potiers locaux dédiés à cette manufacture. Le nombre de ces ateliers est de plus en plus nombreux à mesure qu'avance la centurie. L'on sait aussi par la documentation qu'il y avait des potiers valenciens qui géraient les centres de Barcelone.

Il s'agit d'une production destinée à la consommation populaire, qui n'avait pas une grande qualité technique ni décorative, puisque son objectif était plutôt celui d'atteindre des prix compétitifs. Vers le milieu du XVIème siècle elle a commencé à tomber en déchéance favorisant d'autres productions catalanes, comme celles décorées en reflets métalliques moyennant la technique du « pinceau - peigne ». Enfin, pendant le premier tiers du XVIIème siècle elle ne se fabrique plus[12].

La plus part des tessons trouvés à Callús présentent une pâte rosée qui varie du beige rosé au rose rougeâtre. C'est une pâte poreuse, avec des vacuoles et de petites inclusions, surtout de mica. La glaçure stannifère, brillante et de bonne qualité, est distribuée uniformément sur la superficie intérieure des pièces.

Toutefois, nous présentons aussi deux écuettes qui ne s'adaptent pas à cette description, ayant une pâte beige crème et une glaçure qui couvre la pièce entière. Ces caractéristiques les rapprochent aux productions valenciennes, d'autant plus si nous tenons compte de l'habitude d'acheter de la céramique valencienne déjà glaçurée pour la décorer après, ce qui est documenté au moins depuis 1447[13]. Et pourtant, sa ressemblance avec d'autres exemplaires définis comme productions de Barcelone nous ont fait pencher pour les décrire sous cette épigraphe.

Tous les tessons provenant de Callús appartiennent à des écuettes, plats « d'aile » ou plats coupants. Leur décor est souvent inspiré à celui du valencien, mais plus simple, y prédominant les espaces vides et les traits schématisés :

Rose fermée : souvent à huit rayons recourbés sur eux-mêmes qui remplissent le fond intérieur de la pièce. Nous ne l'avons associée avec aucun autre décor puisque nous n'avons qu'un fragment de la base d'un plat. C'est un motif d'influence valencienne[14], imitée à Barcelone et présentent aussi, au début du XVIIème siècle, des reflets métalliques[15]. Dans notre cas, il date du XVème siècle (pl. I.14).

Etoile à rayons épais : Il s'agit d'un motif qui a déjà des antécédents dans des productions en vert et manganèse[16]. A ce qui concerne à des pièces de Barcelone, il a une fourchette chronologique du XIVème au XVIème siècle[17]. À Callús, il se trouve associé au motif des « alafias » (pl. II.3).

Chevrons opposés : Motif central si bien il puisse aussi apparaître comme bordure, qui est d'influence valencienne[18]. C'est un décor de longue tradition, le trouvant déjà en vert et manganèse[19] et aussi dans quelques exemplaires de Muel[20] et même en reflets métalliques. De nombreuses parallèles le situent entre le XIVème et le XVème siècles[21] (pl. II.5).

Motif héraldique : Blason royal qui est déjà habituelle dans les productions décorées en vert et manganèse[22] et bleues valenciennes[23]. Dans les exemplaires de Barcelone souvent se trouve entouré d'une circonférence et associé à une bordure consistante à groupes de trois ou quatre barres (pl. II.6).

Fleure en bouton : Quoique nous n'ayons pu localiser aucun parallèle, c'est presque sûr qu'il s'agit d'une production valencienne, se trouvant associé aux « alafias » et zigzags. Cet exemplaire est daté de la deuxième moitié du XVème siècle (pl. II.2).

« Alafias » : Motif épigraphique d'influence arabe qui souhaite bien-être au possesseur de la pièce. C'est un motif imité des productions valenciennes[24] très utilisé dans celles de Barcelone et qui comprend, d'après les parallèles, depuis la fin du XIVème jusqu'à la fin du XVIème siècle[25] (pl. II.3 et 8).

---

[12] PARERA, 1998: 75.

[13] SOLER, 1981: 22.

[14] Comme l'on peut déduire de l'existence de différents exemplaires produits à Paterna (AMIGUES, 1987: fig. 44.4; COLL, 1987: fig. 3; NAVARRO, 1986: pl. 4).

[15] SANTANACH, 1987: 26, fig. 2.

[16] AMIGÓ, 1986: 77, fig. 1.9, XIVème s..

[17] PARERA, 1998: 76, pl. XCVIII.2, depuis milieu XVème au début du XVIème s.; CERDÀ, 1991: 161, pl. 6.4, deuxième moitié du XVème s.; MORO, 1994: 21, pl. XXXII. 2, XVIème s.

[18] SOLER, 1992: fig. 26; LERMA, 1992: 110, fig. 62.

[19] COLL, 1979: 270, fig. 945.

[20] ALMAGRO, 1952: 22, pl. XLVI. 4162, deuxième moitié du XVIIème s.

[21] BOLÒS, MALLART, 1986: 62, CD 16, CD 17, XVème s.; CERDÀ, 1991: 161, pl. 6. 5-7, 7, deuxième moitié du XVème s.; PARERA, 1998: 77, pl. XXXII.6, LXVIII.7, CII.2 et CVII.6, XVème s. jusqu'à *circa* 1600.

[22] D'habitude, il s'agit des motifs très schématiques. PARERA, 1998: 70, table I; BARRACHINA, 1983: 109-111, fig. 14.

[23] BARRACHINA, 1983: photo 46.

[24] MARTÍNEZ CAVIRÓ, 1983: 111-112.

[25] AMIGÓ, 1986: 43, 46, 77, fig. 54.531, vers le milieu du XVème s.; BOLÒS, MALLART, 1986: 61, CD15, CD17, fin du XIVème et tout le XVème s.; TELESE, 1992: 113, 118, fig. 57, première moitié du XVème s.; CERDÀ, 1991: 161, 177, pl. 8.2, 10.1-3, deuxième moitié du XVème s.; PARERA, 1998: 78, pl. VI.8, LX.5, XVème et XVIème ss.; MORO, 1994: 21, pl. XXIX.2, XVIème s.; SOLER, 1981: 26, fig. 3.132, XVème s.

LA CÉRAMIQUE CATALANE DE GLAÇURE PLOMBIFÈRE

L'imperméabilisation de la céramique avec une glaçure vitrifiée impliqua une grande avance grâce à sa fonctionnalité. Bien que l'origine de cette production soit très ancienne, ce n'est qu'au bas moyen âge qu'il se trouve de façon généralisée aux gisements catalans. Les premières pièces de cette manufacture eurent une glaçure verte de cuivre qui fut appelée « terre verte de Barcelone », manufacturée pendant le XIVème et la première moitié du XVème siècle [26].

C'est une production de cuisson oxydant, avec des pâtes très compactes. Toutes les pièces ont une glaçure transparente d'oxyde de plomb qui les imperméabilise. Les diverses tonalités de la glaçure étaient obtenues en y ajoutant un autre oxyde métallique : ferre pour le miellé, cuivre pour le vert ou antimoine pour le jaune. Nous présentons ici les exemplaires trouvés à Callús par rapport à sa fonction et aux types auxquels ils appartiennent.

Marmites : Récipients globulaires avec un profil en esse, lèvre sortie et bord élevé. Malgré l'absence des anses de notre ensemble, elles en ont habituellement deux ou quatre. La date attribuée à ce type se remonte au XVème siècle quoiqu'il survive jusqu'aujourd'hui [27] (pl. III. 1-2).

Couvercles : l'utilisation des couvercles avec glaçure est datée, par la documentation écrite, des XIVème et XVème siècles [28]. Le seul exemplaire trouvé à Callús est du type dénommé «d'arc de pont », une variante très rare dans des pièces glaçurées bien qu'elle apparaisse souvent aux productions grises. Nous n'avons trouvé qu'un seul parallèle au site du Bullidor (Sant Just Desvern, Barcelone), qui a une fourchette chronologique du début XIVème jusqu'à la première moitié du XVème siècle [29] (pl. II.9).

Jarre petite : Correspondant à une forme très connue dans des productions en vert et manganèse, elle servait à sortir l'eau, le vin ou d'autres boissons à table. Tous les exemplaires de Callús ont une glaçure verte à l'extérieur, où elle couvre trois quarts de la pièce, et jaunâtre à l'intérieur. C'est un type daté du XIVème-XVème siècles [30] qui, sur notre site, correspond au milieu du XVème siècle (pl. II. 10-11).

Mortier : La première référence écrite de ce récipient date de l'année 1069 bien qu'on n'en sache le matériel dont il était fait [31]. Nous en avons trouvé deux variants différentes, l'une avec des anses et l'autre sans elles. Les deux types ont une glaçure verte à l'extérieur, à l'exception du quart inférieur, et jaunâtre à l'intérieur. C'est un récipient très utilisé pendant le XIVème et XVème siècles, au long desquels la « terre verte » a connu son *floruit*[32] (pl. III. 3,4 et 6).

Seau de puits : Ce sont des récipients fermés ovoïdaux, avec un bord haut, étroit et orné de cannelures. Disposant d'un bec et d'une anse verticale supérieure centrée, où l'on y attachait une corde pour extraire de l'eau du puits. Ce récipient apparaît déjà cité sur la documentation l'année 1347[33], à partir d'où il n'a pas cessé de se produire, jusqu'au XXème siècle (pl. III.8).

LA CÉRAMIQUE COMMUNE OXYDÉE

Malgré la généralisation des glaçures de plomb, pendant le bas moyen âge, l'on n'a pas cessé de produire de la céramique sans glaçure, soit par des raisons économiques, soit par des besoins liés à son utilisation, qui était, notamment, le transport et l'emmagasinage des liquides ou du grain. Très abondant pendant le XIVème et XVème siècles, les caractéristiques techniques de cette production sont semblables à celle avec de la glaçure plombifère : pièces oxydées avec des pâtes rouges ou marrons, quelques vacuoles et inclusions de mica et de quartz.

Amphore : À Callús, nous avons trouvé un grand nombre de fragments appartenant à des amphores –nommées « gerres » en catalan- dont nous avons différencié trois types. Dans les trois cas il s'agit des exemplaires avec une base très étroite, plan et instable, un corps en fuseau et un cou presque inexistant. Il est normal, aussi, qu'ils aient un décor de rainures longitudinales sur les parois externes, lesquels ont servi pour y mettre des cordes pour protéger les pièces pendant leurs fréquents voyages en bateau.

Elles sont produites à tour, en série et par parts séparés : la moitié inférieure, la supérieure et le bord, c'est pourquoi elles apparaissent souvent très nettement fragmentées. Bien que nous n'ayons trouvé des parallèles que par deux des trois types, il s'agit des productions propres d'une fourchette chronologique embrassant la deuxième moitié du XIVème[34] jusqu'à la fin du XVème siècle [35] (pl. III. 7, 9 et 10).

---

[26] BARRACHINA, 1983: 178, XIVème et première moitié du XVème s.; MORO, 1994: 21, XVème s.; VINYOLES, 1984: 232, 233.

[27] PARERA, 1998: 115; BASSEGODA, 1977: pl. XVIIIa, XVIème s.; BELTRÁN DE HEREDIA, 1994: 117, 141, fig. 61, XIVème et XVème ss.; CERDÀ, 1991: 166, pl. 15.1, XVIème s.

[28] PARERA, 1998: 113.

[29] AMIGÓ, 1986: 26.

[30] BARRACHINA, 1983: 191, fig. 21, première moitié du XVème s.; BELTRÁN DE HEREDIA, 1997: 242, n. 23, XVème s., postérieur au 1438; BOLÒS, 1986: 692, XVème s.; CABESTANY, RIERA, 1978: 411, XIVème et XVème ss.

---

[31] ALCOVER, MOLL, 1968: 598.

[32] PARERA, 1998: 114; AMIGÓ, 1986: 28, n° 1154 et 1157, XVème s.; BARRACHINA, 1983: 190, photo 73, première moitié du XVème s.; BOLÒS, 1985: 689, n° 34, XIVème-XVème ss., BELTRÁN DE HEREDIA, 1997: 241, n°. 17 et 18, XVème s., postérieur au 1438.

[33] BASSEGODA, 1977: 117.

[34] DÍES, GONZÁLEZ, 1986: 615, 617, fig. 1, *terminus post quem* 1350.

[35] BORREGO, SARANOVA, 1994: 190-191, depuis la fin du XIVème à la fin du XVème s.

Adresse des auteurs

Ainhoa PANCORBO PICÓ, Alberto LÓPEZ MULLOR,
Àlvar CAIXAL MATA
Diputació de Barcelona
Service du Patrimoine Architectonique Local
187, rue du Comte d'Urgell.
E-08036-Barcelone, ESPAGNE
Email : lopezmal@diba.es

Bibliographie

ALCOVER, A., MOLL, F., 1968, *Diccionari català-valencià-balear*. Palma de Mallorca.

AMIGÓ, J., ET ALII, 1986, *El Bullidor, jaciment medieval. Estudi de materials i documentació.* Quaderns d'Estudis Santjustencs, III. Sant Just Desvern.

AMIGUES, F., 1987, *Un horno medieval de cerámica. El testar del molí, Paterna (Valencia).* Madrid.

BARRACHINA, J., 1983, Estudi arqueològic del jaciment. *El castell de Llinars del Vallès. Un casal noble a la Catalunya del segle XV.* Barcelona.

BASSEGODA, J., 1977, *La cerámica popular en la arquitectura gótica.* Barcelona.

BELTRÁN DE HEREDIA, J., 1994, Terminologia i ús dels atuells ceràmics de cuina a la Baixa Edat Mitjana. *Del rebost a la taula. Cuina i menjar a la Barcelona gòtica*, Ajuntament de Barcelona, Barcelona.

BELTRÁN DE HEREDIA, J., 1997, La ceràmica localitzada a l'extradós de les voltes de la Pia Almoina de Barcelona. *Quaderns Científics i Tècnics, 9: Ceràmica medieval catalana.* Servei del Patrimoni Arquitectònic Local de la Diputació de Barcelona. Barcelona: 235-253.

BOLÒS, J., ET ALII, 1986, Ceràmiques medievals dels museus d'arts, indústries i tradicions populars. *I Congreso de Arqueología Medieval Española, Huesca 1985.* Saragossa: 683-702.

BOLÒS, J., MALLART, L., 1986, *La Granja cistercenca d'Ancosa (La Llacuna).* Excavacions arqueològiques a Catalunya, 7. Barcelona.

BORREGO, M., SARANOVA, R., 1994, Envases cerámicos recuperados de las bóvedas de la iglesia de Santa María. *Alicante, enclave comercial mediterráneo del bajo medievo.* Alicante.

CABESTANY, J.F., RIERA, F., 1980, *Ceràmica de Manresa. Segle XIV.* Barcelona.

CASANOVAS, M.A., 1983, *La ceràmica catalana.* Barcelona.

CERDÀ, J., 1991, Un conjunt de ceràmica del segle XVI procedent de Can Xammar (Mataró). *Laietània*, 6. Mataró: 157-178.

CIRICI, A., 1977, *Ceràmica catalana.* Barcelona.

COLL, J., 1987, *Cerámica española en colecciones mallorquinas.* Palma de Mallorca.

DÍES, E., GONZÁLEZ, R.J., 1986, Las tinajas de transporte bajomedievales y sus marcas de alfarero. *I Congreso de Arqueología Medieval Española. Huesca, 1985.* Saragossa.

LERMA, J.V., ET ALII, 1984, Sistematización de la loza gótico-mudéjar de Paterna/Manises. *La ceramica medievale nel Mediterraneo occidentale. Siena-Faenza, 1984.* Firenze.

LLUBIÀ, L.M., 1967, *Cerámica medieval española.* Barcelona.

LÓPEZ MULLOR, A., 1988, Excavacions a l'ermita de la Mare de Déu de Bellvitge. L'Hospitalet de Llobregat, Barcelonès. Campanyes 1978-1981. *Identitats* (l'Hospitalet de Llobregat), 1: 17-35.

LÓPEZ MULLOR, A., CAIXAL, À., FIERRO, J., 1997, Cronologia i difusió d'un grup de ceràmiques medievals trobades a les comarques de Barcelona (segles VII-XIV). *Quaderns Científics i Tècnics, 9: Ceràmica medieval catalana.* Servei del Patrimoni Arquitectònic Local de la Diputació de Barcelona. Barcelona: 101-142.

MARTÍNEZ CAVIRÓ, B., 1983, *La loza dorada.* Madrid.

MORO, A., 1994, El fossat nord del castell cartoixa de Vallparadís, Terrassa, Vallès Occidental. Memòries de les intervencions arqueològiques a Catalunya, 5. Servei d'Arqueologia de la Generalitat de Catalunya. Barcelona: 6-53.

NAVARRO, C., 1986, Cerámicas valencianas bajomedievales aparecidas en el castillo de la Mola. Novelda (Alicante). *I Congreso de Arqueología Medieval Española. Huesca, 1985.* Saragossa.

PARERA M., 1998, Ceràmica medieval decorada i ceràmica moderna. *Monografies, 4: Torre del Baró (Viladecans). Arqueologia.* Servei del Patrimoni Arquitectònic Local de la Diputació de Barcelona. Barcelona: 69-128.

SANTANACH, J., 1987, Noves aportacions sobre l'obra d'escudellers barcelonina en la transició dels segles XVI i XVII. *Butlletí d'informació ceràmica*, 35. Barcelona: 26-29.

SOLER, M.P., 1992, Valencia. *Mediterraneum. Ceràmica medieval en España e Italia.* Viterbo: 11-90.

SOLER, N., 1981, *Ceràmica valenciana del segle XV trobada a la Pia Almoina de Girona.* Girona.

TELESE, A., 1992, Cataluña. *Mediterraneum. Ceràmica medieval en España e Italia.* Viterbo: 91-119.

VINYOLES, M.T., ET ALII, 1984, Els atuells de terrissa a les llars barcelonines vers l'any 1400. *Acta Historica et Archaeologica Mediaevalia*, annex 2. Barcelona: 200-239.

THE STUDY OF MEDIAEVAL ARCHITECTURE FROM AN ARCHAEOLOGICAL PERSPECTIVE

Rebeca BLANCO ROTEA

Résumé : L'ÉTUDE DE L'ARCHITECTURE MÉDIÉVALE DÉS L'ARCHÉOLOGIE. Depuis les années 80, à l'Espagne on s'étude l'Architecture historique dès la perspective archéologique. Jusqu'à ce moment, les études historiques sont objets exclusifs de l'historie de l'Architecture ou de l'Historie de l'Art, sans prendre en considération que le site archéologique non est seulement le sous-sol du bâtiment mais encore tout ce que s'élève par-dessus. Attendu, donc, que les architectures sont documents historiques susceptibles d'être étudies avec une méthodologie archéologique, on c'est développé l'Archèologie de l'Architecture, qu'étude précisément l'architecture dès une perspective archéologique. À notre Laboratoire, nous avons appliqué cette méthodologie à l'étude de constructions médiévales, sur les études de la stratigraphie de ses parements. Nous diviserons notre communication en deux; sur la première nous ferons une brève explication sur notre méthodologie archéologique ou *Lecture de Parements*; et sur la seconde l'application de cette méthodologie à l'Église de S. Fiz de Solovio (Santiago de Compostela, A Coruña, Spain) liée a la découverte des reliques de l'Apôtre Saint-Jacques et à la fondation et au déroulement de la cité de Santiago de Compostela.

Abstract: The archaeological perspective has been applied to Spanish historical Architecture since the 1980's. Before then, historical buildings had been studied either through Architectural History or Art History. These traditional studies did not consider historical buildings as archaeological sites in the way that we do, including not only the foundations of the building but also what is found on the surface. The Archaeology of Architecture, the study of architecture from an archaeological perspective, considers historical buildings as historical documents which may be analysed through the application of an archaeological methodology. In our Laboratory of Archaeology and Cultural Forms, we have applied this methodology to the analysis of medieval buildings, studying the stratigraphy of the paraments.

Keywords: History of Medieval Art; Archaeology of Architecture; stratigraphic analysis.

We have organised this lecture into two sections. In the first, we will explain the archaeological methodology or Parament Readings. Secondly, we will illustrate our technique using the example of the church of San Fiz de Solovio (Santiago de Compostela, A Coruña, Spain). This church is linked with the discovery of the relics of the Apostle Saint James ('Santiago' in Spanish), and with the founding of the city of Santiago de Compostela.

A BRIEF INTRODUCTION TO STRATIGRAPHIC ANALYSIS AND THE ARCHAEOLOGY OF ARCHITECTURE

Unlike traditional studies about mediaeval architecture which use the perspective of Art History or Architectural History, in this text we propose a way of exploring this architecture from a perspective which is different yet complementary to the first: the Archaeology of Architecture. We propose dealing with mediaeval architecture and the architecture of historical buildings in general (when there is stratification) using an archaeological methodology.

The archaeology of architecture, as its name implies, is a discipline which studies historical constructions from an archaeological perspective, using an archaeological methodology in particular. It first appeared in Italy in the 1970's and 1980's, with its application and development in Spain starting in the mid 1980's, as a result of contacts with Italian sources. In the Laboratory of Archaeology and Cultural Forms (ITR, USC), a line of research has been developed in recent years within Archaeology of Architecture which focuses on prehistoric as well as historical architecture, and essentially deals with the following aspects: the analysis of perception (Mañana Borrazás 1999), spatial analysis (Ayán Vila 2000), and the stratigraphic analysis of ornamental elements (Blanco Rotea 1997; 1999). The last is the subject of this paper.

What is *stratigraphic analysis* or *ornamental reading*? It is important to underline that this is a field which belongs to the much wider discipline of archaeology of architecture, which includes other types of analysis including those mentioned above. When dealing with the study of a historical building (in our case, a mediaeval building) with archaeological methodology, there are two essential conditions; we must consider the building as a site (the first condition), which as such is subject to a process of stratification (second condition) and which as such should be analysed using an archaeological methodology. The building is a prolongation at subsurface level, where the elements which form the subsurface and raised parts of the site are the product of archaeological stratification - of constructive and deconstructive activity, of anthropic transformations or other actions caused by natural agents (Azkarate 1995). The building should therefore be considered as an important part of material culture, a historical document with archaeological attributes that is susceptible to be studied, using an archaeological methodology which in turn supports other types of studies.

The development of this methodology has been directly related to the increase in Mediaeval and post-Mediaeval

Stratigraphic analysis or elevation readings			
Object of study	Protohistoric and historical architecture		
Model	"Harris Method"		
Objective	• Identify, organize and date the different stages of buildings • A detailed analysis of units and stratigraphic groups • To identify the building's stratigraphic sequence		
Methodology	*Nature*	*Instruments*	*Analytical procedure*
	• Instrumental • Flexibility	• Graphic documentation • Sectors • Numeration • Analytical records • Lists • Diagrams	• Graphic documentation. Planimetry
			• Differentiation of sectors • Differentiation, numeration and description of elements • Interpretation of temporal relationships
			• Creation of diagrams • Reduction, periodization and correlation • Identification of activities • Simplification of elements
			• Historical documentation
			• Synthesis and dating
			• Creating an archive for compiling information
			• Publication

archaeology, periods in which the increased and improved conservation of architectonic elements made it necessary to adapt Harris method of stratigraphic analysis to the study of historical buildings. We believe that while on one hand this has been a positive step for archaeology and architecture itself, as it has benefited the development of new analytical methods making it possible to explore the 'life' of a building, contributing to its comprehension, on the other it has led to a direct confrontation with the History of Architecture and Art History.

The methodology for the analysis of ornamental elements is an analytical process through which we obtain the stratigraphic sequence of historical constructions, which in turn makes it possible for us to establish relative chronologies, although we need the support of other types of analysis such as archaeographic, archeometric, typological or chronotypological analyses, in order to obtain absolute chronologies (Quirós 1994: 145-6). All of these types of analysis form part of Archaeology of Architecture, and must be understood jointly and in a complementary manner, although we only deal with some of them.

As we said before, this analytical methodology adapts archaeological stratigraphic study through the so-called "Harris method" to the layout of historical buildings. It consists fundamentally in identifying, organizing and dating the different stages through which the building has passed, from its construction until the time of study, using a detailed analysis of its elements, activities and constructive-destructive processes. The starting premise is that historical constructions are stratified objects which follow stratigraphic principles (Caballero and Latorre 1995: 38-9): buildings are subject to transformations produced by a continuous series of constructive actions which form a stratigraphic sequence, which we have to extract using a suitable archaeological methodology, the *stratigraphic reading of ornaments*.

THE METHODOLOGY OF STRATIGRAPHIC ANALYSIS

There follows a brief explanation of the stages in this process.

Firstly, we must differentiate and define the parts of the building, which contain the historical data we will recover using analytical instruments, data which will be dealt with using the analytical process, in order to both conserve and communicate it (Caballero 1992: 3). We will briefly define the walled stratigraphic elements (WSE) that form a historical construction: a stratigraphic element is the smallest unit with stratigraphic individuality and homogeneity: it may have materiality and volume as an actual element, or simply be a surface, the interfaces which define these elements, both vertical and horizontal. Activity is the group of elements and their interfaces which have the same function, and belong to the same chronological period. The building is the final unit which reaches us, formed by different types of activities.

All of these stratigraphic units are subjected to stratigraphic relationships which we need to identify, as they will define and order the stratigraphic sequence of the building. Firstly, we have physical relationships: one WSE is joined to another, is supported by another, cuts through or divides another; secondly, there are temporal relationships, which may be of contemporaneity or anterior-posteriority; finally, we must consider if these relationships are certain or dubious, direct or indirect (Caballero 1996: 14).

Once the WSE have been defined together with the relationships which exist within them, we then move on to describing the stages of the working process we must follow in order to deal with the study of a historic building. Although here we propose a series of methodological rules

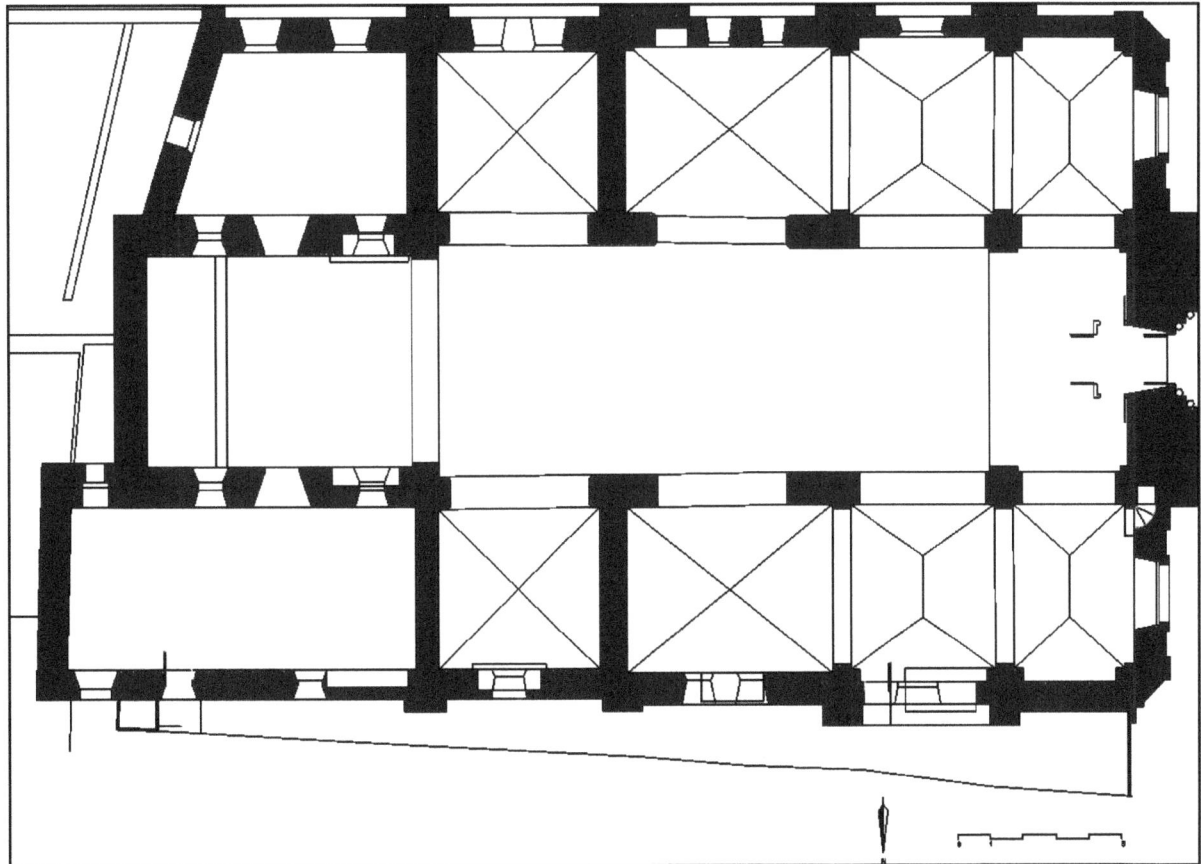

Figure 1.

to be followed if work is to be carried out in an orderly and systematic manner, this method is characterised by its flexibility, with these rules being adaptable to each specific case we analyse. The actual characteristics of the building, the instruments available to the analyst and other details, may make it necessary to adapt the methodology as long as the work is carried out seriously and systematically, and the basic stages of the process are followed.

We should firstly make a graphic documentation of all of the parts of the building, either planimetrically or photographically. In this way it is possible to recover its total volume and be able to act on it. The type of documentation used should be suited to our purposes, the type of building and the resources we have available, although all observable data should be recorded. This phase is essential before carrying out an analytical intervention. The building should then be divided into working sectors, a merely instrumental division which helps make work easier and more agile, particularly in the case of large, complex constructions. The use of direct observation or graphic documentation allows us to make a differential analysis of the units and a reading of their relationships.

In the second phase, we will move on to differentiate elements and interfaces according to stratigraphic criteria, observing the actions which created them or their constructive dimension, the relationships they have with other units or their spatial dimension and their temporal sequence or chronological dimension. We will differentiate the contours of all of the homogenous constructive actions and relationships which existed before, after and during each action. As we gradually differentiate the stratigraphic units, these are given a number, which serves as a code we may use to recover all of the information which exists about the stratigraphic unit, as well as the instruments which correspond to each unit. The next stage is to create the analytical documentation for each WSE. This may be of several different types, although the basic fields which should be covered are: identification and description of the unit; a field which includes the actions and relationships between units, as well as a diagram or matrix; interpretation, and finally references to other instruments, the name of the person responsible for the work, date of creation and some archive data.

Once the WSE have been identified, numbered and described, we should then proceed with the analysis of the stratigraphic relationships which exist between them, in order to produce the diagrams which will give us the final stratigraphic sequence, essential for the interpretation of the building's historical process. This stage of description implies a very important and delicate analytical operation, as here we are attempting to "read" the direction of time in the relationships between constructive parts. These relationships have a spatial-temporal dimension, and it is very important to understand their chronological value in order to be able to interpret them and then produce a diagram which reflects the constructive processes involved

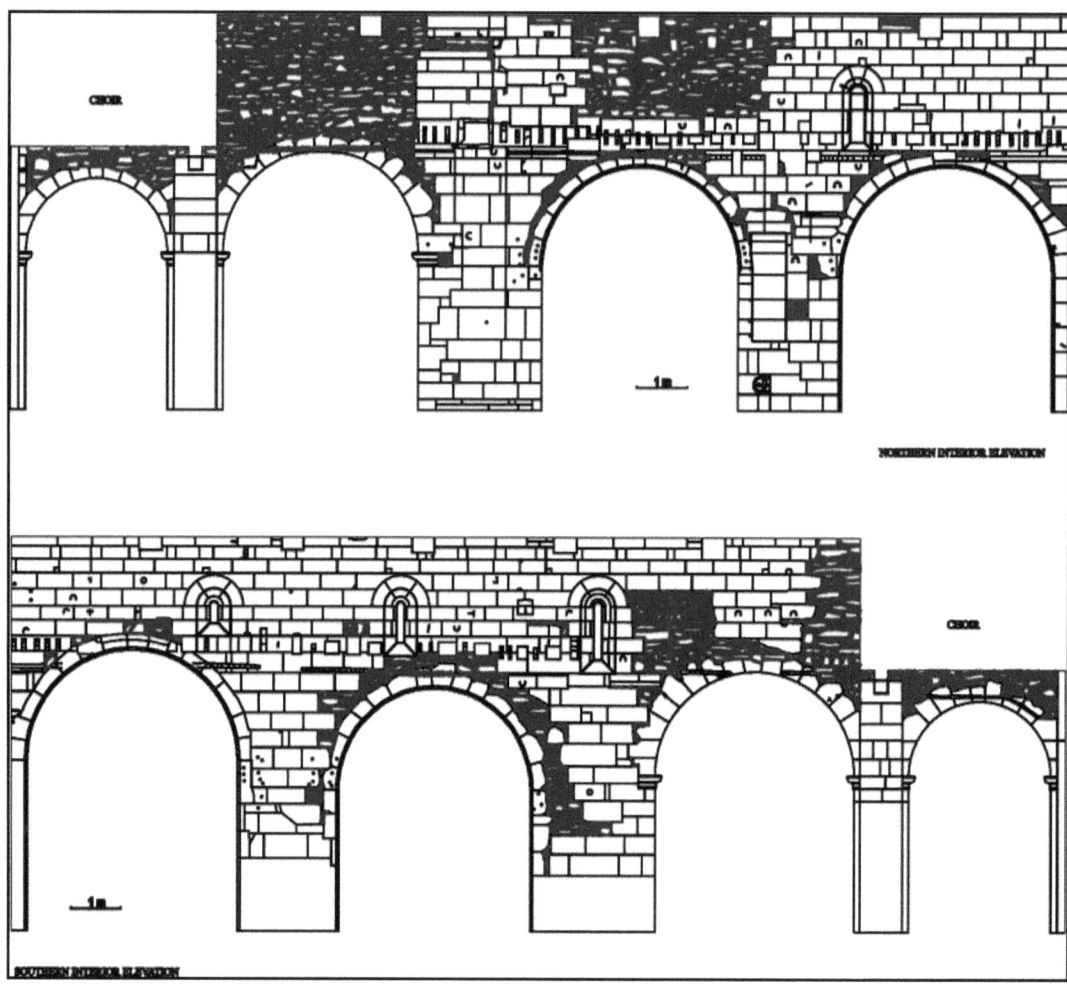

Figure 2.

in the building, together with its historical significance. The synchronic relationships of each original constructive moment are reflected in the horizontal steps of the diagram, with vertical rows showing the diachronic evolution of its reconstruction (Caballero 1992; 15). We should firstly create diagrams of elements, and then diagrams of synthesis.

Next are the processes of synthesis and dating. Here we recover the unity of the building in an attempt to understand its totality, so that the building progressively recovers its character as a constructive unit. We now enter into an interpretative process. We should firstly eliminate the redundant relationships between units, as the diagram should only represent direct relationships, both horizontally and vertically. Then the processes of periodization should be estimated: we deduce the historical periods through the relative chronology obtained for the situation in the diagrams of elements, further assisted by chronological indicators, which will give us absolute chronologies (Quirós 1994: 145-6). Finally, elements should be correlated, grouping them together in increasingly complex units or contexts, until we once again arrive at the main unit, the building itself.

Historical analysis is the final stage of the methodological process. Here, historical data are interpreted, obtained either through the analysis itself or by the application of other disciplines. As we know, Archaeology of Architecture has mainly historical aims: until now we have reduced this finality to basically deciphering the chronological aspects which defined the activities or building itself, but without concerning ourselves with what function these constructive processes had. This is the moment to interrelate the data obtained from the analysis with historical data, as well as with possible architectonic theories which help us to situate the construction within the different historical-artistic periods throughout which it has existed.

PARAMENT READINGS IN THE CHURCH OF SAN FIZ DE SOLOVIO[1] (SANTIAGO DE COMPOSTELA, A CORUÑA, SPAIN)

The first phase of our study in the church of San Fiz de Solovio was a complete documental analysis of the building, which we contrasted in the final stage of the investigation with the data obtained throughout the whole reading process. We reached the following conclusions.

---

[1] This document is a brief summary of the methodological process and results of the reading. For more information see 1997, 1998a and 1998b.

STAGES OF WORK			DIAGRAM OF A 101
Stages	Walled stratigraphic elements	Activity	
101.1	1040, 1044, 1045, 1049, 1050, 1054, 1056, 1057, 1058, 1060, 1061, 1062, 1063, 1010, 1009	Mediaeval parament	
101.2	1057, 1058, 1045	Mediaeval window	
101.3	1068, 1069, 1070?, 1071?	Mediaeval parament	

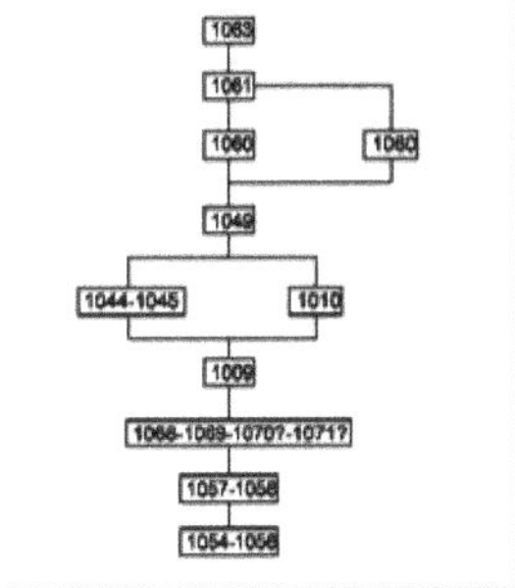

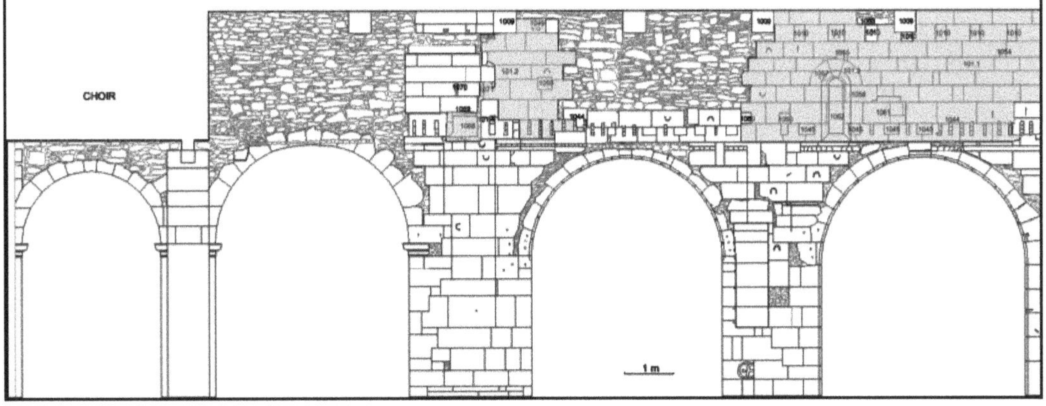

Figure 3.

Some sources believe the church to be the oldest in the city of Santiago de Compostela; we do not know when its foundations were laid, although López Ferreiro (1899: 8-9) estimated between the fifth and sixth centuries. All of the authors we consulted agree that it was erected by the end of the eighth or beginning of the ninth century, and was closely linked with the legend of the discovery of the tomb of St. James the Apostle. We know that subsequently a series of reforms were made up to the eighteenth century, arriving at the building we see today. We also know that there were later additions: in 1952 the Epiphany Tympanum was added to the façade (Perrín 1993); in 1970 the building was restored (Perrín 1982: 140) and again in 1998. The first reform to the initial construction that we know of was the reconstruction of the church by Bishop Sisnando I at the beginning of the tenth century. After having been demolished by the Moorish chieftain Almanzor in 997, it was rebuilt by Bishop San Pedro de Mezonzo (Fernández and Freire 1880: 190). In 1122 Archbishop Gelmírez renewed it "from the foundations up" (Suárez 1950: 337); according to Perrín, at that time it had a nave and apse which were unique. The nave was smaller than it is today, a fact which led to the reforms of the eighteenth century, and it had a covered porch which today contains the choir. There were no further reforms until 1625, when work began on a series of chapels which were added on laterally, and led directly to the reforms in the eighteenth century. In 1701 the architect Simón Rodríguez presented a project to rebuild the church, including the building of a belltower which would introduce a new typology into Galician Baroque architecture. These reforms affected the church as a whole, culminating with the reforms of 1998.

Continuing with the methodological process[2], the next step was to create adequate graphic documentation which differentiated the different constructive elements present in each of the paraments analysed. We also took photographs of the whole church, which were particularly useful when dealing with elevations. Work was divided into two sectors: sector 01 for the northern elevation, and sector 02 for the southern. Visual observation started at this point, when we differentiated units directly on the parament, then including them in the plan. We used the criteria of individualisation and stratigraphic type. We then numbered all the elements and interfaces, starting with 1001 on the northern elevation and 2001 on the southern, indicating this series on the plan. Once this had been done, we started to catalogue all of the differentiated and numbered elements, collecting this information synthetically in lists of elements. Once the individual entries for each element had been completed, we had available the temporal and physical relationships between elements, meaning we were able to move on from elements to activities (hereafter referred to as AA). We were able to identify 4 AA in each elevation, for which an analytical record was also created. These AA also featured different stages of construction work. At this time we defined the stratigraphic sequence and determined the AA that comprised the building. We firstly made diagrams of records, both for elements and AA. To make the process of creating the final diagram

---

[2] The reading refers to the northern and southern interior elevations of what is today known as the central nave, and which in its day was the only nave of the mediaeval church, as because the walls are not covered with plaster, they are the only type where it is possible to carry out a complete stratigraphic analysis.

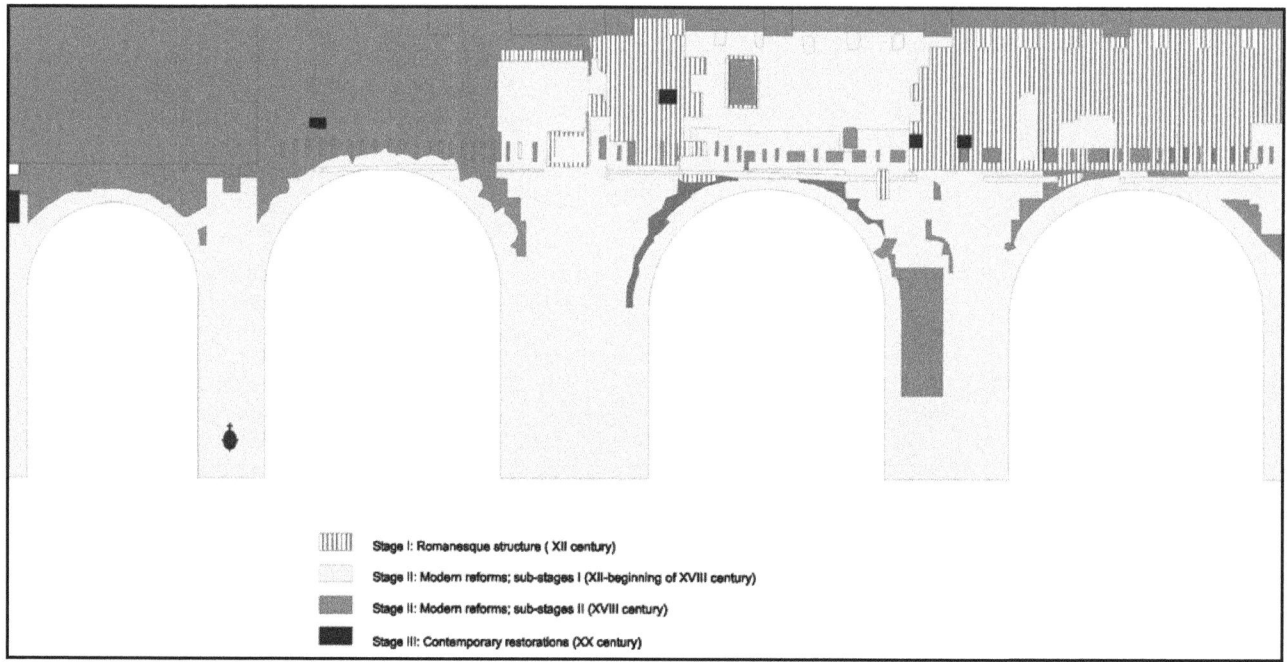

Figure 4.

easier, we made partial diagrams of elements in each AA, and by putting them together we created the final diagram of elements which contains the complete stratigraphic sequence of the building.

We could then differentiate four AA in both elevations, which were: 101 and 102, remains of mediaeval paraments; 102 and 202: different reforms carried out in relatively recently (seventeenth to eighteenth centuries); 103 and 203: restoration carried out relatively recently (eighteenth century); and 104 and 204: modern restoration work (1970 and 1998). Finally, and with the support of the data obtained from the analysis and historical documentation we had available, we could determine the different stages of the building:

STAGE I: ROMANESQUE STRUCTURE OF THE BUILDING

We believe that this structure corresponds to the reforms carried out by Gelmírez in 1122, of which only a few elements remain in the northern and southern elevations which today form the central nave. There are no remains within the building from previous periods included in the bibliography. The walls are made of granite blocks placed in horizontal rows; although it appears to be the same as other parts of the elevations, we know that material was reused from them in the reforms from the eighteenth century. This may be seen in the three processional crosses which are found at the base of two pillars, and which appear to be incomplete, and three more found in other parts of the building. The lack of filling material between the rows of granite blocks which we had thought to be Romanesque, and those from later reforms, was another reason which led us to consider that they did not belong to this period. We believe that the reforms carried out by Gelmírez probably respected the old layout of the church, but since no elements from before 1122 exist, it is not possible to demonstrate this point[3].

The ruinous state of the Mediaeval paraments is the result of a series of reforms which took place in later stages of the building, at times using the same type of material (re-using building materials), or using granite blocks. We also believe that the design of the Mediaeval nave stopped at the point where the choir begins, where there would have probably been a covered portico which was eliminated when the nave was lengthened in the eighteenth century. We base this supposition on the fact that from where the second arch starts (from west to east) until we reach the elevation of the western façade on both sides, we did not find any remains of possible Mediaeval paraments, only granite blocks. Finally, the mediaeval building was lit by slit windows which shed light inwards, with an arch in their upper part. Only three of these remain in the southern section, two of which were split by the opening of archways into the chapels, and one in the northern section. Some of the reforms which we saw in the northern elevation appear to correspond to these windows having been closed. Apart from one placed in the southern elevation, the rest were covered either in the eighteenth century or in the 1970's.

STAGE II: MODERN REFORMS AND REBUILDING

The volume of the present-day building was created in the period between 1625 and the start of the eighteenth century. The changes were the result of different

---

[3] This problem would be solved by excavating in the area of the building, completing the results of the elevation reading with the data conserved in the subsoil of the church.

requirements which created different working stages. In the first stage, it was the need to enlarge the building and adapt it to a new architectonic style, the Baroque (and its sub-stages). In the second stage, there was a change in functionality, when it was annexed as the chapel of the Palace of the Count of Altamira, long-vanished and whose site is now covered by the city's marketplace (leading to the second stage of construction work).

The first stage of construction work involved the opening of a series of lateral chapels[4] which would lead to the ruin and collapse of several parts of the parament, which were either restored with re-used masonry or granite blocks. It also involved the extension of the nave, and its being covered by an unsupported dome, whose remains may be seen in a horizontal groove which divides the northern and southern paraments of the nave from the choir to the chancel (a groove into which the dome was set), as well as in two parallel vertical grooves which meet in the second and third pillar on both sides of the nave, and which descend from the horizontal groove (the remains of the pillars which supported the dome).

In a second stage of work, we have included the reforms which resulted from the church being annexed as chapel to the Palace of the Count of Altamira. At this time a gallery and high choir were also built, and a series of openings added which made access to the church possible directly from the Palace (in the northern elevation of the building). This reform meant it was necessary to destroy the dome so that access was possible from the gallery. Today only the upper choir remains; however, it is possible to see the remains of the gallery from the series of slots carved into the wall to support the beams and crossbeams which exist on both sides of the nave. They start at the height of the choir and continue until the start of the apse. At this time the slit windows in the northern elevation were also destroyed to make way for gateways, and the only one which remains is hidden from view. We also believe that at this time the roof was raised on the central nave, giving it more vertical space needed for the building of the gallery. We corroborate this thesis by the presence of a series of large, covered support slots situated beneath the present ceiling, which we believe supported the beams of a previous covering.

STAGE III: CONTEMPORARY RESTORATIONS

The building has undergone three restorations in recent times, although only the last two, from 1970 and 1998, are visible in the elevations which contain them (the northern and southern interior elevations of the central nave). Neither of them have affected the interior structure of the church, and in both cases are simple 'repairs', which dealt with cavities, the rejoining of building materials, the covering of some parts of the paraments (particularly those with granite blocks), or the covering of some slit windows. These are really reforms rather than rehabilitation work which took place in the church.

To sum up, the reading of paraments has given us a series of data which have helped us to establish the precise limits of each stage, which had been quite confused until now, and to also help with the identification of a series of stages of work which we were not able to identify using historical data, as they were not included in any of the sources we consulted. We would again emphasise that this was only a partial reading, and that a complete analysis of the building is necessary to present more data for this study. This would mean removing all of the plasterwork covering most of its elevations, and excavating an area within the church and outside it.

Author's address

Rebeca BLANCO ROTEA
Laboratory of Archaeology and Cultural Forms
Institute of Technological Research, University of Santiago de Compostela
R.U. Monte da Condesa
Campus Universitario Sur.
15706 Santiago de Compostela SPAIN
E-mail: phrebeca@usc.es.

Bibliography

AYÁN VILA, X., 2000, Una aproximación al problema del espacio doméstico de la Edad del Hierro del NW a través de un proyecto de revalorización cultural. La reconstrucción de un recinto habitacional castreño en el yacimiento de Elviña (A Coruña). Traballo de Investigación de Terceiro Ciclo. Facultade de Xeografía e Historia. USC. Inédito.

AZKARATE GARAI-OLAUN, A., FERNÁNDEZ DE JÁUREGUI, A. Y NÚÑEZ, M., 1995, Documentación y análisis arquitectónico en el País Vasco. Algunas experiencias llevadas a cabo en Álava-España. Informes de la Construcción 435, P. 65-78.

BLANCO ROTEA, R., 1997, Introducción al estudio arqueológico del patrimonio construido: el análisis estratigráfico de paramentos. (Tesis de licenciatura). Grupo de Investigación en Arqueología del Paisaje – Departamento de Historia 1, Universidad de Santiago de Compostela (España). (Inédita).

BLANCO ROTEA, R., 1998[a], La arqueología en el muro: lectura estratigráfica de paramentos en San Fiz de Solovio. Gallaecia 17, p. 481-500.

BLANCO ROTEA, R., 1998b, Las construcciones históricas desde una perspectiva arqueológica. En Actas del Segundo Congreso Nacional de Historia de la Construcción (La Coruña, 22-24 de octubre de 1998), 49-56. Madrid: EFCA.

BROGIOLO, G. P., 1995, Arqueología estratigráfica y restauración, Informes de la Construcción 435, p. 31-36.

CABALLERO ZOREDA, L. (coord.), 1992, Sobre el análisis arqueológico de construcciones históricas. La experiencia llevada a cabo en Santa Eulalia de Mérida, La Torre de Hércules en La Coruña y S. Pelayo de Arlanza. En III Encuentros sobre Arqueología y Patrimonio de Salobreña. Arqueología del monumento (1992). (In press).

CABALLERO ZOREDA, L., 1995. Método para el análisis estratigráfico de construcciones históricas o "lectura de paramentos". Informes de la Construcción 453, p. 37-46.

CABALLERO ZOREDA, L., 1996, El análisis estratigráfico de construcciones históricas. En Curso de Arqueología de la

---

[4] Today only the two chapels closest to the apse remain, one on the northern side and one on the southern. The others have been joined, thus becoming lateral naves.

Arquitectura (Burgos, Junta de Castilla y León, 1996), 55-74. Salamanca: Europa Artes Gráficas, S.A.

CABALLERO ZOREDA, L. & LATORRE , P., 1995b, La importancia del análisis estratigráfico de las construcciones históricas en el debate sobre la restauración monumental. Informes de la Construcción 435, p. 5-18.

CABALLERO ZOREDA, L. & LATORRE, P. (coords.), 1995a, Leer el documento construido (monográfico). Informes de la Construcción 435.

CARRO GARCÍA, J., 1949, La escritura de concordia entre don Diego Peláez, Obispo de Santiago, y San Fagildo, abad del Monasterio de Anteltares. Cuadernos de Estudios Galegos 4: 111-122.

Estracto o razón curiosa de los papeles de la Fábrica de San Félix de de Solobio de Santiago, echo en el año de 1710. Archivo parroquial de San Félix, legajo de diversos papeles y documentos sin paginación.

FERNÁNDEZ SÁNCHEZ, J.M. & FREIRE BARREIRO, F., 1880, Santiago, Jerusalén, Roma: diario de una peregrinación a éstos y otros lugares de España, Francia, Egipto, Palestina, Siria e Italia, en el año del jubileo universal de 1875. Santiago de Compostela.

FOLGAR DE LA CALLE, Mª. C., 1981, Simón Rodríguez y su escuela. Tesis Universitaria (extracto). Departamento de Arte Moderno, Universidad de Santiago de Compostela. Santiago de Compostela: Servicio de mecanización.

HARRIS, E. C., 1991, Principios de estratigrafía arqueológica. Barcelona: Editorial Crítica.

HARRIS, E. C., 1993, Practices of Archaeological Stratigraphy. London: Academic Press.

Iglesia de San Félix (Santiago de Compostela). Manuscritos.

Libro de Cuentas y Visitas de la Fábrica de San Félix de Solobio de la ciudad de Santiago, desde el año 1696 hasta el 1806. Archivo Histórico Diocesano Santiago, Fondo Parroquial, Santiago, San Fiz. Serie Administración Parroquial, 1.

LÓPEZ FERREIRO, A., 1898-1909, Historia de la Santa A. M. Iglesia de Santiago. Santiago de Compostela.

MAÑANA BORRAZÁS, P., 1999, Bases metodológicas para el estudio de la arquitectura tumular. Una propuesta preliminar de análisis formal y su aplicación a un caso gallego. (Trabajo de Investigación del Tercer Ciclo). Departamento de Historia I, Facultade de Xeografía e Historia, USC. Santiago de Compostela. Inédito.

MORALEJO, A., TORRES, C. T., & FEIJOO, J. (trad.), 1951, Liber Sancti Iacobi: Codex Calistinus. Santiago de Compostela.

PARENTI, R., 1995, Historia, importancia y aplicaciones del método de lectura de paramentos. Informes de la Construcción 435, p. 19-29.

QUIRÓS CASTILLO, J. A., 1994, Contribución al estudio de la arqueología de la Arquitectura. Arqueología y territorio medieval 1, p. 141-158.

SUÁREZ, M. (trad.), 1950, Historia Compostelana, o sea hechos de D. Diego Gelmírez: Primer Arzobispo de Santiago. Santiago de Compostela.

YZQUIERDO PERRÍN, R., 1982, Homenaxe ó Pofr. Dr. Hernández Díaz, I. P. 139-512. Sevilla.

YZQUIERDO PERRÍN, R., 1993, La ciudad de Santiago. Patrimonio Histórico Gallego. Pp: 548-564 Santiago.

MORPHOMETRIC EVALUATION OF SOME BONY SEGMENTS IN A CASE OF DWARFISM OF THE LATE MIDDLE AGES (CIVIDALE DEL FRIULI, UDINE)

G. BAGGIERI & M. DI GIACOMO

During archaeological excavations carried out by the Head of Monuments and Fine Arts of Friuli Venezia Giulia at the Longobard necropolis of Cividale del Friuli, a ground level grave bearing two bodies were dug out from soil layers from the Late Middle Ages or the pre-Renaissance period (XII-XIV century). The two buried bodies were lain down in the same position, but in opposite directions. One was probably a male body aged between 25 and 35 and the other female body also an adult. The importance of this burial was immediately grasped because of the presence of a prone skeleton affected by dwarfism. This latter had an unusual bilateral opposition of articular facets on the diaphysis of the tibia and fibula. The interest for these particular alterations led us to an indispensable morphological evaluation. We point out the bending of the inferior segments and the different lengths of femoral segments of the tibia and the fibula (larger on the left), probably caused by kyphosis and scoliosis.

METRIC RELIEFS REFERABLE TO ACHONDROPLASIAC DYSPLASIA

The interest for these particular alterations led us to a necessary morphometric evaluation. The curvatures of the inferior segments are present, as well as the different lengths of the segments of the femur, tibia, and fibula (bigger on the left side), probably caused by kyphoscoliosis. Regarding the height of the subject, the metric relief obtained on the soil shows a height of 1.20 – 1.25 centimetres. This measurement is probably more realistic than the measurement obtained from traditional methods related to non-malformed subjects.

MORPHOMETRY OF AN ACHONDROPLASIAC DWARF

In order to compare the morphometry of the Cividale dwarf? we took into account the work of Charles E. Snow, physical anthropologist at the Alabama Museum, W.P.A. Archaeological Laboratory Birmingham, Alabama; and of J. Michael Hoffman of the Department of Anthropology, University of California (1976).

The measurement of the torsion angle of the right femur diaphysis, taken in the plane of the tibia and femoral joint, is equal to 28°. However, the ideal longitudinal axis of the angle of the diaphysis opening is 155°, thus there is a difference of 25°.

The left femur does not present torsion angles, its longitudinal diaphysis axis is normal and there is no evidence of an angle of diaphysis opening.

The left tibia shows an opening angle on the ideal longitudinal axis of the tibia-malleolar which is 156°, with a difference of 24° from the angle in the plane.

The right tibia shows a curvature of 138° with a difference of 42°, notably reducing the size of the angle from the plane.

We can extend the same considerations and evaluations to the fibulas, of which the one on the right has an opening angle in the middle of the diaphysis curvature which is 150°.

From the measurements of femoral, tibial and fibular segments, we can observe in particular a different maximum length which is the biggest of the segments on the left side. This difference in length of the left limb could favourably confirm the first diagnosis of the corpse by the naked eye which would correspond with the presumed scoliosis.

Also, this could be associated with a probable kyphoscoliosis, already seen in the positioning of the body during the burial.

This could offer an explanation concerning the weight of the body leaning on the right side as the continuous compression contributed to the lengthening of the controlateral limb.

	destra/right	sinistra/left
scapola		
cavitas glenoidalis, diametro trasversale	2,5	2,6
cavitas glenoidalis, diametro longitudinale	2,7	2,9
distanza dal punto estremo dell'acromion, all'angulus inferior	12,5	13,9
omero		
dalla estremità della troclea humeri, al punto estremo superiore del caput humeri	21,8	22,2
diametro alto alla crista tuberculi	2,8	3,3
diametro diafisario	1,9	2,1
diametro massimo caput humeri	4,5	n.r.
Ulna		
Lunghezza fisiologica	18,2	17,9
lung. max dal punto sup. estremo della incisura troclearis, al processo styloideus	19,8	20,2
Radio		
Lunghezza fisiologica		19,5
femore		
dal margine superiore del caput femoris, al condylus lateralis	24,4	26,2
diametro max del caput femoris	4,2	4,4
diametro min del caput femoris	4,0	4,4
diametro del collum femori	2,4	2,5
distanza tra il trocantere major ed il trocantere minor	6,4	6,4
diametro max sottotrocanterico	3,4	3,0
dal punto estremo del caput femoris, al centro del trocantere minor	6,4	7,2
dal punto estremo del caput femoris, al centro del trocantere major	5,5	5,6
fossa intercondilare	1,6	1,8
tibia		
lunghezza fisiologica da facies articularis malleoli, a eminentia intercondylaris	27,6	28,4
distanza estrema tra il condylus medialis, ed il condylus lateralis	5,7	5,7
fibula		
lunghezza estrema incompleta e frammentata di entrambe le fibule della facies articularis	22,9	24,2
diametro max a metà diafisi	3,1	2,2
iliaco		
incisura ischiatica, apertura max di svincolo	2,5	2,5
lunghezza max dalla cresta iliaca al margine estremo del ramus inferior pubis	17,3	17,5

Cranium (in mm.):

Glabello-occipital length	167
Maximun breadth	145
Basion bregma height	141
Minum frontal b.	85
Basion nasion	125
Basion-prosthion	113
Horizontal circumference	502
Nasion-opisthion arc	283
Bizygomatic b.	119
Midfacial (bimaxillary) b.	
Total facial h.	94
Upper facial h.	65
Nasal h.	42
Nasal b.	18
Orbital h. L 36 R 36	
Orbital b.(maxil front)L 35 R 40	
Orbital b (dacryon)	
Anterior interorbital b.	
(maxil-front)	16
(dacryon)	21
Biorbital b.	
Maxillo-alveolar l.	54
Maxillo-alveolar b.	
Foramen Magnum	33
Foramen Magnum	27
Distanza apici mastoidei	104

Mandibola (in mm.):

Lunghezza bicondiloidea	110
Lunghezza bigonionica	82
Altezza alla sinfisi	17
Lunghezza della mandibola	72
Altezza della mandibolaL 60 R 60	
Angolo mandibola	117
Dist. Fori mentonieri	46
Larghezza ramo ascendente L 26 R 24	
Angolo mentoniero	77°

Cranium (in mm.):

lunghezza max gonion-opisthokranion	167
lunghezza basion-bregma	141
Altezza auricolo bregmatica	131
larghezza max	164

Indici secondo Olivier

Indice cranico orizzontale	84,43	iperbrachicranico
Indice cranico verticale	92,80	iperbrachicranico
Indice auricolo bregmatico-larghezza	0,79	tapeinocranico
Indice basion bregmatico-larghezza	0,85	tapeinocranico
Indice basion-bregmatico-lunghezza	0,84	ipsicranico
Indice auricolo-bregmatico-lunghezza	0,78	ipsicranico

Lumbar vertebral Canal Dimensions in mm.
VertebraInterpeducolate distance Anteroposterior/transversal diameter

C2	1619	
C3	15	23
L1	19	12
L2	16	9
L3	15	9
L4	15	11
L5	15	12

A SPECIFIC BURIAL CUSTOM: THE CATACOMB GRAVE

Lívia BENDE & Gábor LŐRINCZY

Resumé : Un rite funéraire particulier : l'enterrement dans une tombe à niche. L'une des tribus du peuple Avar conquérant le bassin des Carpates en 568, a occupé le territoire entre les rivières de Körös et de Maros, à l'est de Tisza. L'un des rites funéraires particuliers de cette tribu était l'enterrement dans une tombe à niche frontale, qui, selon nos connaissances actuelles, n'a pas de précédent en orient. Sur notre tableau nous présentons des différentes variantes de ce type de tombe à l'aide de dessins de tombes et de photos.

Abstract: One of the groups of the Avars occupying the Carpathian Basin in 568, settled at the territory east of river Tisza between rivers Körös and Maros. One of the characteristic burial rites of this ethnic group is a special type of catacomb grave that, according to our present knowledge, have no direct eastern antecedents. In our poster we display different types of this type of grave with the help of grave drawings and photos.

Peoples and tribes of the Great Migration Period in the Carpathian Basin buried their dead into the generally known simple pit-graves, but, beside it, niche-graves, graves with shoulders, so called graves with „ears" (with horizontal grooves on the two long sides) and catacomb graves were in use. The origin and development of the latter type of burial used in the Avarian Age is still to be resolved.

This type of catacomb graves was prepared in the following way: a rectangular pit-grave was dug into the soil from the daily surface (similarly to the simple pit-graves). A long niche was grooved into one of the short sides of this pit directly or oblique downwards. The dead was put into this niche, in most of the cases with his feet forward. After that the entrance of the niche was closed with a wooden plate or animal skin and sacrificial animals (whole or only parts of them: skin, skull, legs) were placed into the pit. That is to say, after the refilling of the pit, the niche could not be noticed from the surface. The utmost common length of the pit and that of the niche could reach 5 m, and even in the case of a child grave the length exceeded 3 m. Catacomb graves were made for one occasion and served as burial place only for a single person. (Sometimes, but rarely, it happened that a woman was buried together with her child).

From the Early and Late Avarian Age (7th–8th century) we know today almost 400 catacomb burials from more than 30 sites. These sites were found in a well definable part of the Great Hungarian Plain: at the left bank of the Tisza, on the territory between rivers Körös and a Maros. Catacomb graves were found as part of cemeteries, mixed with other types of burials. It is widely accepted that this burial rite was in continuos use in the whole period of Early Avarian Age and was also practiced, though not continuously, in the Late Avarian Age.

To-date we cannot refer to any precise analogies of this grave type, appearing in the Carpathian Basin after the Avarian occupation, either from Inner and Central Asia, or from East Europe. On the basis of the burial customs and find material of the early cemeteries with catacomb graves, it can be suggested that people buried in these graves arrived from the South Russian steppe belt. After their appearance in the Carpathian Basin they, for a certain time, preserved their individual customs, but in the Late Avarian Age they were characterized by the same unified material culture as the people living in other territories of the Avarian Empire.

Lacking the precise analogies of the grave type, there are several possibilities for the explanation of the appearance of this burial rite relatively frequent in the Early Avarian Age. From the point of view of the shape they can be related to the Sarmatian catacomb graves (and earth chamber graves also called catacombs by Russian researchers). However, taking into consideration the lack of exact analogies and that of eastern antecedents from the 6th century, we can also suggest that the general custom of this grave shape was brought by the new settlers of the left bank Tisza valley of the Hungarian Plain from the East, but this form of the burial custom – perhaps following the pattern of the niche-grave used also earlier – was started to be practiced only here. It is supported also by the fact that in case of all of the grave types of the Early Avarian left Tisza bank valley cemeteries the custom of separation of the dead from the pit, from the partly buried animals can be observed.

Authors' addresses

Lívia BENDE
Móra Ferenc Múzeum
6701 Szeged
Pf. 474 HUNGARY
Email: l_bende@mfm.u-szeged.hu

Gábor LŐRINCZY
Móra Ferenc Múzeum
6701 Szeged
Pf. 474 HUNGARY
Email: lorinczy@mfm.u-szeged.hu

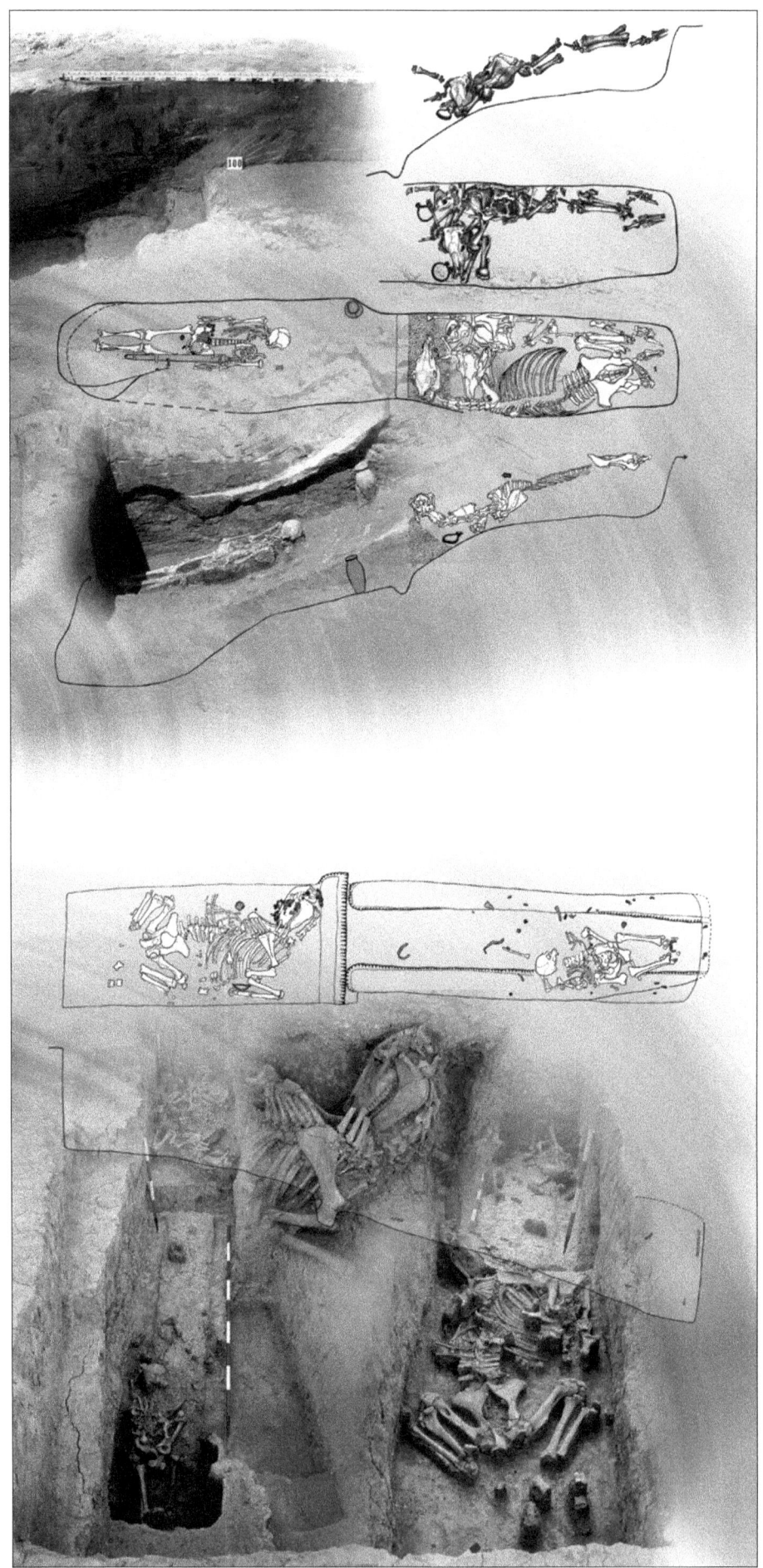

Figure 1. Top: Catacomb grave of early character (Szegvár-Oromdűlő, grave 100, Csongrád county).
Bottom: Catacomb grave of late character (Pitvaros, grave 51 Csongrád county).

Bibliography

BENDE, L., 2000, Fülkesírok a pitvarosi avar kori temetőben. Adatok a fülkés és lószerszámos temetkezések kronológiájához. — Stollengräber im awarenzeitlichen Gräberfeld von Pitvaros. Angaben zur Chronologie der Stollengräber und Bestattungen mit Pferdegeschirr. In *Hadak útján*, edited by L. Bende, G. Lőrinczy & Cs. Szalontai. Szeged, p. 241–279.

LŐRINCZY, G., 1994, Megjegyzések a kora avar kori temetkezési szokásokhoz. (A fülkesíros temetkezés.) — Bemerkungen zu den frühawarenzeitlichen Bestattungssitten. (Die Stollengräber.) In *A kőkortól a középkorig,* edited by G. Lőrinczy, Szeged, p. 311–335.

www.ingramcontent.com/pod-product-compliance
Lightning Source LLC
Chambersburg PA
CBHW061545010526
44113CB00023B/2807